DEBT is a Four-Letter Word
But it Need Not Be!

THE CAR FINANCING EXPERIENCE

By
Richard M. Gutkowski Ph.D. P.E.

ISBN-13: 978-0-9977216-1-4

Cover Design by Jody Zorn
http://www.zornphoto.com/

Printed in the United States of America

17 2 3 4

DEDICATION

For everyone navigating the car financing maze for the first time!

Table of Contents

PREFACE

Formally borrowing money for the first and navigating the unfamiliar territory can be a daunting experience. Indeed, for some it represents a scary challenge. I know. As a young adult, I experienced a bit of it first-hand. In fact, "experienced" is a misnomer. There was little to no prior experience. There were only the first "encounters" with the need to borrow money.

Being wary or afraid of debt can be overcome. As my life moved along, the hard knocks came and went. Learning from my mistakes gradually brought competence and confidence. More passage of time and professional budget management responsibilities at my job further honed my skills and sharpened my strategic capabilities. As a husband, I evolved to having effective techniques and tools to keep the domestic finances in good stead. I figured out how to wisely borrow money and repay it efficiently. As a team, my wife and I manage financial resources attentively and together. We never argue about money, we jointly plan for its utilization.

As a parent, I faced the challenge of teaching my daughter to achieve similar progressions. After all, like many teens, she simply had no interest in learning about money; let alone from her parent. It took time, patience and craftiness. And it took about ten years, from the time she was sweet sixteen to her burgeoning adulthood at twenty-five years old. That quarter-century old daughter was now welcoming, asking for and using my experienced guidance. As she aged another decade or so, there was more to share and for bigger needs. Being able to communicate was a boon to helping out when asked to do so.

With helpful guidance, competent advice and increasing experience with debt matters, a young teen can become increasingly more knowledgeable and comfortable about borrowing money. But you have to make contact first. "Earth to Mars?" "Parent to Teen?" Often, parents are stymied with initiating money management guidance with their adolescent kids. I want to help them start the negotiations. More so, I want to help them mimic my mode of attack and path to progress and eventual success.

DEBT is a Four-Letter Word - *But it Need Not Be!* is an ongoing series of books focused on helping young people learn how to handle newfound debt needs. Each volume covers different aspects of debt needs and issues that occur as a young person grows from about the age of 16 to the age of 35 or so. **THE CAR FINANCING EXPERIENCE** is the second sequential book in the series.

In the first volume, subtitled **THE COLLEGE EXPERIENCE**, the reader walked along as fictionalized high school junior Nicole began considering her interest in pursuing a college degree. The path eventually led to the day she walked down the aisle at her college Commencement. Tagging along was her fictionalized Dad who guided her through the financial aspects of paying for the costs of that education. Nicole graduated with her debt due to the costs of college successfully managed. In between a lot happened and the reader saw the details of all of it.

Nicole's walk began with her enthusiastic, teenaged plea for a credit card. Because some of her high school friends had gotten one, she just had to have one too. She mentioned it to her Dad. "Some of my older friends in the senior class came back this year with a credit card. They were pretty proud, almost bragging about it. I never thought about it but now I'm sort of envious of them. We've never talked about credit cards, so I don't know anything about them. I guess I'll eventually need one, so can you explain them to me? Then maybe I can get one, too?"

Being very anxious to "get one", Nicole presumptively asked her Dad, "How does someone get a credit card? How can I get one?"

While seemingly an episode apart from anything related to college, to her Dad his daughter's inquiry stirred inner thoughts that one day, not far from then, Nicole would be in college and indeed need a credit card. In time she was there and had one, but not until then.

Dad's passage through the inevitable worries about his teenage kid having a credit card, the risks of having one, to her actually getting one was a small part of a larger picture. Initially it was credit cards, later it became student loans. He had a heartfelt desire for Nicole to be accepted into an academic program at a college that best fits her career endeavor. But those costs had to be within the family's financial means. And there was an overarching monetary aspect on his mind. He wanted to teach his teen growing to college graduate age how to effectively handle debt needs. The reader saw in depth how that was accomplished; the calculation procedures, the calculations themselves, the analysis of different options, the decisions made, and the logic and strategies behind the decisions.

Equally important, the reader observed the non-monetary aspects of how Nicole's Dad interacted with her. It was done softly, but no helicopter was involved in doing it. As each monetary task came along, it was addressed together. Dad developed numerical information needed, but made sure Nicole was learning how he calculated it. He implemented careful, detailed analysis of the information and made sure Nicole understood his thinking. In every subsequent step, a strategy was involved before it was taken. Prerequisite to each step was Dad's quizzing of Nicole's understanding of the options and implications. As decisions followed, they moved further along the path, taking each step side-by-side.

How her Dad went about teaching Nicole was as important to observe as the tangible, nitty-gritty monetary items he shared. The reader watched him building a more and more comfortable relationship as he moved his daughter along an invisible parallel path. It led from his understandable initial hand-holding to Nicole's increased self-reliance in handling personal debt.

Nicole and her Dad navigate through her independent need for a credit card for ongoing college expenses, financing her college dreams, considering graduate school, and planning for post-graduation repayment of student loans. Now, Nicole has graduated college and will move further along that path. Nicole and her Dad will proceed through the next stage of her/their development. She will begin to navigate through what the author terms the "post-college experience". So will the reader. **THE CAR FINANCING EXPERIENCE** volume covers the first segment of that path.

In **THE CAR FINANCING EXPERIENCE** and subsequent volumes the reader continues to walk along as Nicole encounters new debt needs. She's just graduated college. Now her path will wind toward and through common post-college debt situations. Increasing complexity and monetary magnitude of the debts ensue. A need for a new car moves into her forefront. Later, purchasing a first condo arises. Further along, moving up to single family residence advances from her horizon. Her Dad will still be accompanying her. His caring teaching approach continues, but with a more mature and independent Nicole walking aside him.

In **THE CAR FINANCING EXPERIENCE** Nicole faces a challenge not uncommon to young college graduates. Ever since her sweet sixteen year-old birthday, she's been driving a parent-provided, low-cost car. Now she needs to replace that long-used, undependable car. And, for the first time, she has to do it herself. As in **THE COLLEGE EXPERIENCE**, her Dad shares his informed, strategic borrowing strategies based on his own experiences and approaches. Together they use them to carefully make important decisions and take vital borrowing steps. In the end, adult Nicole has become more self-reliant and takes those steps alone.

The motivation and approach to each volume of the **DEBT is a Four-Letter Word -** ***But it Need Not Be!*** book series are kept consistent. For my new readers, the preceding ***PREFACE TO VOLUME 1*** **(THE COLLEGE EXPERIENCE*)*** shares those aspects in detail.

Ideally, the new reader should consider first reading **THE COLLEGE EXPERIENCE**, but it is not absolutely necessary. While **DEBT is a Four-Letter Word -** ***But It Need Not Be!*** is a sequential book series, this second volume can be read as a standalone book. To enable that, a few base, generic monetary topics presented in the first volume are covered in condensed lengths.

While continuing Nicole's journey, the material in **THE CAR FINANCING EXPERIENCE** is applicable to anyone wanting to learn more about the car purchasing, car loan, car leasing and car brokering processes. The pros and cons to purchasing a car compared to leasing one are illustrated. Also, purchasing a leased car after the lease ends involves significant overall cost considerations. The author details how to determine those and make a financial decision about that option. Equally valuable, the reader will learn how to monetarily project and compare the option of purchasing a car outright to leasing the same car and purchasing it when the lease ends. Armed with that knowledge, an informed choice can be made before acting on either one.

The author also covers basic aspects about car insurance needed for a purchased car. Critical aspects of insurance needs for a leased car are also detailed. He also covers the financial implications of a leased car either being stolen or being damaged beyond repair in an accident before the lease ends.

DEBT is a Four-Letter Word - ***But It Need Not Be*!** is written in narrative, non-fiction style. It shares the hypothetical, but realistic, evolving fiscal development of a daughter as her Dad teaches her in depth skills in wisely taking on debt. As her abilities for wise decision-making, timely borrowing and effective repayment of debt grow, so does the maturity of their relationship. Nicole's not so secret desire is to, one day, outsmart her Dad. I invite you to the peak in and see how close she comes to achieving that. You can drive along at your own pace and have fun!

Open your mind, sharpen your pencils again and let the **LESSONS** on **THE CAR FINANCING EXPERIENCE** begin!

This is the second volume in the author's **DEBT is a Four-Letter Word,** ***But it Need Not Be!*** *book series. As a means of conveying his motivations for undertaking the book series and insight about the first volume to new readers, the following is a verbatim repeat of its Preface.*

PREFACE TO VOLUME 1 (THE COLLEGE EXPERIENCE)

Borrowing money is an act of getting into **DEBT**. Repaying money is the act of getting out of **DEBT**. The getting into step can occur very easily. The getting out of step is the challenge. But if either step is handled poorly, then trouble will ensue.

When the amount of one's **DEBT** feels like it's becoming hard to repay, that's worrisome. When it actually gets too hard to repay, that's concerning. If the reason you got there was borrowing the money as an act of desperation – that's scary. But **DEBT** need not be scary. The way to avoid this is to be armed with the skills necessary to wisely borrow money and effectively repay it.

THE COLLEGE EXPERIENCE is the first volume in an ongoing series of books; **DEBT is a Four-Letter Word,** ***But it Need Not Be!*** The focus of the books is on individuals who are new or relatively new to debt and are hesitant, nervous or afraid of it. Each volume will cover different aspects of debt needs and issues that occur as a young person grows from about the age of 16 to the age of 35 or so. The format of each book is a set of Lessons written in a narrative style – not as a textbook. But the series is not written in the fashionable style of "Subject for Dummies" primers. It does target basic, beginner subject matter but the content is extensive and thorough.

My underlying purpose in writing this book series is to guide the reader toward avoiding excessive debt and to effectively get out of excessive debt should it happen or already exist. Collectively, the books will help you gain solid technical ability to understand and effectively use debt; not abuse or be abused by it. I will prepare you to be logical and wise in dealing with any loan from the moment you first encounter a need for it. You will learn to conceive, calculate and evaluate options for any loan and make astute, strategic choices.

In my early years, I had some naiveté, unawareness, and a degree of ignorance about formally borrowing money. I had plenty of the negative surprises that debt can and does put into one's life and its consequences to financial well-being. Little by little I learned about the ins and outs of credit cards, bank loans, auto loans, student loans (first when I was a student, later for my daughter), home mortgages and other common types of loans. I learned from my mistakes, omissions and ignorance about exactly how to prepare for and make decisions about borrowing and paying back money. When I learned to dig into and understand the details, I began to make better decisions and do it faster but effectively.

As a professor in civil engineering for almost forty years, teaching and advising young people was a large part of my heart beat. Helping them hone their technical talents and launch professional careers was my endearing commitment. Now retired, it was with that same vigor and caring that I undertook writing this book series. I dedicated myself to developing a valuable guide for young people and their parents to use in managing debt matters as they move through their college experience.

During my career as a university professor I applied for and obtained numerous education and research grants and awards. So maneuvering through the mind-taxing, sometimes befuddling language of government program and application material is in my sweet spot. I am accustomed to deciphering requirements, rules, and regulations that seem overwhelming at first glance.

I managed hundreds of budgets with bottom lines ranging from the low thousands of dollars, to six figures, and beyond. Collectively, I managed millions of dollars. Aside from that, I guided numerous college students to effectively utilize and manage portions of the budget available from my funded research projects. If they ran out of money, they would be in trouble. With proper oversight, that never happened

My evolution in budget management as a professor led me to transfer those highly developed skills into the domestic environment. Computer-based tools I honed at work found their way into managing home finances. They enabled invaluable tracking of income and expenses and producing periodic account summaries, budget status, expenditure projections and so forth. Indeed, those very tools served to produce all of the numerical content of my book series. With these tools at hand, my wife and I grew to manage finances and debt in a strongly cooperative and coordinated way.

The **DEBT is a Four-Letter Word, *But it Need Not Be!!*** book series converts my lifetime of hard knocks, bad and good experiences and subsequent growth in debt management into a powerful sequence of Lessons I learned and now share with you. It reflects my incisive evolution about debt acquisition and management and my developed techniques and strategies to astutely deal with debt needs at all stages of life. It compacts my many years of development into a powerful guide to help you gain that knowledge in the time it takes you to read and learn the content. While pragmatic and detailed, I wrote it in a fun, narrative style so the reader will enjoy learning what otherwise might be unexciting financial matters.

In part, I wrote for parents who want to work with their child to develop his or her skills in borrowing money. I am a parent and worked carefully and effectively to achieve wise debt management and positive outcomes for my daughter's needs as she grew up. In doing that I strove to teach her skills along the way and motivate her to use them. I feel I achieved that to a high degree. Some of the content of **DEBT is a Four-Letter Word, *But it Need Not Be!*** reflects personal parenting steps I used.

The purpose of the books is to help the reader understand and control debt in technically strategic ways. The bulwark is the Situations described in each Lesson which illustrate examples of various loan events with extensive details about them (including needed calculations) based on the considerations taught in the Lesson. Although hypothetical, they realistically mimic circumstances commonly encountered in everyday life. By learning the concepts and examining the Situations described in each volume an adult of any age who desires to leapfrog to greater understanding the ins and outs of loans, expanded ability to negotiate wise loans and confidence to do so, will achieve those needs.

DEBT is a Four-Letter Word, *But it Need Not Be!* is an enjoyable, in-depth written path for both the neophyte and the experienced budgeter to progress to higher skills and confidence about borrowing money and repaying it. I invite you to one of its trailheads. You can walk along at your own pace and have fun!

Open your mind, sharpen your pencil and let the **LESSONS** on **THE COLLEGE EXPERIENCE** begin!

A FEW WORDS ABOUT "Math"

Debt involves money and money involves numbers. I remember my Dad admonishing me (then a kid) "Be sure to know how to count money-yours and others! Getting through life is tough and costly if you cannot do it." All calculations in this Primer are applicable to savings, debt and interest paid on debt. The reader needs to be able to multiply, divide, add, and subtract as learned up to a high school level and to follow formulas.

Many realistic, hypothetical "Situations" are used and involve debt depicted in ways one can and, for many, will encounter. They are written in narrative style to tell the story needed as the main setting for learning. Any mathematics involved is presented in prose style. Calculations are first presented step by step. Once the sequence is shown, further results are summarized and/or tabulated. Formulas are written in worded form matched to words in the text. They don't look like what one sees in a math book, but rather what one might say if spoken as words. So, the need to "memorize" symbols that look like math is entirely avoided. Short, easy to do "Exercises" primarily augment Situations and focus on the reader doing pieces of the same math.

For business matters, monetary amounts are in dollars and cents, e.g. $22.64 or $1024.00. Occasionally a value is written in whole dollars, e.g. $1024, for ease and to help fit tabulated numbers into the page width. In the digital present, numerical information is often presented in printed documents (such as mortgage statements) and computer output, <u>without</u> commas. Almost always tabulated information is so presented. So $1,000.00, $100,000.00, $12,345.67 and $123,456.78 will be written as $1000.00, $100000.00, $12345.67 and $123456.78. It spins one's eyeballs for a while, but they do adjust to it. Please bear with it until you hone in.

Electronic calculators in your cell phone are adequate. Of course, some calculated numbers are extremely and overly precise. For example, 1/3 = 0.33333333 so if it is $ we "round it off" to $0.33. But some number must be precise when part of a calculation. A number like 0.02178467 might be rounded to 0.02178 or 0.021785 or might be used as is. The less it is "rounded" the more "precise" it is. Sometimes "very precise" is needed, mostly not. Don't worry! The author had to do that, not you, and mostly behind the scenes.

If you repeat a series of the author's calculations on a calculator your results can be somewhat different. Where he gets $20.61 you might get $20.63, $20.67, $20.70, or even something more different! When reading, just follow the numbers, even if you get slightly different ones if you try to confirm them. That way you avoid the weeds and see the forest. Sometimes you need to see individual trees, too. So in each Situation, read to see the flow of numbers to and look again to see the details of the trickling stream. It is not vital that you absorb every number. Watch enough to know how the water got from point A to point B to point C and onward to the faucet which gives you the results.

INTRODUCTION

Background

In my days as a college student, upon graduating and "finding a job", for most graduates their next wish list item was buying a **NEW** car. After driving a cheap **USED** car or even what was then referred to as a "jalopy" during college years, the urge to get brand **NEW** "wheels" was irresistible. So once employed most went ahead and purchased a car. They easily qualified for a car loan.

Well, times have changed! The high cost of cars is one factor. Indeed, these days many students "bike" as their mode of transportation. Some have only that means, in some cases also as a social preference as well. Typically, as graduates begin looking for jobs they are saddled with significant student loan debt.

If significant student loan debt is one's circumstance, then the opportunity to qualify to borrow funds needed for purchasing a car can be very limited, if not unworkable. Almost certainly the individual will need to be employed and have sufficient income. If not, then that graduate would possibly be still in the market but for a **USED** car. With a well-paying job in a career in high demand, dependable profession student loan debt at the average level will not prohibit one from qualifying for a car loan for **NEW** cars.

At higher student debt level, say approaching an amount similar to a home mortgage for a condominium that debt would be a factor. Basically, one's financial ability to carry additional debt is the main factor in qualifying for any loan. Having an existing high student loan debt is little different from carrying a modest home mortgage debt. It's likely one can get a **CAR LOAN** in either case. But with a car loan atop high student debt, it likely the person will be driving a **USED CAR** into the parking space of a rented residence.

For the preceding reasons the author chose to write **THE COLLEGE EXPERIENCE** as the first volume in the **DEBT is a Four Letter Word - *But It Need Not be*!** book series. Primarily, it concentrated on effectively handling student loans. It was written to help the reader minimize or avoid an unaffordable student loan circumstance. With that accomplished, the reader is better prepared for oncoming new loan matters.

My fictional Nicole has graduated and chosen to start a career path. She is beginning to encounter the usual financial needs of normal life. She has entered the professional work force as an entry level journalist. She has a salaried income and is supporting herself financially. Based on her college record and having past experiences related to journalism she was hired with a fairly high starting salary. Although very good for an entry level journalist, it's not that high an income, compared to many other professions. Financially, she's basically an average, self-supported young person. Although her student loan debt is manageable, she will encounter new debt needs common to newly independent young people.

Nicole's present day version of a jalopy is her nearly decade old VW. She's beginning to imagine herself in a new car. As she will be doing on her own for the first time, she going to need advice from her Dad. Neither she nor he realizes that acquiring a new car has changed dramatically since the time the first time-buyer shoes were on Dad's feet. In this volume you will observe as they work through the ins and outs of acquiring a new car in today's setting. Borrowing money has not changed, but the paths to that new car are varied. Dad will help on both fronts.

How this volume will help you

THE CAR FINANCING EXPERIENCE volume provides my focused insight and effective strategies about the debt aspects involved in a young person acquiring a car independently for the first time. Learning its content will significantly help young adults be well informed about the basics of purchasing or leasing one. Readers will learn how car loans and car leases are undertaken and repaid. Parents wanting to advise a young adult child how to do these effectively will benefit from observing how Nicole's Dad accomplishes that. If as a parent you are relatively new to the above types of debt yourself, then **THE CAR FINANCING EXPERIENCE** will bring you to a comfort level about them. For all readers the ultimate aim is to prepare you to strategically finance such debts. Moreover, you will be well armed to monetarily complete **THE CAR FINANCING EXPERIENCE** on good financial terms.

THE COLLEGE EXPERIENCE covered several needed and important base topics at length. They include the basics of loan repayment, the amortized loan process, and the loan acceleration process. For readers of this volume who have not read **THE COLLEGE EXPERIENCE** I begin **THE CAR FINANCING EXPERIENCE** with abbreviated versions of them. The content is sufficient to establish the needed understanding, but fewer numerical examples are presented. Readers who feel a need for more depth and application are referred to **THE COLLEGE EXPERIENCE**.

In **THE CAR FINANCING EXPERIENCE** I teach you the nuts and bolts involved in obtaining a loan to purchase a car. If it is a **NEW CAR**, then it can be one of the most expensive purchases most people will make in their entire life time. Atop the high cost, it's a psychological process of cat and mouse maneuvering right to the very day you're handed the key. The flow of the process ebbs between slow worries and necessary fast steps. The main concern is can I make my financial decision before the car is sold to another customer? I share vital behind the scenes information on how lenders determine the rate of interest charged on a car loan. You will learn how your credit standing significantly affects the outcome. Then I walk you through the details and costs of repaying the loan. I arm you to be able to plan for these things before you ever speak to a salesperson.

It is now commonplace for people to lease a car instead of purchasing one. While advertisements make it appear simple, it is actually very complex. Leasing a car is even more complex and mindboggling than purchasing one. Unlike renting a car for a short term, the longevity of a long-term lease can involves very high initial and/or final costs. There are subtle pitfalls and I show you how to handle them, allowing you too alertly and carefully negotiate the lease terms you are offered. Then I show you how to calculate and compare the overall costs of leasing a car compared to purchasing one. For first time car leasers, it can be intimidating and a lot like a leap of faith. In **THE CAR FINANCING EXPERIENCE** I slowly and thoroughly explain all of this. I walk you through the gamut of information, documents, decision making and timeline you will confront. Because of that, you'll have a lot less worry and a lot more confidence about being well informed and prepared for that leap of faith and everything before it.

For readers wary or uncomfortable about purchasing or leasing a car directly at a dealership, there are contemporary alternatives. Purchasing cars on-line via dealership websites or independent on-line service providers is a burgeoning approach. Many websites avail the car buyer of that opportunity and I describe the main ones and how they work. I also cover how you can hire a car broker to locate desired cars and handle the purchase for you. Functionally, it is similar to using a real estate broker to locate potential homes to purchase, that meet your parameters. There are pros and cons of using one and I will cover them in detail.

All the above is extensive alone. But, Surprise! Surprise! It does not end there. You might have an existing car to consider as a possible trade-in toward purchasing a new one. Should you trade it in, or sell it privately instead, or just keep it? You will learn how to monetarily compare those options and make a financially preferable choice. A trade-in can be done as part of a car lease as well. I cover handling the added complexities involved.

Finally, there is the consideration of insuring the car in case of theft or excessive cost of severe damage in an accident. What happens if either occurs before a car loan is paid off or before a car lease has ended? You are still responsible for that debt. I cover these serious risks and how to protect yourself monetarily should they happen to you, I detail the special insurance needed, as well as the basics of normal car insurance for a purchased or leased car for less impact occurrences.

How to read this volume

THE CAR FINANCING EXPERIENCE is comprised of 14 chapters, termed LESSONS. The first three Lessons review base topics previously covered in **THE COLLEGE EXPERIENCE**. *E*nsuing Lessons cover typical car-based debt matters sequentially encountered by young people soon after **THE COLLEGE EXPERIENCE** ends. The format used in **THE COLLEGE EXPERIENCE** volume is continued. In each Lesson, the text content guides the reader through the basic monetary aspects of each debt circumstance. For needed "math" it is covered in general prose terms and readily readable large font equations. Then, SITUATIONS are described and used to illustrate actual calculations involved in assessing different components or scenarios of the debt circumstance taught in that Lesson. The facts involved in each SITUATION constitute a monetary setting which the author uses to teach the reader either a good or a bad aspect of entering into and/or handling debt. In each SITUATION, closing observations are made about the main points to be learned from the example.

As the reader progresses through the LESSONS, the text and SITUATIONS illustrate increasingly more involved debt needs and circumstances. Typically, a prose description of a particular sequence of the applicable calculations with embedded illustrative numerical work precedes the SITUATION(S). Each involves re-use of the ordinary mathematical methods and equations covered in that preceding text. Some SITUATIONS either extend the illustrative material to a longer debt repayment time frame or re-do them for different numerical values for the circumstance, such as a change in the annual rate of interest involved.

The reader should attentively read the precedent text and numerical illustration and then read through the SITUATION once quickly. Avoid delving into the weeds of the particular numbers being processed. Simply observe the flow of the calculations involved and the gist of what observations they lead to. Then learn how to do the calculations involved by going back and tracing the actual numbers. If you prefer to trust the author's math that is perfectly fine. If you can take time to confirm each calculated number, all the better.

Periodic short Exercises are included. They constitute check points to confirm understanding of the subject matter and see if you can do the specifics of the calculation steps involved. I encourage you to try them. Whether you do them or not, the given answers (or partial answers) provide additional learning and insight into the subject matter. If you try hard and cannot confirm one of my answers, then don't hesitate to contact me about it.

The Setting

As Nicole's proceeds in life following college, she confronts desire and the need to acquire a car to replace her aging present car. It's a new circumstance for her to being doing that. When asked, her Dad intervenes to help. In a caring, knowledgeable and wise way her Dad teaches Nicole how to manage each SITUATION and the numerical work involved. They identify the issues and work together to resolve them. Increasingly, Nicole learns to handle aspects of her impending debt need by herself. In the end, she and her Dad have managed **THE CAR FINANCING EXPERIENCE** successfully. My hope and belief is you will do so as well; in your own version of it.

The personal interaction of Nicole and her Dad and their dialogue is invaluable to the reader. The debt matters Nicole face are old hat to her Dad. Caringly but craftily he gradually builds a mutual comfort zone and uses it to effectively share his knowledge. For parent readers wanting to develop a similar relationship with their daughter or son, their example helps.

The time has come. Nicole and her Dad are about to embark on their next journey. Put on your traveling shoes and tag along for a very informative ride and a lot of fun along the way,

LESSON 1 Loans and Loan Repayment – A Look Back at a Past Episode

Winds were howling and roads were impassable. It was a blinding blizzard. Snow drifts were piled so high only an NBA center's head could stick out. School was out because of it. Trapped with nowhere to go, 16-year old high schooler Nicole asked her equally marooned Dad, "Hey Dad! Maybe this is a good time to talk about that **amortization** loan process you mentioned to me a while ago. I don't know where the word comes from, but at least I know how to say it and spell it now."

He had replied, "That's a great idea. I've already been preparing to do that since we last talked before Thanksgiving Day. I'm free right now. Let's go to my office and get started. I have lots to explain but it'll be a slow careful walk not a sprint."

That was the setting when Nicole learned about the most common method of loan repayment. The topic of **amortization** has a little bit of fancy math involved in it, so they had come to that point progressively. When Nicole first asked her Dad about student loans he mentioned the **amortization** process of loan repayment. But then he deflected Nicole from it and introduced the subject of loans and loan repayment at a more basic level. At the end of it he asked, "Peanut. Is there anything else on your mind?"

"I haven't forgotten about that process you called 'ammutization' or however you say it, Dad. You were going to explain that to me and how the darn word is spelled." She had indeed mispronounced the word. Dad corrected her off target "ammutization" to the actual "a-m-o-r-t-i-z-a-t-i-o-n".

Using that past conversation, the author now takes the opportunity to review important subject matter from his first volume. By doing so, he provides a vital backdrop to this intended stand-alone second volume. Assume Nicole has just stepped into her Dad's office on that snow-locked day. Let's go through parts of their conversation again; sometimes augmented, sometimes shortened, sometimes reworded, and somewhat reordered. Basically, let me use author's privilege to unfold it in a somewhat different way than last time.

"Well Nicole, I'm not sure who's got who trapped. I'm glad you want to learn about **amortization**. The **amortization** process is a very common way to repay a loan. As I said last time, it can be a little intimidating at first. It's particularly true at your age. That's why, back when you first asked about that loan process, I diverted you to a more basic discussion of it. Why don't we start by going through that again?"

"That'd be great Dad. It's been quite a while since you explained it to me. I generally remember it, but could use a refresher"

"Ok, let's go back to the starting line. It's not going to be a race, but a gradual walk along the same track.

Loans and Loan Repayment

"As you know, when you borrow money from a lender to buy something, like a computer, you have to pay it back. Not all at once, but in incremental payments. Predominately those partial payments are made monthly. The **terms** of the loan can be anything the lender and borrower agree to. Do you remember what I mean by 'the **terms** of the loan'?"

"I actually do, Dad. It means what each person says they will do in lending/borrowing the money. The guy giving the money can make you do anything, if you agree to do so."

"Can you be more specific, Nicole?"

"You taught me the **terms** of a loan include three main things. One is the amount of money involved. Another is how long it will take to pay the money back. Third is the amount of interest to be paid."

"In general words, that's it, Sweetie. In financial words, the amount of money involved is the **LOAN AMOUNT**. The length of time to pay it back is called the **TERM** of the loan. The interest to be paid is based on an **ANNUAL RATE OF INTEREST**. Do you remember that terminology?"

"Yeah, Dad, I remember my confusion about how the **terms** of a loan include the **TERM** of the loan. You said it was confusing to everyone, but it is what it is. The **terms** of the loan are all the conditions and you spell it in small letters. The **TERM** of the loan is one specific condition and has no 's' at the end. You put it in capital letters."

"OK. I remember your confusion about that and my saying that a lot of other people have it.

"The **TERM** of the loan is usually expressed as how many months it will take to repay the loan. That's because it is repaid by paying an agreed portion of the **LOAN AMOUNT** each month, plus **MONTHLY INTEREST** on the unpaid amount. The **MONTHLY PAYMENT** is the sum of the two.

"How is the **MONTHLY INTEREST** calculated? Can you write it in math form, Nicole?"

"I think so, Dad. I remember you telling me that lenders use an **ANNUAL RATE OF INTEREST** in the terms of the loan. But, in repaying it, we need the monthly value. We need to divide **ANNUAL RATE OF INTEREST** by twelve to get the **MONTHLY RATE OF INTEREST**." Nicole scratch writes the equation."

MONTHLY RATE OF INTEREST = ANNUAL RATE OF INTEREST/12

"That's right. And how do we get the amount of interest charged each month?"

"Well, amount of money left unpaid at the end of that month is multiplied by the M**ONTHLY RATE OF INTEREST**."

"What's the unpaid amount of money called?"

"When you taught me about credit cards, you called it the **OUTSTANDING BALANCE**?"

"Right again, Nicole. 'Outstanding' does not mean 'it's a great thing'. It means it's the amount remaining unpaid. Because you are charged the interest on that amount, it's not 'a great thing'. If you paid the entire amount owed at the end of a month then there would be no interest charged on the **OUTSTANDING BALANCE**. Because it would be fully repaid, the loan would end. Loosely, some people say the loan has been 'paid off'.

"Can you write the math equation for calculating the amount of **MONTHLY INTEREST**?"

"I think so."

MONTHLY INTEREST = (MONTHLY RATE OF INTEREST/100) x OUTSTANDING BALANCE

"Great! Peanut. That's correct. Why is the 100 in there?"

"I know the **ANNUAL RATE OF INTEREST** is a value with a percent sign. Way back in school I learned that when you find the percentage of something you need to divide the value given in percent by 100. Then you multiply the result times the something to get the percentage of it."

Smiling softly, Dad replies, "Whew! That's sort of going in circles. But, you are correct. What's the 'something'?"

"Here it's the **OUTSTANDING BALANCE**? Like I showed in the equation for **MONTHLY INTEREST**"

"Perfect! Smarty Pants."

"Dad? You're always calling me that."

"I only say it because it's true. Let's move along.

"Let's say you borrow a certain **LOAN AMOUNT**. Each month a specified portion of borrowed money is paid back at the end of the month. It could be either the same amount or a different amount each month. Call it the **SCHEDULED MONTHLY PAYMENT**. Again, the **MONTHLY INTEREST** is an additional charge and is also owed at the end of each month."

Monthly Statements

"Each month the entire **SCHEDULED MONTHLY PAYMENT** amount is to be applied to reduce the amount of money owed. A **MONTHLY STATEMENT** is received showing those monetary actions and resulting amounts."

"Dad, you mean I get a statement similar to a credit card **MONTHLY STATEMENT**?"

"Yes, it is similar. Since there are no ongoing purchases, it's a lot shorter in length.

"Once a loan is initiated, at the end of the first month a **MONTHLY STATEMENT** is received. The initial **OUTSTANDING BALANCE** is the **LOAN AMOUNT**. Then the **OUTSTANDING BALANCE** is reduced by the **PAYMENT RECEIVED**.

"**MONTHLY INTEREST** is obtained by applying the **MONTHLY RATE OF INTEREST** to that **REDUCED BALANCE**. The result is added to the **REDUCED BALANCE** to get the **NEW OUTSTANDING BALANCE**. It is also added to the **SCHEDULED MONTHLY PAYMENT** to get the **AMOUNT DUE**."

"Wow! Dad. That sure is a mouthful."

"Let me show all that as math equations. Let's look at my monitor."

<u>MONTHLY STATEMENT 1</u>

OUTSTANDING BALANCE = LOAN AMOUNT

REDUCED BALANCE = OUTSTANDING BALANCE – PAYMENT RECEIVED

RATIO = MONTHLY RATE OF INTEREST/100

MONTHLY INTEREST = RATIO x REDUCED BALANCE

NEW OUTSTANDING BALANCE = REDUCED BALANCE + MONTHLY INTEREST

AMOUNT DUE = SCHEDULED MONTHLY PAYMENT + MONTHLY INTEREST

"If the **AMOUNT DUE** is paid on time, then in the next month it is the **PAYMENT RECEIVED** amount.

"Are you following this OK, Sweetie?"

"Yeah, mostly I do recall those things. Remind me, Dad, what is that **RATIO** term?"

"You actually know what it is. You said it and wrote it earlier. It's the **MONTHLY RATE OF INTEREST** divided by 100. Now, I just gave it a name."

"Hmm, I didn't notice that before. I see it now."

"That's good, Sweetie. **RATIO** is actually a common math term used when the percentage is written in decimal form. The decimal form comes from dividing the percentage by 100."

"I kind of recall my math teacher using that term. She didn't spend a lot of time on it. I sort of understand your equations. Like last time, all the different names of balances are starting to spin my head a bit."

"Peanut, as I describe it, my mind spins a little bit, too. Later, I'll make them clearer by using a numerical example."

"Dad, I understand the meaning of the **NEW OUTSTANDING BALANCE**. I tend to be confused about why the **AMOUNT DUE** is not equal to it."

"Recall that the **LOAN AMOUNT** is being repaid by incremental amounts each month. The **AMOUNT DUE** is that incremental amount of money plus any interest charged for any amount of money left unpaid that month. You'll also see that more clearly in my numerical example. Bear with me for a little longer."

"OK. But please don't growl at me."

"I'd never do that to you. You'd laugh at me too much.

"After the end of Month 2 the second **MONTHLY STATEMENT** arrives. The **NEW OUTSTANDING BALANCE** is carried forward as the **PREVIOUS OUTSTANDING BALANCE.**

"The **PREVIOUS OUTSTANDING BALANCE** is reduced by the **PAYMENT RECEVED. MONTHLY INTEREST** is obtained by applying the **MONTHLY RATE OF INTEREST** to the **REDUCED BALANCE**. Then the rest is like Month 1.

"Let's look at that in equation form."

<u>MONTHLY STATEMENT 2</u>

REDUCED BALANCE = PREVIOUS OUTSTANDING BALANCE
– PAYMENT RECEIVED

MONTHLY INTEREST = RATIO x REDUCED BALANCE

NEW OUTSTANDING BALANCE = REDUCED BALANCE + MONTHLY INTEREST

AMOUNT DUE = SCHEDULED MONTHLY PAYMENT + MONTHLY INTEREST

"This pattern continues each month until the loan is fully paid off, that is until all **SCHEDULED MONTHLY PAYMENTS** and calculated **MONTHLY INTEREST** amounts have been paid. Are you still with me?"

"I still am, Dad. It does seem similar to credit card statements."

"Let's look at an example with actual numbers. As you're too young to legally make such a loan, I'll use a hypothetical individual named Melissa."

SITUATION 1

"Melissa takes out a bank loan for $1500.00 to buy a sofa. The local furniture store accepts a $300.00 down payment and agrees to give her a year to repay the remaining $1200.00. **MONTHLY PAYMENTS** of $100.00 are to be made at the end of each month. An **ANNUAL RATE OF INTEREST** of 6.00% is to be applied on a **MONTHLY INTEREST** basis in the manner I just described.

"Nicole, what's all that information called?

"I suppose those are the **terms** of the loan?"

"That's right.

"Assume Melissa makes all payments, including **MONTHLY INTEREST**, on time."

"Dad, when are the **MONTHLY INTEREST** charged and the **AMOUNT DUE** paid?"

"Good question. Looking at the flow of my monthly equations, the **MONTHLY INTEREST** is charged when the **MONTHLY PAYMENT** for the preceding month is received. On that day, the **MONTHLY INTEREST RATE** is applied to the resulting **REDUCED BALANCE**. The **MONTHLY INTEREST** is part of the **AMOUNT DUE** right at the end of the month. Other ways could be used, but let's assume that's what is stated in the **terms** of Melissa's loan.

"As is usual, assume Melissa pays by mailing in a bank check. Usually a so-called **grace period** is included. That means she would have a few days into the following month to have her check received by the lender. Typically, the grace period is between five to ten days. The **AMOUNT DUE** is actually due up to the end of that period."

"That makes sense, if she is using snail mail."

"Yeah, a lot of people in your generation would do it electronically by computer. So far, I don't see any banks shortening their grace periods because of that.

"Let's get the **MONTHLY RATE OF INTEREST** and look at the outcome after the first month of repayment."

MONTHLY RATE OF INTEREST = ANNUAL RATE OF INTEREST/12 months
= 6.00%/12 months = 0.50% per month

RATIO = 0.50%/100 = 0.005

MONTHLY STATEMENT 1

OUTSTANDING BALANCE = LOAN AMOUNT = $1200.00

REDUCED BALANCE = OUTSTANDING BALANCE – PAYMENT RECEIVED
= $1200.00 – $0.00 = $1200.00

MONTHLY INTEREST = 0.5% of $1200.00 = 0.005 x $1200.00 = $6.00

NEW OUTSTANDING BALANCE = REDUCED BALANCE + MONTHLY INTEREST

= $1200.00 + $6.00 = $1206.00

SCHEDULED MONTHLY PAYMENT = $100.00

The AMOUNT DUE = $100.00 + $6.00 = $106.00 and is paid on time.

<u>SITUATION 1 - CONTINUED</u>

"Do you understand those calculations, Sweetie?"

"I'm beginning to remember things from the first time we talked about it, Dad. I do mostly understand it. Why is the **PAYMENT RECEIVED** zero dollars?"

"Because it's the first **MONTHLY STATEMENT** there is no previous month. No payment has been made. Nothing is due until after that first statement is received."

"Ok, I realize that now."

"Let's look at the next month's outcome."

<u>MONTHLY STATEMENT 2</u>

PREVIOUS OUTSTANDING BALANCE = $1206.00

PAYMENT RECEIVED = $106.00

REDUCED BALANCE = PREVIOUS OUTSTANDING BALANCE
= $1206.00 - $106.00 = $1100.00

MONTHLY INTEREST = 0.005 x $1100.00 = $5.50

NEW OUTSTANDING BALANCE = REDUCED BALANCE
+ MONTHLY INTEREST
= $1100.00 + $5.50 = 1105.50

SCHEDULED MONTHLY PAYMENT = $100.00

The AMOUNT DUE = $100.00 + $5.50 = $105.50 and is paid on time.

SITUATION 1 - CONTINUED

"Are you still following this?"

"I sure am, Dad. It's just a repeat of the process with different numbers."

"Right. What happens next?"

"It keeps repeating each month with different numbers."

"Exactly. The monthly progression with a **MONTHLY PAYMENT** of $100.00 repeats ten more times. Since we've seen the pattern, I've skipped the calculations and condensed those results. Here are the results for the next nine months. To save space I wrote it in text."

MONTHLY STATEMENTS 3 through 11

The sequence of results for REDUCED BALANCE, MONTHLY INTEREST is:

Month 3: $1000.00, $5.00; Month 4: $900.00, $4.50**;** **Month 5: $800.00, $4.00:** Month 6: $700.00, **$3.50; Month 7: $600.00, $3.00;** Month 8: $500.00, **$2.50; Month 9: $400.00, $2.00;** Month 10: $300.00, **$1.50; Month 11: $200.00, $1.00.**

Adding the two values will give the NEW OUTSTANDING BALANCE for each month.

SITUATION 1 - CONTINUED

"Still following me?"

"It takes a bit of eye attention, but yes, Dad. I see you give the values of those two items for each of the next nine months. That's through Month 11. What happens next?"

"I understand the eye strain. If you want to do the calculations as voluntary homework, then you can fill in the details all the way through. But, whoa on what happens next. Before I show that, tell me what's happening to those values as the months pass?"

"Well they both keep getting lower."

"Why, Sweetie?"

"I guess it's because the **MONTHLY PAYMENTS** are reducing what is owed each month. So the amount of **MONTHLY INTEREST** is less each month."

"Very good!

"At the end of Month 11 the **REDUCED OUTSTANDING BALANCE** is $100.00. What's interesting about that, Nicole?"

"I guess since the last **MONTHLY PAYMENT** is $100.00 the loan will be paid off that month?"

"That's right. There will also be **MONTHLY INTEREST** charged added to that $100.00. That's why I held off on showing Month 12. Let's look at that last month."

<u>MONTHLY STATEMENT 12</u>

PREVIOUS OUTSTANDING BALANCE = $200.00 +$1.00 = $201.00

PAYMENT RECEIVED = $101.00

REDUCED BALANCE = $201.00 - $101.00 = $100.00

MONTHLY INTEREST = 0.005 x $100.00 = $0.50

NEW OUTSTANDING BALANCE= $100.00 + $0.50= $0.00

SCHEDULED MONTHLY PAYMENT = $100.00

The AMOUNT DUE = $100.00 + $0.50 = $100.50 and is paid on time and the loan ends.

<u>SITUATION 1 - CONTINUED</u>

"Indeed the loan has now been paid off. What's the total amount of interest paid over the twelve months, Nicole?"

Pondering for a few moments, Nicole replies, "It would be the sum of the twelve **MONTHLY INTEREST** amounts."

"Exactly! The **TOTAL INTEREST** equals $6.00 + $5.50 + … + $0.50. Those amounts add up to $39.00. What's that as a percentage of the **LOAN AMOUNT**?"

"Hmm? I think I should know how to get that? It escapes me right now."

"Here's how we calculate it. Peanut."

RATIO = TOTAL INTEREST/LOAN AMOUNT = $39.00/$1200.00 = 0.0325

PERCENT TOTAL INTEREST = FRACTION/100 x 0.0325 x 100 = 3.25% (rounded)

SITUATION 1 – CONTINUED

"Yeah, now I remember. Like I said before, to get the percentage something is of something else you divide the something by the something else and multiply by 100. It's sort of the reverse of calculating the something when you know the percentage and the something else. Seems like sort of the reverse of the **RATIO** term you used before."

"Well, Nicole, that is sort of an expanded mouthful and earful of what you said before. But you do know it. To be specific, what are the something and something else?"

"Let me think. The something is the **TOTAL INTEREST**. The something else is the **LOAN AMOUNT**."

"Now you've got it, Peanut. Notice the **PERCENT TOTAL INTEREST** is significantly less than the **ANNUAL RATE OF INTEREST** of 6.00% stated in the terms. That's due to the **OUTSTANDING BALANCE** declining each month. Similar to credit cards, the lesson here is to pay off your entire **AMOUNT DUE** each month and on time."

"Sweetie, the example of Melissa's loan gives you the basics of how the terms of a loan dictate the repayment and how the numbers flow each month. Here are some voluntary homework exercises."

Exercise 1: *Repeat the first three months of SITUATION 1 for an* ***ANNUAL RATE OF INTEREST*** of *12.00%.*

Your <u>partial</u> results should be: *At the end of Month 2,* ***MONTHLY INTEREST*** *= $11.00,* ***NEW OUTSTANDING BALANCE*** *= $1111.00. At the end of Month 3,* ***NEW OUTSTANDING BALANCE*** *= $1010.00.*

For readers wanting to carry on through to the last month, the results for Month 12 are ***MONTHLY INTEREST*** *= $1.00 and* ***NEW OUTSTANDING BALANCE*** *= $101.00. That amount is paid and the loan ends. The* ***TOTAL INTEREST*** *= $78.00.*

Exercise 2: *Repeat the first three months of SITUATION 1 for a* ***LOAN AMOUNT*** *of $2100.00, a* ***DOWN PAYMENT*** *of $600.00 and an* ***ANNUAL RATE OF INTEREST*** *of 3.00%. Melissa makes twelve equal* ***SCHEDULED MONTHLY PAYMENTS*** *of $125.00.*

Your <u>partial</u> results should be: *At the end of Month 1,* ***NEW OUTSTANDING BALANCE*** *= $1503.75. At the end of Month 3,* ***NEW OUTSTANDING BALANCE*** *= $1253.13.*

For readers wanting to carry on through to the last month, the results for Month 12 are ***MONTHLY INTEREST*** *= $0.31 and* ***NEW OUTSTANDING BALANCE*** *= $125.31. That amount is paid and the loan ends. The* ***TOTAL INTEREST*** *= $24.39.*

"Nicole, if you do the voluntary homework, then also consider redoing it for different values of the **LOAN AMOUNT** and **ANNUAL RATE OF INTEREST**. You can try a longer **TERM** too, but that adds a lot of lines of calculations."

"I'd like to do that Dad, but I'll have to see how it fits in my school time."

"Of course you should. Whatever you do, I gave you some answers to check your results. If yours don't agree with mine, let me know. We can walk through the math together."

"That's great, Dad.

"And maybe I will try that voluntary homework when I have the time to do it. At least for the example you've shown me, I already have the correct answers to check my work."

"Great! If you try the other variations, then let me know the specifics. I'll email you the answers for them."

"I can't promise to try variations, Dad. Having the answers will be helpful and push me a little."

"Ok, Nicole. Why don't you take time today and tomorrow to try what you can before we move on to **amortization**? Then we can get into that on Saturday."

"**Amortization** sounds pretty scary, Dad. Let's do that so I can be sure I've got these basics down."

LESSON 2 Amortized Loans = Getting Out of Debt Faster and Faster!

Saturday has rolled around. The blizzard has tapered off, but some lingering snowflakes are slowly finding their way to the ground. Typical to teens, Nicole slept as long as she could. She did not have to meet her Dad until the afternoon anyway. Hopefully, she did not have nightmares about the Ghost of Amortization. Her long snooze without jumping awake suggests she did not. In a short while, her Dad would be the only spirit that would visit her. And he isn't scary at all.

At lunch Dad greets her with, "Hi Nicole! In a while we'll meet and tame the monster of **amortization**. How did you do with all that voluntary homework?"

"Good morning Dad! I did alright. I also tried some variations and got the same results as the answers you sent me. It took me a long time, but in the end I felt pretty good about it."

"That's wonderful, Nicole. You did it by calculator?"

"I sure did and it seemed to take forever. But it was worth it. I feel very good and am ready to tackle that **amortization** beast."

"Ok. We'll get to that right after lunch. I'll try hard to tame any monsters that are involved as they come along. Oh, I do my calculations using computer routines. It takes fraction of the time you took, but I feel strongly that one needs to first do things the long way before depending on a computer. Then you are sure you know what you are doing, not being helped by invisible computer methods. Down the road I'll show you how to use my computer routines."

"I'm glad to hear that and cannot wait. I'm wearing out my pencils."

Amortization

With lunch over, it's **amortization** time! That's nowhere near as beckoning as a snowball fight, but unavoidable.

"Nicole, since you did all that homework I want to note two characteristics of those loans. Each month you make a **MONTHLY PAYMENT**. It is comprised of a **SCHEDULED MONTHLY PAYMENT** plus the **MONTHLY INTEREST**. The **SCHEDULED MONTHLY PAYMENT** is the same amount each month. That's due to the specific terms of the loan. The lender could have broken up the repayment into any sequence that totals $1200.00. For example, $50.00 per month for six months ($300 total) followed by $150 per month for six months ($900 total). The other characteristic is that the **MONTHLY INTEREST** is an add-on; that is, it is <u>additional to</u> the **SCHEDULED MONTHLY PAYMENT**.

"In the loan we talked about Thursday, and in your homework, in each month the debt was reduced by the amount of the **PAYMENT RECEIVED**. For a loan payment sequence developed by **amortization**, the **SCHEDULED MONTHLY PAYMENT** is called the **AMORTIZED MONTHLY PAYMENT**. The amount is always the same each month, too. However, the **MONTHLY INTEREST** is <u>not</u> an add-on. Instead, the **AMORTIZED MONTHLY PAYMENT** is split into two portions. One portion is applied to pay the **MONTHLY INTEREST** charge. The other is applied to reduce the debt, the amount owed. The former is calculated first and taken out of the **AMORTIZED MONTHLY PAYMENT.** Then, the remaining amount is subtracted from the debt.

"The way **amortization** works out is the portion of the **AMORTIZED MONTHLY PAYMENT** that is used to pay interest decreases each month. As a result, the portion used to reduce the debt increases each month. Consequently, the borrower is getting out of debt faster and faster!

"Do you understand this distinction, Nicole?"

"Dad, I understand there is a difference in what happens in each case. I get that in one case the **MONTHLY INTEREST** is paid in addition to the **SCHEDULED MONTHLY PAYMENT**. In the other case it is part of it, not an extra amount. I'm clueless as to how **amortization** works in actual numbers. You'll have to show me. And I still have no idea why it has that awful sounding name."

"That's Ok, Sweetie. All I was expecting was that you sort of get the nature of the difference. I'm just about to cover the numbers part. Before that, here's where the word **amortization** comes from.

"Since you wondered about the source of the word last time, I looked into it. It actually comes from the Latin words for 'to' and 'death', which are 'ad' and 'mortem'. In common terminology when the **amortization** process is to be used, one says they are going to 'amortize the loan'. Albeit a scary translation the phrase 'to amortize' means 'to die'. I suppose the terminology came about because the amount of interest being paid each month from the fixed **AMORTIZED MONTHLY PAYMENT** amount gets less and less. And when the loan ends, it goes away."

"Wow! It really does have an eerie meaning, Dad."

"I'd call it a morbid meaning, myself, Sweetie.

"Let's move on to what might actually be a scary part. That's the math involved. I promised not to be a ghost. I'll go slowly, too."

Amortization Equation

"In practice, the **AMORTIZED MONTHLY PAYMENT** amount is determined by the lender using a specific mathematical equation. It's called the **AMORTIZATION EQUATION**. The lender only gives the borrower the resulting amount. It is very useful and important for the borrower to be able to use that equation, too. Let's call the **AMORTIZED MONTHLY PAYMENT** amount, **MPAYMENT**. Here's the mathematical equation for it."

$$\mathbf{MPAYMENT = (PRINCIPAL\ x\ MRATIO\ x\ (MRATIO + 1)^{TERM})/((MRATIO + 1)^{TERM} - 1)}$$

"Holy cow! I can see why a lender does not show it to anyone and only gives the result."

"It does look a bit intimidating, Nicole. Nonetheless, I'll show you how to use it. I'll make it more palatable by applying it step-by-step."

"Hopefully you can use baby steps, Dad."

"That's my intention, Peanut.

"Looking at the right side of the equal sign, you see three words: **PRINCIPAL**, **MRATIO** and **TERM**. They are called the 'variables' in the equation. To use the **AMORTIZATION EQUATION** one needs to specify their numerical values.

"Dad, I'm familiar with what is meant by the variables in the equation. I just had that in my algebra class."

"Ok, I figured you probably were.

"In this case, **PRINCIPAL** is the financial terminology for the amount of money to be borrowed. It's what I called the **LOAN AMOUNT** before. **MRATIO** is the **MONTHLY RATE OF INTEREST** in ratio form. **TERM** is the agreed-to number of months to pay off the loan. In other words, these variables are the main numerical terms of the loan."

"Ok, I understand that part."

"That's good. The equation for **MPAYMENT** is more readily used if written in another way."

$$\textbf{MPAYMENT} = \textbf{NUMERATOR/DENOMINATOR}$$

where

$$\textbf{NUMERATOR} = \textbf{PRINCIPAL} \times \textbf{MRATIO} \times (\textbf{MRATIO} + 1)^{\textbf{TERM}}$$

and

$$\textbf{DENOMINATOR} = (\textbf{MRATIO} + 1)^{\textbf{TERM}} - 1$$

"It does look a little less intimidating Dad but not by much."

"That's true. This only breaks it into two main calculations. The ease of the actual sequence of calculations is best illustrated by a numerical example. Let me do that using another imaginary actor to keep it interesting. To start we'll make the loan terms the same as for our prior Melissa."

Calculation Process

SITUATION 2

"Consider a young man named Ron. He needs to take out a loan from a bank to pay for a set of pots and pans. He needs $1200.00 and wants to repay it over a period of one year.

"Based on Ron's very good credit and current loan rates, his bank agrees to amortize the loan and offers him the loan at an **ANNUAL RATE OF INTEREST** of 6.00%. The loan officer indicates that the **AMORTIZED MONTHLY PAYMENT** amount will be \$103.28. He obtained the amount by using computer software. Let's confirm that ourselves by using a calculator.

"I've already done the actual calculations. Let's look at them step by step."

MONTHLY RATE OF INTEREST = 6.00%/12 months
= 0.50%/month

MRATIO = 0.50/100 = 0.0050

TERM = 1 year x 12 months/year = 12 months

$$\textbf{(MRATIO + 1)}^{\textbf{TERM}} = (1+0.0050)^{12} = (1.0050)^{12}$$
= (1.0050)(1.0050)(1.0050)... twelve times!
= 1.0617 = 1.06 (rounded)

NUMERATOR = PRINCIPAL x MRATIO x (MRATIO + 1)TERM
= 1200.00 x 0.0050 x 1.06 = 6.00 x 1.06
= 6.36

$$\textbf{DENOMINATOR} = \textbf{(MRATIO+1)}^{\textbf{TERM}} - 1 = 1.06 - 1 = 0.06$$

MPAYMENT = NUMERATOR/DENOMINATOR = 6.36/0.06 = \$106.00

SITUATION 2 - CONTINUED

"Do you follow my calculations?"

"Everything, except the calculation using the **TERM**, is easy, Dad. I know that the number 12 is an **exponent**. It means that 1.0050 is being raised to a power of 12. And that means multiplying 1.0050 times itself twelve times. At least those are the type of words I remember my teacher used back when I learned it. We used our calculator to raise a number to a power of 2 or to a power of 3. We just multiplied the number two or three times but never twelve times. That takes a while and I probably would make mistakes."

"Calculations involving exponents require the use of a scientific calculator of the type used by high school students or via smart phones with such a calculator capability. You probably were taught to use functions on a calculator. Maybe you just don't do it often or forgot?"

"Yeah, you're right Dad. I have my smart phone. Can you remind me how to do it?"

"Go to the calculator on your phone."

"Ok. Now what?"

"Turn your phone horizontally."

"Why, Dad?"

"You need to do that to get to a scientific calculator."

After doing so Nicole excitedly says, "Wow, I didn't know I had one on my smart phone. It's great to know that and how to find it."

"It's great I could show my teen how to do something on a smart phone."

"Now, can you find the function y^x?"

"I have it."

"Ok on your keypad, enter 1.0050, then select y^x, then enter 12 to get 1.061677..."

"Got it!"

"In my calculations I first showed it rounded to 1.0617. Then I rounded that to 1.06.

"Ok, now what about the final result of $106.00? It's not the $103.28 that the bank officer stated to Ron is it?"

"I noticed that. What's wrong?"

"Actually, nothing's wrong. As I went along in my calculator, I rounded some of the numbers. A bank officer's software would not round off numbers so roughly.

"I recalculated the results using a consistent round-off pattern of four decimal places. Here are the revised results."

MONTHLY RATE OF INTEREST = 6.00%/12 months
= 0.5000%/month

MRATIO = 0.50/100 = 0.0050

TERM = 1 year x 12 months/year = 12 months

(MRATIO + 1)TERM = (1+0.0050)12 = $(1.0050)^{12}$
= (1.0050)(1.0050)(1.0050)... twelve times!
= 1.0617

NUMERATOR = PRINCIPAL x MRATIO x $(\text{MRATIO} + 1)^{\text{TERM}}$
= 1200.00 x 0.0050 x 1.0617 = 6.00 x 1.0617
= 6.3702

DENOMINATOR = $(\text{MRATIO}+1)^{\text{TERM}}$ – 1 =1.0617 – 1 = 0.0617

MPAYMENT = NUMERATOR/DENOMINATOR = 6.3702/0.0617= \$103.24

SITUATION 2 – CONTINUED

"The answer of \$103.24 is very close to the bank loan officer's result. It's only off by \$0.04. When I increased the round-off to 5 decimal places, I got these results."

$(\text{MRATIO} + 1)^{\text{TERM}} = (1+0.0050)^{12}$
= (1.0050)(1.0050)(1.0050)…twelve times!
= 1.06167781 = 1.06168

NUMERATOR = 1200.00 x 0.0050 x 1.06168 = 6.37008

DENOMINATOR = $(\text{MRATIO}+1)^{\text{TERM}}$ – 1 = 1.06168 – 1 = 0.06168

MPAYMENT = NUMERATOR/DENOMINATOR = 6.37008/0.06168
= \$103.27827 = \$103.28

SITUATION 2 - CONTINUED

"Bingo! Now we have the loan officer's result exactly.

"The approximate value based on rounded numbers is \$2.72 higher than the precise value."

"Dad, it's sort of tedious and anal to use so many decimal places. Isn't it?"

"Sure is! That's not my intent. Nobody would keypunch numbers to that many places. It would drive them bananas. I used my computer and got them.

"The main reason to calculate it yourself, using very rounded numbers like I did, is to roughly know the **AMORTIZED MONTHLY PAYMENT** before you go to the lender. That way you know beforehand if you can afford it or not. In this case the \$106.00 is close enough to know that. If you grin and bear it through more decimal places you get closer, but it's a waste of time. Or you can use a computer to do it.

"These days you can even find an app to get the precise result. Without my lesson you would be getting it blindly. The same dilemma exists. Can you trust the result of an app? Chances are you will want confirm it too, at least the first few times."

"Dad, I didn't think you even knew about apps."

"Surprise, surprise! I do, but having a whole bunch of those to access just drives me crazy. So I leave those to you young people. As time goes on you can teach dear old Dad more about them. As I said before, mainly I want you to know how the value is manually calculated. If you do that you begin to be confident the computer and/or app result is correct.

"More important, I want you to get into the habit of always wanting to know how money-related calculations are actually done. Once you do then the computer is standing by to save you time. The rub is you have to be able to make it do that. In time you'll learn that in school. As for apps it's a total act of faith to use them. By first doing things manually and comparing, you can take that leap of faith knowing there's a safety net in place."

"When we talked about general loans, a **LOAN AMOUNT** or **PRINCIPAL** of $1200.00 and an **ANNUAL RATE OF INTEREST** of 6.00% were also used. The **SCHEDULED MONTHLY PAYMENT** used was $100.00.

"For our Ron's loan, the **AMORTIZED MONTHLY PAYMENT** value is $103.28, which is similar to the $100.00. Again, a portion of it is applied to pay the interest owed. The rest of it is applied to reduce the amount of money owed. That's why it is a bit higher than $100.00. Let me illustrate the contrasting computations of the sequence of payments involved in the **amortization** process."

SITUATION 2 - CONTINUED

"Let's say that the entire funds for Ron's loan are disbursed on the first day of a month. The first **AMORTIZED MONTHLY PAYMENT** is due on the first day of the next month and subsequent payments are due on the first day of each month thereafter. There is a five-day grace period.

"The loan papers are signed. The money is disbursed and the payments ensue. Ron makes every payment on time. The grace period does not come into play. Let's trace the first two monthly outcomes."

For Month 1:

PRINCIPAL = $1200.00.

MONTHLY INTEREST owed = 0.50% of $1200 = 0.0050 x $1200.00 = $6.00

AMORTIZED MONTHLY PAYMENT = $103.28 is paid on time.

Portion APPLIED TO INTEREST = $6.00

Portion APPLIED TO PRINCIPAL = $103.28 - $6.00 = $97.28

OUTSTANDING PRINCIPAL = $1200.00 - $97.28 = $1102.72

For Month 2:

MONTHLY INTEREST owed = 0.50% of $1102.72 = 0.0050 x $1102.72 = $5.51

AMORTIZED MONTHLY PAYMENT = $103.28 is paid on time.

Portion APPLIED TO INTEREST = $5.51

Portion APPLIED TO PRINCIPAL = $103.28 - $5.51 = $97.77

OUTSTANDING PRINCIPAL = $1102.72 - $97.77 = $1004.95

SITUATION 2 - CONTINUED

"Do you follow this sequence of calculations?"

"Some of the names of terms are different, but I see what's happening. The **OUTSTANDING PRINCIPAL** is like what you called the **OUTSTANDING BALANCE** before. Like it, the **OUTSTANDING PRINCIPAL** gets lower each month. Why are different names used?"

"It's because, in amortized loans from a lender like a bank, they call the **LOAN AMOUNT** the **PRINCIPAL** and then say the amount of **PRINCIPAL** owed is declining. The amount currently owed is the **OUTSTANDING PRINCIPAL**. It's sort of standard wording.

"Did you notice the amount of **MONTHLY INTEREST** is lower in Month 2 compared to Month 1? Why is that?"

"I did notice that. It's because the money owed in Month 2 is less than the amount owed in Month 1."

"Yes, that's correct. What happened to the portions of the **AMORTIZED MONTHLY PAYMENT**?"

"I see the portion **APPLIED TO INTEREST** got lower and the portion **APPLIED TO PRINCIPAL** got higher."

"Exactly, that's the key feature of the amortization process. It happens each month. Let's look at the next month."

For Month 3:

MONTHLY INTEREST owed = 0.50% of $1004.95 = 0.0050 x $1004.95 = $5.02

AMORTIZED MONTHLY PAYMENT = $103.28 is paid on time.

Portion APPLIED TO INTEREST = $5.02

Portion APPLIED TO PRINCIPAL = $103.28 - $5.02 = $98.26

OUTSTANDING PRINCIPAL = $1004.95 - $98.26 = $906.69

SITUATION 2 - CONTINUED

"I see the trend now Dad."

"That's good. This continues for nine more months. Here are the rest of the results."

The AMORTIZED MONTHLY PAYMENT remains $103.28.

The sequence of portion APPLIED TO INTEREST, portion APPLIED TO PRINCIPAL, and OUTSTANDING PRINCIPAL amounts will be:

Month 4: $4.53, 98.75 and $807.95; Month 5: $4.04, $99.24 and $708.71**; Month 6: $3.54, $99.74, and $608.98;** Month 7: $3.04, $100.23 and $508.74**; Month 8: $2.54, $100.74 and $408.01;** Month 9: $2.04, $101.24 and $306.77**; Month 10: $1.53, $101.75 and 205.02;**Month 11: $1.03, $102.25 and $102.77**; and Month 12: $0.51, $102.77 and $0.00.**

SITUATION 2 - CONTINUED

"For homework, you can confirm these results. Because, I'm sure you would do it correctly, it's voluntary, too."

"I'm pretty sure I would, Dad. If I find the time, then I might do it anyway."

"At the end of Month 12 the loan has been paid off. The **TOTAL INTEREST** paid = $6.00 + $5.51 + … + $0.51 = $39.36. The original signed loan agreement would be returned to Ron by the bank and he could 'tear it up'. He is excited to be done with his payments, almost jumping with joy. It is best that Ron not 'tear it up' until the document is no longer needed for either legal reasons or possible tax considerations."

"I'm sure I would enjoy 'tearing it up' too, Dad."

"These results confirm my earlier general statement about an amortized loan payment process getting you out of debt faster and faster! As you observed, the portion of the fixed **AMORTIZED MONTHLY PAYMENT** that was **APPLIED TO PRINCIPAL** got larger and larger each month; starting at $97.28 in Month 1 and gradually increasing each month to being $102.77 at the end of Month 12.

"To reiterate, for Melissa's loan the **SCHEDULED MONTHLY PAYMENT** was $100.00 and the portion applied to reduce the **OUTSTANDING BALANCE** was the <u>entire</u> amount! Each of the twelve payments was actually greater than each of the corresponding portions of the $103.28 payments **APPLIED TO PRINCIPAL** involved in the amortization process. For example, for Month 1, $100.00 is greater than $97.28. However, the **MONTHLY INTEREST** charged on the **OUTSTANDING BALANCE** was <u>additional</u> to those $100.00 payments. When the loan ended the **TOTAL INTEREST** paid was $39.00."

"Well, Nicole, I hope I eased you through the edgy math gently. Once the **AMORTIZED MONTHLY PAYMENT** amount, **MPAYMENT**, is known, the computations of monthly changes to **PRINCIPAL** are repetitious and comprised of ordinary multiplication and subtraction operations."

"Actually it was fairly painless, unless I decide to try that voluntary homework."

Amortization Schedule

"Again, it isn't necessary for the borrower to do the math. The lender does it all. Detailed results are provided in the loan documents to be signed the bank. They are organized into what is called the **AMORTIZATION SCHEDULE** for the loan. An ability to do that math yourself is vital to being knowledgeable enough to confirm or to check the entries in the **AMORTIZATION SCHEDULE**. It also allows you to independently calculate different loan option scenarios before actually beginning to seek a loan. Then you can compare options, assess affordability, and choose the best option."

"Ok, Dad. Now you've got me curious about what an **AMORTIZATION SCHEDULE** looks like."

"I'm glad your curiosity is peaked once again. My next part was to do exactly that. With those merits in mind, let's look at the process again as it would be provided by a lender in the **AMORTIZATION SCHEDULE** format.

Loan Terms: PRINCIPAL: $1200.00, 6.00% ANNUAL RATE OF INTEREST (0.50% monthly), TERM: 12 months.

AMORTIZATION SCHEDULE:

							Principal = $1200.00	
Term in Years	Annual Rate of Interest	Month	Amortized Monthly Payment	Applied to Interest	Applied to Principal		Outstanding Principal	Cumulative Interest
1	6.00	1	103.28	6.00	97.28		1102.72	6.00
		2	103.28	5.51	97.77		1004.95	11.51
		3	103.28	5.02	98.25		906.70	16.54
		4	103.28	4.53	98.75		807.95	21.07
		5	103.28	4.04	99.24		708.71	25.11
		6	103.28	3.54	99.74		608.98	28.66
		7	103.28	3.04	100.23		508.74	31.70
		8	103.28	2.54	100.74		408.01	34.24
		9	103.28	2.04	101.24		306.77	36.28
		10	103.28	1.53	101.75		205.02	37.82
		11	103.28	1.03	102.25		102.77	38.84
		12	103.28	0.51	102.77		0.00	39.36

SITUATION 2 - CONTINUED

"For each month the **AMORTIZED MONTHLY PAYMENT** is $103.28. It's called that because it is assumed the full scheduled amount will be made. For Month 1, the listed portion **APPLIED TO INTEREST** is $6.00 and the remaining $97.28 is the listed portion **APPLIED TO PRINCIPAL** by the bank to reduce the **OUTSTANDING PRINCIPAL** to $1102.72. Those are the values I calculated before. The narrow seventh column will be needed later, but for now it is void.

"In Month 2 the listed **OUTSTANDING PRINCIPAL** of $1102.72 for Month 1 is used to compute the $5.51 listed as the portion **APPLIED TO INTEREST**. The remaining $97.77 is the listed portion **APPLIED TO PRINCIPAL**. It reduces the **OUTSTANDING PRINCIPAL** to $1004.95. The **CUMULATIVE INTEREST** listed in the rightmost column is a running total of the interest paid as it accumulates each month. After Month 2 it is $6.00 + $5.51 = $11.51. After twelve months it is the $39.36. Those are the values I calculated before.

"The next ten lines of the **AMORTIZATION SCHEDULE** follow by repetition. Do you follow them?"

"I sure do, Dad. If you had not shown me the manual calculations and I had only gotten this table, then I would have been really scratching my head."

"Probably so, Sweetie. That's why I did it.

"The tabulated results were done by computer using very precise calculations. If you check all the numbers you may see very slight, insignificant differences values compared to the results you get if you use rounding throughout.

"Let's look at the results if the approximate **AMORTIZED MONTHLY PAYMENT** value of $106.00 is used."

AMORTIZATION SCHEDULE:

							Principal = $1200.00	
Term in Years	Annual Rate of Interest	Month	Amortized Monthly Payment	Applied to Interest	Principal		Outstanding Principal	Cumulative Interest
1	6.00	1	106.00	6.00	100.00		1100.00	6.00
		2	106.00	5.50	100.50		999.50	11.50
		3	106.00	5.00	101.00		898.50	16.50
		4	106.00	4.49	101.51		796.99	20.99
		5	106.00	3.98	102.02		694.97	24.97
		6	106.00	3.47	102.53		592.45	28.45
		7	106.00	2.96	103.04		489.41	31.41
		8	106.00	2.45	103.55		385.86	33.86
		9	106.00	1.93	104.07		281.79	35.79
		10	106.00	1.41	104.59		177.20	37.20
		11	106.00	0.89	105.11		72.08	38.08
		12	106.00	0.36	105.64		-33.56	38.44
		12	*72.44*	*0.36*	*72.08*		*0.00*	*38.44*

SITUATION 2 - CONTINUED

"As the **AMORTIZED MONTHLY PAYMENT** is $2.72 per month higher than the precise bank value two things occurred.

"First, the last month results in a $33.56 overpayment. That's because $2.72 per month more was being than required; i.e. $2.72/month x 12 months = $32.64 in total. The $33.56 results because the all monthly values in the table were rounded to two decimal places.

"The bank would adjust the last **AMORTIZED MONTHLY PAYMENT** to equal the preceding **OUTSTANDING PRINCIPAL** plus the **MONTHLY INTEREST** on that amount, that is to $72.08 + 0.0050 x $72.08 = $72.08 + $0.36 = $72.44. I added the adjusted line to the **AMORTIZATION SCHEDULE** in italics.

"Is this all clear, the flow of the numbers and the adjustment for Month 12?"

"Yes, it's all just slightly different numbers from the precise answers. And the adjustment makes sense to me."

"The second thing to notice is that the **CUMULATIVE INTEREST** paid is $38.08 + $0.36 = $38.44 which is $0.54 less than the precise result."

"What's do these results suggest to you, Nicole?"

"You made your point, Dad. I can see that I don't have to make it tedious and anal by using a whole lot of decimal places manually to get **AMORTIZED MONTHLY PAYMENT**. Once I learn how to do an **AMORTIZATION SCHEDULE** by computer, I won't have to worry about it."

"It seems that way, Peanut.

'Ok, why don't I give you some homework to try?"

"Is it voluntary?"

"Sorry, but it is very important for you to know how to calculate amortized loan repayment. I've written it as an Exercise. To reduce the amount of pencils, I am giving you some partial results as well. That way you don't have to do a complete **AMORTIZATION SCHEDULE**. You can manually check any or all of the partial results and, then, fill in the missing numbers along the way"

Exercise 3: *For Ron's loan, calculate the* ***AMORTIZED MONTHLY PAYMENT*** *amount using a consistent rounding to two significant decimal places. Then produce the* ***AMORTIZATION SCHEDULE*** *using that value.*

Your <u>partial</u> results should be:

MRATIO = 0.01

MPAYMENT = NUMERATOR/DENOMINATOR = 13.56/0.13
= $104.31 (rounded)

AMORTIZATION SCHEDULE:

							Principal = $1200.00	
Term in Years	*Annual Rate of Interest*	*Month*	AMORTIZED *MONTHLY PAYMENT*	*Applied to Interest*	*Principal*		*Outstanding Principal*	*Cumulative Interest*
1	*6.00*	*1*	*104.31*	*6.00*	*98.31*		*1101.69*	*6.00*
		2	*104.31*	*5.51*	*98.80*		*1002.89*	*11.51*
		3		*5.01*	*99.30*			*16.52*
		4	*104.31*	*4.52*	*99.79*		*803.80*	*21.04*
		5	*104.31*				*703.51*	*25.06*
		6	*104.31*	*3.52*	*100.79*		*602.72*	*28.58*
		7	*104.31*	*3.01*	*101.30*		*501.42*	*31.59*
		8	*104.31*	*2.51*	*101.80*			
		9	*104.31*	*2.00*	*102.31*		*297.31*	*36.10*
		10						*37.58*
		11	*104.31*	*0.97*	*103.34*		*91.15*	
		12	*104.31*	*0.46*	*103.85*		*-12.71*	*39.01*
		12	*91.60*	*0.46*	*91.14*		*0.00*	*39.01*

"In case you want more homework, here are some additional exercises. They are voluntary. Again, I've given you most of the results."

Exercise 3A: *For Ron's loan in Exercise 3, calculate the **AMORTIZED MONTHLY PAYMENT** amount using and an **ANNUAL RATE OF INTEREST** of 12.00% and rounding to two decimal places. Then produce the **AMORTIZATION SCHEDULE** using that value.*

Your partial results should be:

MPAYMENT = NUMERATOR/DENOMINATOR = 13.56/0.13
= $104.31 (rounded)

***Alert**: As a consequence of using only two decimal places in the calculations the result for the **MPAYMENT** is the same as for an **ANNUAL RATE OF INTEREST** of 6.00%. However, the **AMORTIZATION SCHEDULE** is entirely different.*

AMORTIZATION SCHEDULE:

							Principal = $1200.00	
Term in Years	Annual Rate of Interest	Month	AMORTIZED MONTHLY PAYMENT	Applied to Interest	Principal		Outstanding Principal	Cumulative Interest
1	12.00	1	104.31	12.00	92.31		1107.69	12.00
		2	104.31	11.08	93.23		1014.46	23.08
		3	104.31	10.14	94.17		920.29	33.22
		4						42.42
		5						50.68
		6	104.31	7.29	97.02		632.11	57.97
		7	104.31	6.32	97.99		534.12	64.29
		8	104.31	5.34	98.97		435.15	69.63
		9						73.98
		10						77.33
		11	104.31	2.34	101.97		132.27	79.68
		12	104.31	1.32	102.99		29.28	81.00
		13	104.31	0.29	104.02		-74.74	81.29
		13	29.57	0.29	29.28		0.00	81.29

Observation: *Although the **AMORTIZED MONTHLY PAYMENT** is only slightly different than for the **ANNUAL RATE OF INTEREST** of 6.00% in Situation 2 and Exercise 2 the **CUMULATIVE INTEREST** is about doubled. That's due to the portion **APPLIED TO INTEREST** being about twice as much.*

Exercise 3B: *For Ron's loan in Exercise 3A, produce the **AMORTIZATION SCHEDULE** using the precise value of $106.62 for the **AMORTIZED MONTHLY PAYMENT**.*

Your <u>partial</u> results should be:

AMORTIZATION SCHEDULE:

							Principal = $1200.00	
Term in Years	Annual Rate of Interest	Month	AMORTIZED MONTHLY PAYMENT	Applied to Interest	Principal		Outstanding Principal	Cumulative Interest
1	12.00	1	106.62	12.00	94.62		1105.38	12.00
		2	106.62	11.05	95.56		1009.82	23.05
		3	106.62	10.10	96.52		913.30	33.15
		4						42.28
		5						50.44
		6	106.62	7.17	99.45		617.91	57.62

7	*106.62*	*6.18*	*100.44*		*517.47*	*63.80*
8						*68.97*
9						*73.13*
10	*106.62*	*3.14*	*103.48*		*210.08*	*76.27*
11	*106.62*	*2.10*	*104.52*		*105.56*	*78.37*
12	*106.62*	*1.06*	*105.56*		*0.00*	*79.42*

***Observation**: The **CUMULATIVE INTEREST** of $81.29 for the approximate **AMORTIZED MONTHLY PAYMENT** in Exercise 3A is only $2.81 higher than the precise result of $79.42.*

"Well, Peanut, does that tell you enough about **amortization**?"

"It's plenty enough and I'm glad some of the exercises are voluntary. I'll try the first one for sure. If I can manage the time and pencils, I'll try the other ones, too."

"Do you have any other curiosities?"

"Nothing I can think of right now. Maybe later something will hit me."

"Ok. Let me leave you with one to think about. What would happen if each month you paid more than the **AMORTIZED MONTHLY PAYMENT**? I do not want a reply from you right now. It's called **acceleration** of the loan repayment. It's a very important topic, We should discuss it at next time."

"After trying your homework, I'll think on that one. Since we're still totally snowed in and I am on school break, how about tomorrow?"

"That's fine with me. I can get some things ready."

LESSON 3 Acceleration = Getting There Faster and Faster and Faster!

Nicole is up and already waiting in her Dad's office. She actually did her Dad's homework and can't wait to tell him she got all the same answers. Beaming as her Dad comes in, she proudly exclaims, "Hi Dad! Guess what, I got all the way through your exercises. There were some tricky parts I had to work through a few times. It took a while, but I kept getting the correct answers and it made me charge right along. I can show you all of it. I have the papers with me."

"That's terrific, Nicole. I'll look it all over closely later and undoubtedly put my big A+ on it."

"Maybe I'll show that to my Physics teacher to put a sub-conscious prompt in her mind to do the same when she gives me her grade."

"I'm pretty sure you won't have to do that and will still get that A+, Smarty Pants.

"Now, I'm ready to go and looking forward to explaining the process and effects of **accelerating** loan repayment. You seem to be raring to go, too."

"I am, Dad. It sounds a lot more interesting than that **amortization** stuff."

"Actually, you haven't escaped that entirely, Nicole. I'll be using it today, too. You're A+ tells me it will go just fine. Before I do that, and in order to understand how that works, you need to know what the word **acceleration** means. To do that I want to describe something you will study in Physics."

"That's sound neat. I'm in already in Physics class at school. It's kind of a challenge but I find it interesting to learn how some things we take for granted work. Like why a helium-filled balloon wants to float away."

"Oh, that's good. Have you studied the behavior of moving objects?"

"Not yet, I think we're doing that soon."

"Well, Nicole, when you reach that point your teacher will explain the concepts of velocity and acceleration. You'll learn about them in detail, but that can wait. What I'll do is illustrate their meaning in simple terms using an everyday example."

"Ok. It will be new to me but I'll do my best to follow."

What's Acceleration?

"Nicole, we've all felt the thrill and/or fright of pressing the gas pedal of our car to the floor. The driver feels an exhilarating sensation as the pedal is pressed down and the car surges forward faster and faster. If you press it all the way too quickly you pick up speed really fast. Hopefully, you're not doing that."

"No, Dad. I drive very carefully."

"It's great that you do drive safely. Let's look at why a car speeds up.

"When you're pressing the car's peddle you are actually pushing on an accelerator. The result is the gas gets into the engine faster and faster. The car begins to move and pick up speed. We say it begins to accelerate. That's why we call the accelerator by that name. But, I don't want to discuss the details of auto parts, Sweetie. I want to explain the resulting movement of the car."

"I'm not ready for a lesson on car parts either, Dad. I just began driving one a few months ago and am far from being a mechanic."

"Don't worry Sweetie, so am I. In simple terms, the car is gaining speed over time. Initially the car is moving at zero miles per hour and in a few seconds it is moving at some velocity. Velocity is physicist's term for speed, the rate at which the car moves. In common words, as you push on the accelerator the car is picking up speed.

"Let's say the speed of the car increases from a speed of 0 miles per hour to a speed of 60 miles per hour and it takes 10 seconds to do that. The speed of the car was increasing at an average rate of 6 miles per hour each second. That physical phenomenon is called acceleration. In simple terms, the speed is getting <u>faster</u> each second. Following me?"

"The 'miles per hour each second' is a little fuzzy, Dad."

"Let me say it another way. If, for each second, the speed increases by the same amount than it did in the previous second, then a physicist would say the acceleration is constant. For every second it is accelerating, the car gains 6 miles per hour in the speed at which it is moving. In 1 second the car is moving 6 miles per hour; in 2 seconds the car is moving at 12 miles per hour; in 3 seconds it is moving at 18 miles per hour; and so on."

"That's clearer."

"Great, Sweetie. Because the car is getting faster by the same amount each second, its speed is said to be increasing 'linearly'. Let's instead say the speed of the car increases from 0 miles per hour to 0.5 miles per hour after 1 second, then to 2 miles per hour after 2 seconds, then to 5 miles per hour after 3 seconds, and so on. As time passes the speed is getting faster but is also doing it faster each second! For this circumstance the acceleration is not constant, not linear. Compared to linear acceleration for which the speed is getting <u>faster</u> each second, in this case the speed of the car is getting <u>faster and faster</u> each second. A physicist would say its speed is increasing 'nonlinearly'."

"Whew! That linear and nonlinear stuff goes over my head, Dad."

"I'm not surprised it does. Let's look at it visually. I made some plots that show it."

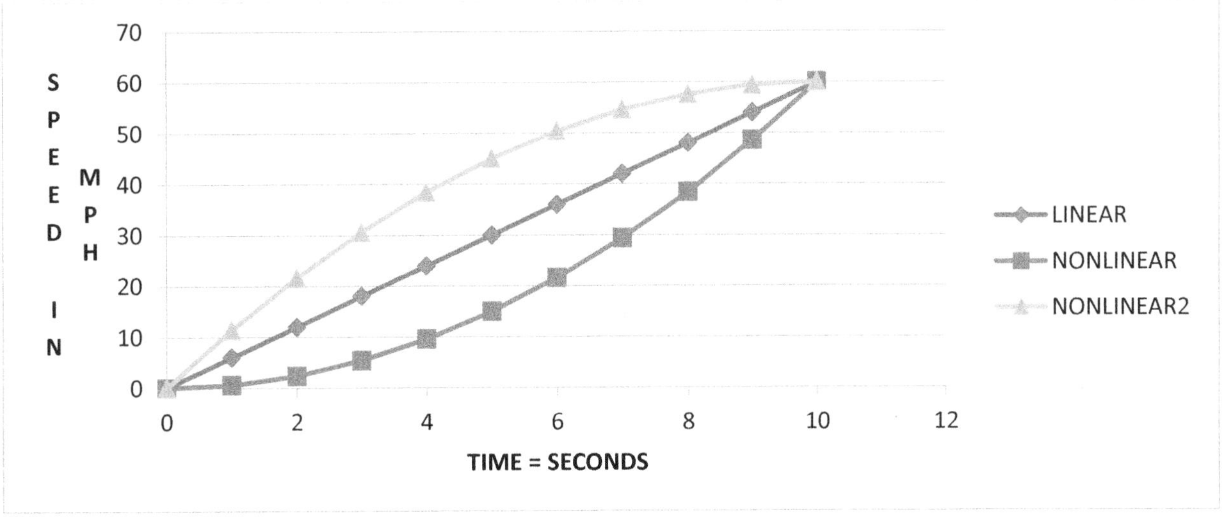

"Two of the plots are based on the numbers I described. The straight line is for the linear changes in speed. The upward curvy line is for the nonlinear changes in speed. The downward curvy line is for another possible nonlinear speed pattern leading to the same end result.

"How's this all look to you, Nicole."

"It helps a lot to see it graphically, Dad. So, there are different ways to get the car up to 60 miles per hour?"

"Exactly, Peanut. It all depends on how you press the pedal. For our purposes, the three I have shown will do.

"And there is a more important thing that happens. It's neither felt nor noticed. The distance the car travels increases even faster than its speed. During each second it will travel a greater distance than the one before. That's how a race driver catches up with a car ahead of him or her that is not accelerating as fast.

"I won't go into the physics and math of how to calculate it, Sweetie. I'll leave that as a subject for your teacher. I calculated it for the car accelerating at a constant 6 miles per hour per second. During the first second: the car travels 4 feet; during the next second it travels another 13 feet; during the third second it travels another 22 feet; during the fourth second it travels another 31 feet and; and so on. After 4 seconds it will have traveled a total of 70 feet. After 10 seconds it will have traveled a total of 440 feet!

"My main point is that in each second, the car has moved by a different and higher amount. I've done a plot of the distance the car is traveling in 10 seconds."

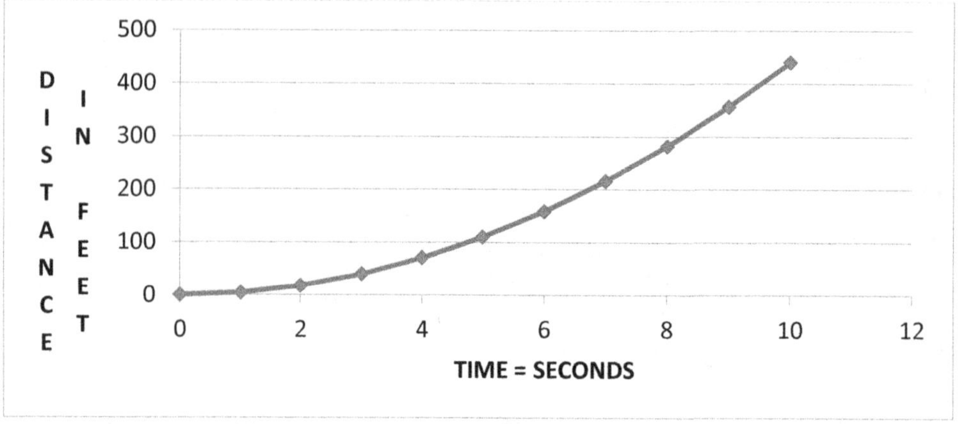

"Do you understand the plot?"

"I do, Dad. It's nonlinear."

"Indeed it is Smarty Pants. That means it is getting to its destination 'faster and faster and faster'."

"Now consider the accelerating car as you getting into debt. The feeling of rapidity is there, but not the exhilaration. If, instead, you're getting out of debt, then it is exhilarating. That's what accelerating repayment of your debt accomplishes. You are paying it off faster and faster and faster! As a result the debt ends sooner than the **TERM** of the loan. It will save you money. The more you accelerate, the more you will save. That's a much more exhilarating sensation than speeding up a car's movement!

"Have I explained the analogy well enough for you?"

"Dad, I do generally get the physics of the car aspects. I'll wait to learn more about it from my teacher. At least I have a leg up on it. I don't get a feeling for how you apply it to loan repayment. And why will it save me money?"

"You do that by paying an extra amount above the **AMORTIZED MONTHLY PAYMENT** each month. You add as much as possible and consistently do it. One way to do that is to take any cash that is burning a hole in your wallet and pocket and use some of it to pay that extra amount. It saves you money because each month the **OUTSTANDING PRINCIPAL** is getting smaller by a larger amount than if you did not pay the extra amount. Since the **MONTHLY INTEREST** is charged on it, those amounts will also be smaller each month. You'll see that when I show you a numerical example.

"Now let's monetarily examine how to accomplish acceleration of loan repayment and the benefits of doing so. It can be done for any kind of loan, but let's look at it for an amortized loan."

With a smirk on her face, Nicole grimaces, "At least you've warned me that was coming."

Acceleration of Amortized Debt Repayment

"With an amortized loan, a <u>fixed</u> **AMORTIZED MONTHLY PAYMENT** amount is established. Indeed, for such loans the loan is already being paid off faster and faster. That's because the amount of the **AMORTIZED MONTHLY PAYMENT** that is **APPLIED TO INTEREST** gets lower and lower each month, resulting in the amount that is **AMOUNT APPLIED TO PRINCIPAL** getting higher and higher each month. Do you remember that from last Thursday, Sweetie?"

"Yes, it's still in my mind, Dad."

"In the context of acceleration of loan repayment, the **AMORTIZED MONTHLY PAYMENT** is 'fixed' only in the sense that the amount is the same each month. It does not mean one cannot pay more than that amount.

"Essentially, the **AMORTIZED MONTHLY PAYMENT** is the 'minimum' amount due each month. If the terms of the amortized loan permit it, then the borrower can pay any amount above the minimum payment each month. Doing that accelerates the repayment. Indeed, if the terms of the loan permit it, then the entire **OUTSTANDING PRINCIPAL** can be paid off in full at any time."

"Dad, you said that 'if' they let me do it I can accelerate the repayment of an amortized loan? Why wouldn't they let me?"

"It's not a very common step, but the lender might want to have the loan in place for a satisfactory length of time to collect more interest on it. The lender might want to collect enough interest to justify the time and effort and cost of making the loan in the first place. An extreme is someone borrows money for several years, but pays it back in one month. The lender might want to prevent that."

"That kind of makes sense Dad."

"Good, Nicole. The qualifier 'if the terms of the loan permit it' is very important. One should assure oneself that such terms exist before accepting the loan. It is important to have a clause present that allows one to 'prepay the loan in full, without any prepayment penalty'. If the loan is for buying a home, then it is especially critical and crucial. Otherwise, selling the property in order to move to another home has a financial constraint to overcome before it can be down. The severity of the constraint depends upon the specific prepayment penalty clause in the terms of the loan. However, home buying is well down the road for you."

"It sure is Dad. I'll try to remember that when that day comes."

"When it does come, I'll be around to help you go about it. You just have to ask me, Sweetie."

"I'm pretty darn sure I will want to do that, Dad."

"Ok, now let me further illustrate the concept of accelerating the repayment of an amortized loan by reexamining a SITUATION we looked at previously."

SITUATION 3

"Let's return to SITUATION 2 of Ron taking out an amortized loan from a bank for $1200.00, for a **TERM** of 1 year, at an **ANNUAL RATE OF INTEREST** of 12.00%. You solved that one for homework. The **AMORTIZED MONTHLY PAYMENT** amount was $106.62. The resulting **CUMULATIVE INTEREST** was $79.42. It took one year to pay off the loan.

"Assume that Ron receives a pay increase at his job and can afford to pay $145.00 per month. Here's the resulting **AMORTIZATION SCHEDULE.**"

							Principal = $1200.00	
Term in Years	**Annual Rate of Interest**	**Month**	**Amortized Monthly Payment**	**Applied to Interest**	**Principal**	**Additional Amount Applied to Principal**	**Outstanding Principal**	**Cumulative Interest**
1	12.00	1	**106.62**	**12.00**	**94.62**	**38.38**	**1067.00**	**12.00**
		2	**106.62**	**10.67**	**95.95**	**38.38**	**932.67**	**22.67**
		3	**106.62**	**9.33**	**97.29**	**38.38**	**797.00**	**32.00**
		4	**106.62**	**7.97**	**98.65**	**38.38**	**659.97**	**39.97**
		5	**106.62**	**6.60**	**100.02**	**38.38**	**521.57**	**46.57**
		6	**106.62**	**5.22**	**101.40**	**38.38**	**381.79**	**51.78**
		7	**106.62**	**3.82**	**102.80**	**38.38**	**240.61**	**55.60**
		8	**106.62**	**2.41**	**104.21**	**38.38**	**98.02**	**58.01**
		9	**106.62**	**0.98**	**105.64**	**38.38**	**-46.00**	**58.99**
		9	***99.00***	***0.98***	***98.02***	***0.00***	***0.00***	***58.99***

SITUATION 3 - CONTINUED

"Nicole, notice that the **AMORTIZATION SCHEDULE** has an additional column labeled **ADDITIONAL AMOUNT APPLIED TO PRINCIPAL.** I had that column in before but it was narrow and void of contents. I said it would have a purpose."

"I remember you saying that, Dad. What's it for?"

"The difference between the actual monthly **AMOUNT PAID** and the **AMORTIZED MONTHLY PAYMENT** is entered in that column. That difference is $145.00 – $106.62 = $38.38. As the **MONTHLY INTEREST** amount due has been met by a portion of the $106.62, this $38.38 is entirely used to further reduce the **PRINCIPAL** due the next month. Do you see that?"

"I understand the point Dad. How does that amount come into the calculations?"

"Let's walk through that for the first two months of the table entries. Ron pays the $145.00 on time each month. Here's the monetary outcome."

For Month 1:

PRINCIPAL = $1200.00.

MONTHLY INTEREST owed = 1.00% of $1200 = 0.01 x $1200.00 = $12.00

AMORTIZED MONTHLY PAYMENT = $106.62

Portion APPLIED TO INTEREST = $12.00

Portion APPLIED TO PRINCIPAL = $106.62 - $12.00 = $94.62

ADDITIONAL AMOUNT APPLIED TO PRINCIPAL = $38.38

OUTSTANDING PRINCIPAL = $1200.00 - $94.62 - $38.38 = $1067.00

For Month 2:

MONTHLY INTEREST owed = 1.0% of $1067.00 = 0.01 x $1067.00 = $10.67

AMORTIZED MONTHLY PAYMENT = $106.62

Portion APPLIED TO INTEREST = $10.67

Portion APPLIED TO PRINCIPAL = $106.62 - $10.67 = $95.95

ADDITIONAL AMOUNT APPLIED TO PRINCIPAL = $38.38

OUTSTANDING PRINCIPAL = $1067.00 - $95.95 - $38.38 = $932.67

SITUATION 3 – CONTINUED

"What's happening in the flow that is different from before, Sweetie?"

"The only difference I notice is that in each month the **OUTSTANDING PRINCIPAL** is being reduced by that $38.88 in addition to the amount from the **AMORTIZED MONTHLY PAYMENT**."

"That's right. Compared to before, will the sequence of **OUTSTANDING PRINCIPALS** be lower or higher amounts?"

"Well Dad, they would all be lower than before?"

"That's right. And what effect does that have on the amounts of **MONTHLY INTEREST** being charged?"

Thinking for a moment, Nicole replies, "Like you explained before, because interest is charged on the lower **OUTSTANDING PRINCIPAL** amounts, the **MONTHLY INTEREST** amounts would all be lower, too."

"That's right, Sweetie. This sequence continues for seven more months, producing the rest of the **AMORTIZATION SCHEDULE**. As a result the **CUMULATIVE INTEREST** paid should be noticeably lower than in the previous example when acceleration was not in play. Let's examine the outcome.

"How long did it take to pay off the loan as compared to before, Peanut?'

"I can see the loan has been paid off after 9 months, instead of a full year. It looks like in Month 9 and adjustment is made to the final payment? I see that because there is an adjusted Month 9 line shown in italics."

"Indeed there is, Nicole. In the original results for Month 9, an overpayment of $46.00 occurred. The last **ADDITIONAL AMOUNT APPLIED TO PRINCIPAL** of $38.38 is not needed. Even with that omitted, the debt is still overpaid by $46.00 - $38.38 = $7.32. The bank would adjust the last payment to be the **OUTSTANDING PRINCIPAL** after Month 8 plus the **MONTHLY INTEREST** due on that amount. That's $99.00, of which only $0.98 is **MONTHLY INTEREST**. The rest of it is $98.02. That's **APPLIED TO PRINCIPAL** and pays off the debt."

"Nicole, at that point what's the amount of **CUMULATIVE INTEREST**?"

"It's $58.89, Dad."

"Right. That amount compares to the **CUMULATIVE INTEREST** of $79.42 when only the **AMORTIZED MONTHLY PAYMENT** of $106.62 was paid.

"While the dollar amounts involved are small, the relative benefit is clearly evident. By paying an extra $38.38 each month, Ron reduced the time to pay off the loan by three months and the **CUMULATIVE INTEREST** by $79.42 - $58.89 = $20.53. That's a reduction of $20.53/$79.42 x 100 = 25.84%. It's exhilarating to reduce the cost of a loan debt by nearly 26%."

"It sure is Dad."

Exercise 4: Ron of SITUATION 3 is able to pay $60.00 as an ADDITIONAL AMOUNT APPLIED TO PRINCIPAL. Calculate the first three lines and the last line of the AMORTIZATION SCHEDULE.

Your partial results should be:

Term in Years	*Annual Rate of Interest*	*Month*	*Amortized Monthly Payment*	*Applied to Interest*	*Applied to Principal*	*Additional Amount Applied to Principal*	*OUTSTANDING PRINCIPAL*	*Cumulative Interest*
1	*12.00*	*1*	*106.62*	*12.00*	*94.62*	*60.00*	*1045.38*	*?*
		2	*106.62*	*10.45*	*96.16*	*60.00*	*?*	*22.45*
		3	*106.62*	*?*	*?*	*60.00*	*731.49*	*31.35*
		-	-	-	-	-	-	-
		8	*106.62*	*0.85*	*105.77*	*60.00*	*-81.12*	*51.83*
		8	*85.50*	*0.85*	*84.65*	*0.00*	*0.00*	*51.83*

"Sweetie, I'll make one last point.

"For the base amounts being **APPLIED TO PRINCIPAL**, the amortized loan was already being paid off 'faster and faster'. That's because those amounts were getting larger and larger each month. The consistent **ADDITIONAL AMOUNT APPLIED TO PRINCIPAL** hastens the repayment even more. For that reason ***Acceleration = Getting There Faster and Faster and Faster!***"

"It sure looks that way, Dad."

"Great, Sweetie. And unless you have even more curiosities, we're done!"

"Awesome! I can't think of anything else. Thank you very much!"

"It's been my pleasure. Ok, let's relax and continue to enjoy being snowed in."

LESSON 4 I'm Dreaming of My New Car

Jumping forward in time, at the end of volume 1 (**THE COLLEGE EXPERIENCE**) our Nicole had graduated and was employed as an entry level journalist. She graduated with her student loan debts successfully managed, but still owing some money. She's about to face new debt needs. Older now and wiser about debt, she is better able to face the challenges it will present. One of them is buying and financing a **NEW CAR**. It will be new territory and she will seek her Dad's experienced advice and guidance, as needed.

Let's face it, before you can hit the road with a **NEW CAR** you will hit the reality of how much they cost. **NEW CARS** are expensive. Prices in the common range of $20000.00 to $40000.00 hit you in the face first, and then in your wallet. Add high end luxury cars with all the so-called 'bells and whistles' to the mix and prices soar toward $50000.00 to $80000.00 and even higher. Buying a **NEW CAR** is serious business. If you're dreaming of a **NEW CAR**, then it could be more of a nightmare than a pleasant dream.

Even **USED CARS** are not as inexpensive as they used to be. The law of supply and demand is in play. High prices for a **NEW CAR** have increased the demand for **USED CARS**. Car owners are holding on to **NEW CARS** for as long as practical. That affects the supply, quality and condition of **USED CARS**. **USED CARS** in good to excellent condition are harder to find, thus commanding higher prices than before.

For most car buyers, a significant **CAR LOAN** comes into the picture. If you have a car to trade-in toward another one, that reduces the burden somewhat. For first-time buyers the need to borrow a lot of money is normally in play. One such population of buyers is college graduates. Nicole is one of them.

Indeed, these days many students 'bike' as their mode of transportation. Some have only that means, while in some cases also as a social preference as well. Nicole biked too, but also had her **VW NEW BEETLE**. Bought for her by her parents, she's had it since just after turning sixteen. Now, Nicole and her car are each eight years older.

Typically, as college graduates begin looking for jobs they are saddled with some amount of student loan debt. They average amount is approaching $30000.00. In volume 1**,** the content was concentrated on preparing for and handling those loans. If significant student loan debt is one's circumstance, then the opportunity to qualify to borrow funds needed for purchasing a car can be very limited if not unworkable. Almost certainly the individual will need to be employed and have sufficient income. If not, then that college graduate would possibly be still in the market but for a **USED CAR**.

With a well-paying job in a career in a high-demand, dependable profession; having student loan debt at the average level will not prohibit one from qualifying for a **CAR LOAN** for a **NEW CAR**. Nicole was in that circumstance, but decided try to wait a couple years before buying her next car. She wanted to pay off her student loans for a little while, first. She also wanted to be sure she can readily handle paying normal costs of life herself alongside her student loan payment. With a reasonable pay increase, she anticipated being fine by then.

Because she has a very manageable student loan debt, Nicole very likely could finance the purchase of a residence. She elected to rent an apartment, anyway. She plans to wait until she knows she is happy with her job and settled into it enough to consider purchasing a condo.

Preparing to Buy a Car

***ASIDE**: The aim of this Lesson is to explain the many paths to purchasing a car and determining a fair price. It details how to be sure your loan interest rate is correct and fair, calculate loan costs, and compare alternatives. It helps you make a strategic monetary choice once you have decided upon a car to purchase. It does not cover the psychology and challenges of getting an honest and fair deal from a car salesperson. That can be a heavy duty mental endeavor. That's why a lot of people loath having to buy a car. You can get better peace of mind on the mechanics of how to go through it and dealing with the persuasive maneuvering that occurs at a dealership. The author notes some websites that will help you get that. Now, follow along as Nicole moves down the car buying road and her Dad helps her reach the comfort level needed to reach its end.*

Now two years into her job as a journalist at the Evening Gazette, Nicole is extremely pleased with her career start. She's performed her work well and has been promoted to greater responsibilities. Accordingly, she has had good salary raises. Her career telescope sees her staying put for at least five years as a wise option.

Fortunately, Nicole's VW has had no major problems and is in good condition. She has her mind on replacing it with another one. The usual dilemmas have come to mind as well. Will it be a **USED CAR** or a **NEW CAR**? How much cash can she afford to use? Will she have to borrow money atop that?

Friends who have done it have told her the process is pretty intimidating, especially going to dealerships and encountering a car salesperson for the first time. They had worried about the possibility of having to go to a **USED CAR** lot and facing the infamous 'used car salesman'. In the end, each said that before they knew it they had bought one. It happened so quickly and without fully understanding everything that transpired at the dealership. They needed to borrow part of the money and encountered the aspects of a getting a **CAR LOAN** for the first time. Each was not looking forward to the next time either.

Facing those consternations, on a Sunday afternoon, Nicole contacts her Dad for guidance. She lives far away, so chooses to Skype with him. It's a lot different than actual face-to-face, but at least it will be visually as close to that as possible.

"Hi, Dad! It's wonderful to see your face again, even though it is only the virtual you."

"Hi Nicole! It's very nice to see the virtual you, too, despite it being a lot different than sitting here in my office. How is everything going?"

"I'm settled in. I like my job and have gotten used to living away from home. I like living here and keep making more and more friends. Recently, I got a promotion and nice increase in pay along with it."

"That's great, Peanut. In your email asking to Skype with me you mentioned buying a **NEW CAR** was on your mind. You seemed to have some nervousness, even cold feet, about having to do so?"

"You're right, Dad. My car is getting really old. Despite its good condition, I don't want to keep it much longer. I feel I need to buy one, but am uncertain about how much I need to pay for it. Affordability is my key concern. Being a journalist at a newspaper, I see car ads all the time. I know that decent cars are expensive, even for a **USED CAR**.

"And yes, it is a bit scary to have to do it for the first time. Some of my friends did and they say they felt overwhelmed. They're not very anxious to have to do it again one day. That kind of makes me worry about what I will be facing. Yeah, I do feel something between nervousness and feet so cold that I would just avoid doing it. That's why I want to get your advice on it for now. Then when I have to do it, I can use your guidance in making the best financial choices."

"Nicole, it's safe to say that a lot people find car buying to be an anxiety-filled experience. Between trying to purchase within one's affordability range and maneuvering through the selling process at a dealership, it can be a nervous to scary process in a buyer's mind. Trying to decide on the best car to fit one's needs and budget takes time and effort. Then, trying to negotiate the best deal possible comes to the forefront. Sometimes it might feel smooth and other times it may feel as if a salesperson is only maneuvering hard to get the best deal possible for the dealership."

"I sure hope it goes smoothly for me. With you helping me I will feel a lot less wary about doing it. How should I go about getting the best deal possible?"

"That's what everyone hopes to achieve. It's likely more people don't, than do. Since I have bought a few cars in my lifetime, I have a decent understanding of it all. Here's my broader perspective on it to start.

"Getting the best deal begins with knowing how car dealerships and their salespeople make a profit from the sale of the car. The profit made relies on all aspects of the sale. It comes from the combination of the final sale price of the car; the interest earned if a loan is dealer financed; the gain made on reselling your trade-in car; extra fees like vehicle preparation; extra or upgraded features like tinted windows or an upgraded media player; extended warranties; a dealer long-term service and maintenance contract; and factory-to-dealer incentives."

"Dad, that's a lot of things to consider and some of it's all new to me. How do they play into what I will end up paying for the car?"

"It sure is a lot to consider. Let's go through all the typical aspects of how a dealership establishes the price of the car. It's a very involved process, so we'll walk along slowly."

Pricing a Car

- New Cars -

Manufacturer's Suggested Retail Price

"One basic aspect you, as the buyer of a **NEW CAR**, must be aware of is the difference between the **MANUFACTURER'S SUGGESTED RETAIL PRICE, MSRP** for short, and what the dealership actually pays the manufacturer for it. The **MSRP** typically appears on the lengthy decal found on the car window. The price of the car is broken into a **BASE PRICE** plus the cost of all the standard and other features of the specific car you are gazing at on the lot. The **MSRP** is the price the manufacturer specified when that make, model became available. It includes the standard equipment. It excludes taxes, transportation and destination charges. Those additional costs plus the cost of the extra features shown in the decal list are part of the price."

"Dad, why is it called a suggested price?"

"It is not like buying groceries or books, where you pay the exact price that is shown on the shelf or on the item. When buying a car, the **MSRP** shown on the decal is not a fixed price. It is sort of a starting point for negotiations. The actual price you pay is what you and the dealership agree to after negotiating everything involved. It's important to know and understand how the dealership goes about their side of the pricing."

Invoice Price

"The dealership has to purchase the car from the manufacturer. They pay a factory **INVOICE PRICE** which includes a 'holdback' and advertising costs. It does not include any additional equipment installed by the dealership or any **DESTINATION CHARGE**."

Factory-to-Dealer Incentive

"What's a holdback?"

"The holdback is an amount of money the manufacturer might pay to the dealership once a particular car is sold, sort of a bonus. It amounts to a small percentage of the **MSRP**. In a way it is extra profit. For that reason, it's often referred to a **FACTORY-TO-DEALER INCENTIVE**."

"Why is that done?"

"The factory does it to encourage sale of the particular make, model, and year of the car. It can bias the price the dealership sets on that particular car you are looking at. It can also influence what other cars they suggest to you. Those other choices could involve a better holdback amount."

"I see your point and how I can be maneuvered away from the car I asked about to another car."

"Indeed. It's commonly called 'bait and switch' and you have to be wary of that possibility."

Asking Price

"Ultimately, the dealership sets an **ASKING PRICE** for the car, the amount they aim to get for it when it's sold. That price reflects any holdback that is in play. Knowing there is one gives the dealership, via the salesperson, leeway to let you negotiate downward in the price. The **ASKING PRICE** is always noticeably less than the **MSRP** and is always negotiable. The buyer must then work toward reducing it to what they are willing to pay for the car.

"For example, you might be able to negotiate some, or all, of the holdback out of the **ASKING PRICE**.

You won't know the amount of the holdback, but the salesperson's flexibility will be evident. You might show lower comparable prices offered by another dealership to reduce the **ASKING PRICE** at your dealership. You can request repairs or modifications to fix any identified defects such as scratches, malfunctioning lights etc. For a **NEW CAR** it's highly unlikely any are needed. For a **USED CAR** it's not unusual to need a few minor ones. If a **USED CAR** needs anything major fixed, I would not even consider buying it."

"That holdback seems kind of sneaky, too, Dad. But, I can see how it can be to my advantage. That is, if I play it smart."

"Yes, it can be. And, I know you are smart, Smarty Pants."

Destination Charge

"Dad, what's a **DESTINATION CHARGE**?"

"That's a charge for getting a **NEW CAR** from the factory to the dealership, even if the car is already on the lot. It's a several hundred dollars or more; maybe even $1000.00 for a luxury car. A lot of people don't like to pay that charge. Typically it is non-negotiable."

Buyer Incentives

"**NEW CARS** often come with **BUYER INCENTIVES** offered to the customer. One incentive might be a low financing rate; the **ANNUAL RATE OF INTEREST** to be applied if you finance through the dealership. Another incentive might be a factory **CASH REBATE**. A **CASH REBATE** is basically a discount available to the buyer. Despite being factory-originated it is credited to you at the time of the sale. A **CASH BONUS** might be included. It is similar to a **CASH REBATE**, but you are required to apply it toward the dealership's financing. Accepting one requires that you use their financing."

"At least there are some potential goodies out there, now that I know about them."

"Righto! That's why I mentioned them.

"Those are basics of how a dealership goes about setting their **ASKING PRICE** for a car. Again, that's the target price they will set for the car once a customer engages them about a specific car he or she has in mind. Rarely is it the price you actual end up paying. That's where the selling process and negotiation enter the picture. The end result is the price you actually pay."

"Yeah, Dad. That's what really worries me; what happens when I actually go to a dealership to consider buying a car."

"Ok, let's cover that."

Selling Process

"Let's assume you have a general idea of the kind of car you are interested in. Before settling in on an actual purchase, you likely will visit more than one dealership. In each case, unless you have a brand or model or particular car in mind, the salesperson who greets you will quiz you about it. Then he/she will take you around the lot showing you different cars that meet your description.

"Usually, you are either interested in a few cars you either saw advertised or found by looking around the dealership when it was closed. If, so, then the salesperson will show you those and discuss them. Over a few visits you may narrow it down to a choice at one of those dealerships. Then the selling process ensues."

"How does that process work, Dad?"

"You have to be aware that a salesperson, a finance person, a 'closer' and others will be involved. Each has a role. They can collectively maneuver you to get a final desired maximum profit. The salesperson's task is to motivate you to buy a car. The finance person's task is to get you do any needed financing via a loan from that dealership. The closer is usually the sales manager but may be another veteran salesperson. The closer is there to close the deal and get you to sign the **PURCHASE AGREEMENT**. The closer will try to sell add-ons and will settle any negotiation issues. The outcome is an agreed to **SELLING PRICE** plus **OPTIONS**.

"What exactly is involved in getting to that point?"

"It involves all those factors I mentioned about how the dealership makes a profit from selling you a car. Everything from interest earned if a loan is dealer financed to those factory-to-dealer incentives. A lot of it was new to you. Let's cover those mysteries. Just pluck one off to start."

"Ok, what exactly do you mean by **SELLING PRICE** and **OPTIONS**?"

- Selling Price and Options

"The **SELLING PRICE** covers the **BASE PRICE** plus the cost of all the standard equipment and extra features listed on the decal. **OPTIONS** include the prices of any extra or upgraded features such as rear view camera and designer wheel caps. They will be an additional cost."

"Ok, how about the dealership financing? Can't I just use a bank?"

- Dealership Financing

"Besides selling you a car, the dealership is interested in handling any financing needs you might have. If you plan to take out a **CAR LOAN** and have reasonable creditworthiness or better, then they want to be the lending party. That's because you will be paying them a lot of interest on the loan. Before you even show up at a dealership to buy a car, it's important for you to consider bank and credit union sources for the loan to find out the terms you would be offered. Do that once you have your mind on a particular car and likely amount of the **CAR LOAN** needed. Then you are prepared to compare those results with any dealership terms offered to you."

"Ok, Dad. What about service and maintenance plans? It seems sensible to have one."

- Service and Maintenance Plans

"The dealership makes a lot of money if they can get you do all that work done at their service department. Typically, they try to sell you a plan in which you agree to do that for a period of years, as many as possible. Be particularly wary. Service and maintenance plans are commonly based on mildly to highly exaggerated prices for the individual service involved – and you get locked into them. You might unknowingly agree to higher prices than if you shop around. Even if you don't buy a plan, they can get your business other ways. For example, they might include 'free' oil changes with the purchase. It's a way to get your vehicle into their repair shop for possible other maintenance or repair needs they might find. In the worst case, you might not actually need them."

"That sounds pretty sneaky, Dad"

"It can be. You need to be watchful."

"How does trading in my car come into play?"

-Trade-In

"The dealership profit on your trade-in is the amount above what they pay you for your **PRESENT CAR** and what the amount they will resell it for. If any work on the car will be necessary before they resell it, then they subtract the cost from what they would normally offer you. You want to get a fair price for that car, recognizing the dealer has to make a profit when it is resold as **USED CAR**. The big worry is unknowingly accepting a low-ball offer."

"What's a low-ball offer?"

"It's an odd terminology. I don't know the source. It means they offer you the lowest possible price for your car. It's a price which is at or near the bottom of the range of values that a car like yours would sell for. At the extreme low-ball offer, you make the least possible on the trade-in and they make the maximum when they resell it."

"How do I find out how much my car is actually worth?"

"There are a lot of sources for estimating that fairly closely. Before moving to that, are there other glaring aspects about pricing the car?"

"I don't think so. Maybe how all those profit paths come together to affect what I finally pay for the car I want?"

"How they get you to the final price and sale depends on what transpires with any given customer. Where cost breaks might be given on some items they will try to add other costs. To offset a low final sale price, one buyer might be persuaded on extra features. Another buyer might be sold a long-term service and maintenance plan. If the buyer has a car to trade in, the offered value comes into play.

"You need to carefully negotiate so that each bucket and the total of them is a fair and acceptable outcome. You must also understand the dealership needs to make a reasonable profit. Somewhere between what they are bargaining for and what you want to pay 'as the absolute best deal' is a price that is fair both ways."

"Gee, Dad, I can see why my friends seemed to feel they bought a car 'before they knew it' and were not looking forward to the next time. Maybe I need you to come along with me when I have to do it."

"I can consider that when the time comes. For now, I want to help you to become well informed about how it all works. Armed with that, you will be much more able to stand on your own two feet. Then you can decide if you need me at all."

"Dad, I've seen some television ads for cars saying they offer a **NO HAGGLE PRICE**? That's sounds to me like a fixed price and that there are no negotiations possible. If I take that route, I could avoid all the headaches."

"I've seen those ads myself. I've never actually done it. My read on it is that if you're willing to pay the **NO HAGGLE PRICE** then they will sell it to you at that price, end of shopping. I would not do that myself without checking out the numbers based on everything I've just covered. To me, it's like any other price on a decal. It's wise to assess if it's a fair **SELLING PRICE**. If I'm satisfied it is and can afford it, then I probably would go ahead and accept it to avoid the haggling. Even so, I would still have to go through the finance person and the closer, and consider their possible influences.

"On the other hand, if I think the **NO HAGGLE PRICE** is not a fair price, then I wouldn't hesitate to haggle anyway. Of course, that's only if I decided I was still interested in the particular car."

"Well, Dad, there sure is a lot involved in getting a fair price for a car. And atop that I have to be so watchful in how to pass through all the way to that closer. How can I prepare myself to handle that gauntlet?"

On-Line Resources

- General

"I certainly understand your nervousness and have never forgotten the first time I did it myself. Each time is different with different people and patterns of events in play. For me, it was the school of hard knocks because it was way back when computers were just burgeoning. Fortunately, these days there are lots of useful websites.

"By searching the web, you can find an exhaustive amount of information and guidance on what the negotiating process for buying a car involves and how to work through it calmly, wisely and more effectively. There are some particular ones I have used myself.

"One excellent source is auto.howstuffworks.com/buying-selling/car-buying.htm. In it, Allison Klein walks you through all the steps, precautions and woes of purchasing a car, be it **USED** or **NEW**, bought at a dealership or via the Internet. If you are in need of a 'wake-up call' on the bad apple aspects of car buying, Ms. Klein rings you up loud and clear."

"Sounds like she's as caring as Mom."

"I wouldn't quite say that. But, she does have the consumer at heart.

"Another helpful source is www.edmunds.com. Under its Car Buying section, the very helpful beginner topic www.edmunds.com/car-buying/10-steps-to-buying-a-new-car.html pragmatically describes the main aspects of the car buying process.

ASIDE: *The author found the article actually only has eight steps described.*

"For an exhaustive guide on the possible ruses and trickery in car buying, I found the website www.carbuyingtips.com to be an excellent source. It is particularly helpful on awareness of and how to negotiate downward and to secure some of the **FACTORY-TO-DEALER INCENTIVE**.

"You can find many others, but those are the ones I found most informative."

"Ok, Dad. I appreciate that and will look into them when I get a chance. You seem to have concentrated on **NEW CARS**. What about **USED CARS**? Depending on what I can afford, it could be I buy one. I am aware that if I do, then I have to be very careful."

"Spot on!, Nicole. I have prepared some information about that, too."

- Used Cars

"Purchasing a **NEW CAR** is not fraught with condition issues. While the infamous 'lemon' does come along once in a while, a **NEW CAR** is fully warrantied for a period of time from the moment of purchase. After that, some major components are warrantied for additional time. An **EXTENDED WARRANTY** can also be purchased to continue coverage for a longer time. Recalls for equipment defects do come along. However, they too are infrequent, albeit sometimes widespread over many models and years. It can take some time to get them done, but you do eventually get the things fixed. By and large, a sound vehicle comes with that **NEW CAR** smell."

"Yeah, Dad, I still remember that smell from when your car was **NEW**. The one you bought me was **USED**. If I can afford one now, then I will get to smell it in my own **NEW CAR**."

"**USED CARS** are a different ball game. If purchased from a dealership, then you might have a **LIMITED WARRANTY** attached to the sale. Perhaps more often than not, it comes with a purchased '**AS IS**' tag attached to it. That means the second it becomes your car you own it and any deficiencies associated with it. If the transmission drops out of it one inch down the road, you now own a car moving in the slowest of motions – no motion."

"That would be horrible. Now, I really want to know more about buying a **USED CAR**."

"Whether it's being purchased from a private party or a dealership, you must do your best to determine the '**AS IS**' condition of a **USED CAR** before you do. Once you are negotiating a specific car, you should take it to your own mechanic and have it inspected. Knowing you are that interested in the car, the dealership should let you do that. A private party should, too; but would have some conditions, perhaps giving them the keys to your car when you do it. Then either negotiate a total cost fitting the car's age and condition, or walk away. Do not drive it away.

"If you do reach what you consider a fair and reasonable total cost, then don't buy it, just yet. Your lender is just as interested as you in the determining the correct value of the car. Maybe more so! The terms of your loan will depend on it. If the age and condition are problematic, then your loan will not be approved. How do you and your lender make the determination of condition? Fortunately, there is help; and lots of it!

"Several broad sources exist. Perhaps the most commonly known source is the **Kelley Blue Book**, located at www.kbb.com. Using its on-line tools, you reach an estimated range of value for a **NEW CAR, CERTIFIED CAR** or **USED CAR**. I visited it this week to refresh myself."

"What's a **CERTIFIED CAR**, Dad?"

"I figured you would ask that. I jotted down the details.

"The **CERTIFIED CAR** descriptor is loose terminology. It actually refers to a **CERTIFIED PRE-OWNED CAR** or for short, a **CPO** car. Dealers offering **CPO** cars have to be certified. And **CPO** cars have met strict conditions. Originally it was mostly intended for luxury cars but less so now. **CPO** cars must: a) be less than 5 years old, b) have less than 100,000 miles, c) no major body work from accidents, d) be refurbished by the dealer, and e) include an extended warranty. One should be cautious that the dealership has indeed taken the actions such that c) and d) actually are the case. The **CARFAX REPORT** should show that."

"What's a **CARFAX REPORT**?"

"Oops! I did slide that in. A **CARFAX REPORT** is an invaluable means of finding the history of a **USED CAR**, sort of its life story. In a moment, I'll cover how you get one.

"For a **USED CAR**, the website *www.kbb.com* for the so-called **Kelley Blue Book** leads you through information requests for: a) year, make, model and mileage; b) style of car; c) all features of the car from air conditioning to braking system to steering, color, air bags etc.; d) are you trading to a dealer or selling to a private party; and e) condition of the car. Item e) offers five choices (Excellent, Very Good, Good, Fair, Poor) and each is accompanied by a detailed list of specific conditions that dictate the choice (e.g. extent of rust if any, tire wear). A quiz is available to help you assess the correct choice for the car of interest. Once all you select a condition option, BINGO! The estimated price for the cars of that description in your region pops up! You can repeat the process as many times as you wish to see how variations in condition choices affect the result."

"That's sounds like a great tool for the consumer."

"Yes, it's invaluable. It's especially so when you are new to buying a car and nervous about **USED CARS**. That's the situation you're in. Let's walk through an example. Do you have your computer handy?"

"Yes, I have my laptop right here."

"Ok, let's each go to *www.kbb.com*."

"Ok, Dad. I've gotten there."

"I'm there too."

SITUATION 4

"Assume you are interested in the market pricing of a **USED CAR**. For example purposes, let's say you seek a **2010 Dodge Charger, four door sedan**. We start on the website home page. As we go through the prompts, let's have you make the choices for each one and enter them. To stay on the same track, just tell me your choices and I'll also enter them at my end. We can jot down the choices as we go through it. Are you ready?"

"I am, Dad."

"Ok, let's start."

NOTE: Starting on the home page the following are sequence of Nicole's choices and the results. Choices she makes are italicized. Otherwise the wording is either a request shown on the site or a result of a choice.

ASIDE*: Before continuing, read Exercise 5 which follows this SITUATION.*

I want to ... Price New/Used Cars

Price Your Next Car

USED 2010 Dodge Charger

Sedan 4D

"Nicole, notice the result indicates that typical mileage for this age of the car is 87297 miles. Also we could choose to price it without options. To see how it works, why don't you pick some options?"

"Ok, let me make some wishes."

Power train

Engine: *V6-2.7 Liter, Transmission: Automatic 5-Spd w/ overdrive, Drivetrain: AWD*

Options

Braking and Traction: *ABS (4 wheel) and Traction Control*

Comfort and Convenience: *Keyless Entry, Air Conditioning, Power Windows, Power Door Locks, Cruise Control*

Steering: *Power Steering, Tilt Wheel*

Entertainment and Instrumentation: *AM/FM Radio, CD (Multi-Disk)*

Safety and Security: *Dual Air Bags, F & R Side Air Bags*

Seats: *Dual Power Seats, Leather*

Roof and Glass: *No choice made*

Lighting: *No choice made*

Wheels and Tires: *Alloy Wheels*

Color: *Gold*

"Now I see I can **choose a price type**, either **Buy from a Dealer** or **Buy from Private Party**. I'll select *Buy from a Dealer*.

"Now it indicates that it will find cars **Based on Good Condition or Better** and lists ten things defining what that means.

"Now I see I have to click on *Get used car price.*

"Very interesting results, Dad. It shows a **Fair Market Range** of **$8989 - $10562**, a **Fair Purchase Price** of **$9776,** and a **Suggested Retail Price of $10292**. It indicates I can browse 11 cars near me and that 2 of them are within the fair market range. It gives me an option to click **Free Vehicle Record Search** to get the history of that vehicle."

ASIDE: *The interested reader can click on* ***definitions*** *to get the lengthy details of what these pricings mean and how they are determined. The main outcome aim of this example is to see what specific cars choices result and their prices.*

"Go ahead and try that, Nicole."

ASIDE*: The current website page also allowed one to click and get* ***Buy from Private Party Pricing****. The author did that and results are cited subsequently.*

"Hmm, I see I need a **VIN** number, which I don't have. I don't even know what it means. What should I do?"

"Skip it, for now. Instead, click on that **Browse** button and see the available cars."

"OK, done. Now that's interesting. Not all of the cars listed are a **Dodge Charger**. Some **Dodge Charger R/T** cars are listed and some others. I guess those are similar but fancier models.

"It only lists two specific **Dodge Charger** cars. One is priced at **$16287** and has **94524 miles** used. The other is priced at **$12287** and has **60430 miles** used. Neither is **Gold** in color. The first one is **Black** and the second one is **Red**.

"It also lists a **Dodge Charger SXT** with a price of **$11287** and **72103 miles** used. It lists another one for **$6500** with **150000 miles** used. Even I know that car is a risk. It lists a **Charger SRT8** for **$26599** with **73155 miles** used. That must be a fancy, upscale model, I suppose."

ASIDE: *The result for* ***Buy from Private Party*** *was a* ***Private Party Value*** *of $7769 for cars in* ***Good***

Condition. *No specific private party car choices were given. However, the above results of dealership cars were given.*

"As you saw Nicole, the website provides a wide range of choices for cars available near you. If you were actually doing this, which one do you lean toward, if any?"

"If I had I would go for the *Dodge Charger* that is priced at *$12287* with *60430 miles* used."

"Ok, now what do you do next?"

"I see I can click on ***Quick View***. Ok, it gives me a photo of the car.

"If I click on ***Get Full Details*** I get a set of color photos showing the car from different angles and lots of its physical details. It also gives a list of worded specifics about the car. I can also click on ***Get an AutoCheck Vehicle History***. I'll do that.

"Wow, it says it found 14 records on this car. Even more Wow, I have to pay $24.99 to get a look at them. I guess free isn't free?"

"I guess not, Sweetie. If you were very interested in this car you might do that, but I would first go see the car, maybe on a Sunday sneak trip. Then you decide about getting the reports before talking to a salesperson."

"Actually, I see it looks like a super sporty car and is red. It's not what I would want to be driving. It looks like a sure target for police trying to catch speeders."

"Nicole, let's look at one of the listings again. I meant to point out that the listings also provide the **VIN** number."

"I see that, Dad. What's a **VIN**?"

"**VIN** is short for **Vehicle Identification Number**. As you see it is a very long number. Each car has one of its own imprinted somewhere on the car. It's also listed in the registration material. All those numbers are coded to identify the car and its specific features in great detail.

"Let me cut and paste the **VIN** into that previous page where we saw the price range for this model and make of car.

"Interesting, it pops up the same mention of the 14 records and the $24.99 cost to get them. I guess what's free is the search they do just to find out those records exist. Where does that leave you, Sweetie?"

"I don't have to do anything. This was only a trial run on an arbitrary choice of specifications. Anyway, I sure see how extremely helpful this website is in finding targeted cars. If I had the time, then I guess I could look at dozens of cars, even hundreds. In real life, I probably would research different types of cars fit to my liking, maybe looking around car lots and at ads. Then, I'd try to narrow it down to a few types and use this website to examine them in detail."

"And in the end, Sweetie, you have to handle the actual purchase of the car, yourself. That cannot be done using **Kelly Blue Book**. They only point you in the direction of available cars. The follow-up is in your hands and feet."

Exercise 5: *Repeat Nicole's search of* <u>*www.kbb.com*</u> *for the same* ***2010 Dodge Charger, four door sedan*** *car specifications as in SITUATION 4.*

Your results should be: *The list of cars that resulted in SITUATION 4 is what came up at the time of writing this Lesson (early December, 2016). It is highly unlikely the same list will occur when the reader does it. After all, time has passed and most, if not all, of them will have been sold. But you can do the same or similar kind of choices at prompts, as done by Nicole. It is also is of interest to see what the new list will contain. If some of the same cars remain or closely similar ones, then the pricing of now somewhat older cars is of interest, too.*

<u>SITUATION 5</u>

Being curious about it, Nicole and her Dad redid SITUATION 4 for a **2012** Model Year.

The **Dodge Charger** choice did not appear. Instead the **Dodge Charger SE** and others appeared. Evidently the **Dodge Charger** model did not exist in 2012, having been replaced by the **Dodge Charger SE** as the low end model. Also, some differences in optional features available arose. Those chosen were made as close as possible to those made for the **2010 Dodge Charger**.

The result for typical mileage was **66565 miles** used. **Fair Market Range** was **$12876** to **$14929**. **Fair Purchase Price** was **$13903** and **Suggested Retail Price** was $14487. Only 4 choices resulted, 3 of them being a **Dodge Charger SE** and the other being a **Dodge Charger R/T**. One **Dodge Charger SE** was priced at **$13489** with **90303 miles** used. Another **Dodge Charger SE** was priced at **$16487** with **50591 miles** used.

Exercise 6: *Repeat Situation 5 for a* ***2014 Dodge Charger SE*** *specifications.*

Your results should be: *As in Exercise 5, specific results cannot be given. The purpose is to compare the difference in type and number of cars available and their prices for a newer model. The interested reader can also try several different model years, to see trends.*

"Nicole, for a more extended investigation of the vehicle history of a specific car, the prominent means is to access a **CARFAX VEHICLE HISTORY REPORT**. That's what I loosely called a **CARFAX REPORT** earlier. You can get one via <u>www.carfax.com</u>. The site is operated by **CARFAX, Inc.**"

"Is it free, Dad?"

"There is a fee for obtaining a detailed report for any specific car or multiple cars. When I looked it up, the cost was $39.99 for a single report, $49.99 for three reports, or $99.99 for six reports. Then, the reports can be requested over a 60 day period flowing purchase of a plan. It's well worth it. The car you are checking out could turn out to be a loser."

ASIDE: *The preceding were the costs at the time of writing.*

"It seems that if I intend to check our several cars, then I should pay for unlimited reports."

"That's what I would do, Nicole.

"A few free services are available via the **CARFAX** website, such as a 'Lemon Check', a 'Recall Check' or a 'Sample Report'. The latter shows the very extensive content of a typical report. It illustrates a Price Calculator, Ownership History, Title History, Additional History (such as structural damage, airbag deployment, accident/damage, manufacturer recall, status of warranty), Detailed History (such as normal maintenance and repairs, sale of the car, specifics of accidents)."

"That's an amazing resource. What if I am looking at **NEW CARS**?"

"An alternate use of the website is to estimate a fair price for and to locate **NEW CARS** or **USED CARS** at nearby dealers to meet specifications you input for the specific type of car you are considering purchasing. Again, the follow-up is left to you and cannot be done online.

"The sample I viewed was eight pages, including some Glossary information. It wasn't for a car of my choice, just an arbitrary sample. To get that, you have to pay the fee. I'll leave it to you to go to the website and view the free sample as homework.

"Another use of the above sources is to find information about your own car if you plan to either sell it or do a trade-in toward the purchase of another one. **Kelley Blue Book** can be used to asses a fair value range for your specific car. If you want to pay for it, you can even get a **CARFAX REPORT** for your own car. Dealerships and private buyers are likely to do that before purchasing your car. It might be wise to see the same information yourself."

"That makes whole lot of sense, Dad. You said they only point me in the direction of available cars. The follow-up is in my hands and feet. The on-line stuff really helps me use my hands. It's the feet part that worries me. Walking on to a car lot for the first time alone feels really scary."

"Yes, Sweetie. I was really apprehensive the first time I had to do it, too. Nowadays, you can really soften the situation. If you want, I can share some of that with you?"

"That sounds really good, Dad. I'd like to play around on-line a little bit first. Maybe we can meet an hour or so after lunch?"

"Terrific, Nicole. I'll see you then."

LESSON 5 How Car Buying Has Really Changed

"Well, Dad, I played around with on-line searching. It's kind of fun, actually. When the time comes, it will really help. Now, I'm anxious to hear about how I go about purchasing a car I want to buy, without going to a car lot."

Contemporary Car Buying

"Yes, it's actually possible to do that. First, let me cover softening the blow of actually having to go to one. Not so long ago, car buying involved an awful lot of drive time and walk time. Most people looked around at many dealership lots on several Sunday afternoons when they were closed, so no salespeople are around. If someone found a car to their liking, they would research it before going back to speak with a salesperson. That was a tedious and tiring hunt for the right car for one's need. The complications and worries involved with the purchase of a car, particularly a **USED** car, directly at a dealership probably contributed to that activity. People still do that, but the longevity of it can be shortened by using contemporary online tools like *www.kbb.com*.

"In past years, hundreds of cars would be listed in printed newspaper ads. Now, relatively few are. Printed newspaper ads are headed toward being pre-historic. Wherever there is a need then in America someone comes along to provide for it. In this case, the opportunity for an individual to research cars via the Internet has flourished. At the basic level, newspaper printed ads are now augmented by digitally formatted ads. You'll find them readily for almost any dealership, photographs included. Indeed, some sites include a 3-D virtual image of the car which you can manipulate to pan and view it as if you were walking around it. Maybe someday, you'll even be able to virtually kick the tires, open the hood, etc."

"That's fantastic, Dad!"

"The picture is even much bigger than that! Nowadays, there are ways to purchase cars on-line."

"That really interests me. My generation does that for buying almost everything, not just cars. We let our fingers do the walking for us at our computer. I'm all ears, Dad."

"I know that Sweetie, my generation is still catching up with yours. Some of us are not very nimble, but we do our best. Numerous dedicated websites now exist to assist an interested car buyer to search commercial inventory. By 'dedicated', I mean they are tied to the actual seller of the cars. Searching online at various dealership websites allows you to pare down available inventory to cars of interest and affordability. Best of all, you can do that all alone on any day, not just Sunday. Then you can visit the targeted dealerships to begin a closer look, eventually leading to a purchase. In some cases one can negotiate and make the purchase electronically. More likely you do both, eventually seeing the potential car on Sunday and following up at the dealership itself on another day if you want to test drive it etc. Then, you can negotiate with the dealership on-line and complete the purchase at the location."

"I'll start to look into that, Dad, to get the general lay of the land."

"Nicole, you're probably aware of **Craig's List**?"

"I am Dad. I haven't actually used it for anything. I know some people who have, though."

"One can search **Craig's List** for **USED CARS** being sold by individuals. That's basically the counterpart of buying one from an individual locally or in nearby locales after reading newspaper ads. The range of 'locally' expands to anywhere in the country. Using **Craig's List** has risks associated with it as the seller is hidden from view and the validity of the person and ad can be questionable. That concern is true to the seller regarding the buyer. One must consider the safety of the location in initial face-to-face meetings. The same is actually true for newspaper ads."

"I agree Dad. As a journalist I have seen news articles about some bad, even criminal outcomes that occur now and then."

"In an even bigger picture, larger websites not dedicated to an individual dealership are available to you. Two popular ones are www.nada.com and www.edmunds.com. The first one is hosted by the **National Auto Dealers Association (NADA)**. The second one is hosted by **Edmunds, Inc**.

"For consumers, the **NADA Consumer Site** is free and primarily locates available **NEW CARS** and **USED CARS** that meet the general specifications input by the user. It works somewhat like the **Kelley Blue Book** website. For example, inputting a make (Buick) and year (2013 **USED**), style (sedan), trim level (Leather I4), mileage (200000) and a few non-standard features (for example, a sunroof) results in prices for cars available (through **NADA**) overall and near your zip code.

"The **NADA** site also provides options to compare prices with others cars of similar make and model etc. they have located. For most **USED CARS** they also post a **CARFAX** report. If you have **VIN** for a car you are looking at yourself, it has options to investigate the vehicle history. If you are interested they also provide insurance quotes.

"For dealers and lenders, the **NADA Business Site** is available to enrolled, paying entities. It provides substantial tools for estimating the value of a **USED CAR**. I find the **Kelly Blue Book** website much more versatile and user friendly. Many lenders prefer the **NADA Business Site** over the **Kelly Blue Book** site. Lenders pay a membership fee and have access to much more exhaustive information than for the **NADA Consumer Site**. If you use the **Kelly Blue Book**, then you might find that a lender using **NADA** arrives at a different outcome than you do.

"**Edmunds, Inc.** is primarily for users seeking to purchase a car. In reality, it is a dealer network. While you can use their site for free to investigate car values, they are available to find and sell you a car. It is a huge corporation with access to millions of **NEW CARS**, **USED CARS** and **CERTIFIED CARS**. Using your input as to requirements, the **Edmunds** website will enable you to find dealerships in your locale offering the make, model and year of car you seek. Then, they offer you quotes for one or more cars and you go from there to purchase it via **Edmunds** on-line.

"Typically, it works like this**.** One visits the site, which automatically locates your locale. You then can find cars within 10 to 200 miles of your locale. You filter choices by Year, Base Price Range, Features,

Mileage Rating, Make, Model, Type, Transmission, and Engine. Click and up pop your available choices. For example, 2014 Toyota Avalon Sedan, $31590.00, sunroof, exterior camera, traction control, stability control, heated seats, side/curtain airbags, mpg 21/30, automatic, 6-cylinder.

"If you're interested then you follow-up further on the site. With more clicking you can see photos, color choices, interior views, etc. You can get average sold price in your selected 'within x miles' range, operating costs, insurance estimates etc. If stock is available in their inventory, you can buy the car. You ask for specific quotes etc. If not, they can refer you to dealers."

"Dad, maybe you ought to be a car salesman?"

"Yeah! I know I am sounding like a sales representative. Of course, I am not. I just gave you a look see at some basics of how the website works. The rest is up to you."

"I'll certainly be doing so when the time comes, Dad."

"**Edmunds, Inc.** is not the only place to buy on-line. Other accessible car pricing/sales websites are www.Cars.com, www.truecar.com, and www.CarClearanceDeals.com. And **Car Buying Tips** at www.carbuyingtips.com which I mentioned before also offers a **Car Buying Service**. All of these websites involve a network of dealerships which serve as the pool for locating available cars. Also, lenders will use one or more of the websites to assess the value of the car for which their customer is seeking a loan. Dealers can also use the websites to help them set a price for a car you seek to trade in. They also have the opportunity to actually directly inspect your trade-in vehicle, as well, and usually do, to the extent needed in their view."

"Gee, Dad, I really see the savings in time and effort. With all these websites, it looks like searching for the car of my dreams is possible just sitting at my desk."

"In a lot of ways, it is. In my world, because you don't have to drive and walk around, we say it saves a lot of 'tire rubber and shoe leather'. But it still can take hours and hours of time, sitting at a computer. And it might turn out your dream car is unavailable anywhere close to you. Or it might turn out the car costs too much. Whatever, you can search and search until your heart's content. Your generation seems to love doing so, for almost any need."

"You're right about that, I suppose. And you've given me a wealth of leads regarding searching for cars online, Dad. Thank you for all your help."

"I appreciate that and hope it helps you get started. Being a journalist you'll surely look at every nook and cranny. There's one more option I want to mention."

Car Brokers

- What's a Car Broker?

"These days, for timid buyers, it gets even easier to avoid the hassles of buying a car directly at a local dealership. One can access a **CAR BROKER** to do all leg work for you."

"What's that all about Dad? I'm always doing a lot of leg work in my job, so any leg work avoided in having to find a car I like is a boon."

"In general a **BROKER** is an individual who works as a middleman to organize, negotiate and arrange contracts for selling something a client wants to purchase from a third party. A **BROKER** either works alone or as an employee of a **BROKERAGE FIRM**. The **BROKER** represents the client and acts as his/her agent and charges a fee for providing brokering services. Familiar examples are stock brokers, bond brokers, and real estate brokers. A **BROKER** must be licensed in the state where he or she is doing business."

"Similar to a **REAL ESTATE BROKER** being paid a fee to assist a homebuyer find and purchase a home, a **CAR BROKER** is paid a fee to locate and arrange the purchase of a car for an interested party. A particular **CAR BROKER** might broker either **NEW CARS** or **USED CARS** or both."

"That sounds great, Dad. How does a **CAR BROKER** do that?"

"A **CAR BROKER** acts as your personal shopper. Whether you are looking for a **NEW** or **USED CAR** (**CPO** or not) he or she does all the walking and talking for you and brings the potential car to you to look at. If you have a trade-in to offer, the car broker handles that aspect too. In the end you sign a contract via the **CAR BROKER** to purchase the satisfactorily located car. Technically, and legally, car buying/leasing internet sites are **CAR BROKERS**, too. But I am talking about the use of a local **CAR BROKER,** whereby you physically visit the broker and interact as he/she acts as your agent to find a car for you to either buy or lease.

"**CAR BROKERS** principally find cars via car dealers. They also find them via car websites and others (for example **Craig's list**). For **NEW CARS** they also can obtain them by factory-order from car companies either directly or by using a dealership."

- How a Car Broker Earns Money

"Dad, how does **CAR BROKER** make money? And how much would it cost me to use one?"

"A **CAR BROKER** will earn money in either of two ways. A **CAR BROKER** will arrange the deal and contract signing for a fee charged to the client. Some **CAR BROKERS** buy the desired car and resell it to the client after adding a profit margin. That's perfectly fine if the resulting **SELLING PRICE** to you is fair and for a quality car that meets your general requirements and particular specifications. Some brokers might do both, buy the car and add a profit margin plus charge a small fee to the client. Any way it is done, you will know the fee and/or cost of the car before you agree to purchase it. By researching the value of the car beforehand you can roughly judge how much of the price is the profit margin. There are some precautions involved, too.

"If you purchase a **NEW CAR** from the **CAR BROKER** after he/she has bought it to resell it to you, then it has becomes a **USED CAR** before you purchased it. Any legal rights specifically related to purchasing a **NEW CAR** are lost. If you do buy a **USED CAR** that way, then be sure any available **REBATES** are either paid to or credited to you.

"One has to be wary that the **CAR BROKER** might also be paid a fee by the source and charge the client only a small or no fee. You want a **CAR BROKER** who only earns a fee from you and only if you purchase the car. For example, for a **NEW CAR** that fee could be a small percentage; perhaps 1-2% of the **MSRP**. With the fee set and being contingent on the purchase, the **CAR BROKER** is motivated to get you the fairest price. If, instead, the fee is based on the **SALE PRICE** to you, then it can be maneuvered to be favorable to the **CAR BROKER**. You likely will be asked to pay a portion of the fee to the **CAR BROKER** in advance, as an indicator of serious intent. If it is not refundable, I wouldn't agree to it."

- Advantages of Using a Car Broker

"Gee, Dad, even though there is no physical legwork for me, it has the same sort of feel as buying a car at the dealership yourself. You have to be careful how they treat you. Right?"

"Being careful is always applicable when buying a car. But, skilled, effective **CAR BROKERS** are a key to providing their clients with a quality auto at a good price. They provide volume to dealerships and car manufacturers. As a result, they can obtain discounts for that productivity. They have become very familiar with different trends in a large pool of dealerships about turnover time to sell cars, consequence of a car being on the lot too long, when new inventory comes in, when pricing flexibility accelerates etc.

"Many **CAR BROKERS** are former car salespersons and are well experienced and tuned to the pricing of cars, margins and maneuvering involved at dealerships to gain a larger profit from the individual customer. They can use that experience to improve the pricing they obtain for their client. Most valuable, you don't get engaged in that process at all. You don't even have to walk through the door to the dealership. You don't have to deal with a sales person, finance person and closer. Neither does your **CAR BROKER**. They deal with bosses and fleet managers. In the end, your **CAR BROKER** conducts the purchasing or leasing transaction with you in his or her own office."

"I can see that now. In the end I have to judge the value of the car compared to the price I pay for it, including fees. The big difference here is that if I use a **CAR BROKER**, then I have much, much less legwork to do. It seems like it would save me a lot of time and energy."

"You're right about that. **CAR BROKERS** with strong activity are constantly seeking cars and examining availability and sources. As a result, they know where all kinds of cars are. And they have a sense of comparative affordability of the prices at various places. In a blink of their eye they may even know places where your dream car is more likely to be found.

"Indeed, there is a great savings in time. Time is money for the **CAR BROKER** and it is for you, too. They find and assess stock far more quickly than you shopping around on your own via ground and via the Internet. If you do that, then it can involve weeks to months of time. By using a **CAR BROKER** that time saved for the client has significant indirect value. That's especially true if you are a busy professional person such as a realtor or sales representative always on the go. You can use your saved time to earn money. Just not having to do the extensive and tiring shopping around is worth paying the **CAR BROKER** to do it, even if the car ends up costing a bit more than if found otherwise.

"Regardless, for any client, the use of an **CAR BROKER** frees up time to enjoy life and its pursuits instead of driving to and fro - from lot to lot, and walking the pavement of each peering at stock and prices, trolling the Internet and, most of all, the later intense time negotiating individual with a salesperson etc. at a dealership once you have found a desired car."

"Well, Dad, I feel a little bit like you have me walking on a cloud. Like I can sit back, relax and let the **CAR BROKER** do almost all the work."

- Precautions

"In a way you're right. But, not to be completely buoyant, one must wisely select a **CAR BROKER**. After all, you are still 'purchasing a car'. Not all have the client first in mind. Bad apples, unethical actions and unscrupulous behavior can occur. If you do decide to consider that route, consider experiences that any relatives or friends might have had with a **CAR BROKER**. Verify licensing with issuers. Check with the **Better Business Bureau** as to the performance and complaint track record. Ask about longevity and experience in the profession. Ask how he or she goes about locating cars and if he or she is being reimbursed for services from sources. Ask about typical timing and number of potential cars shown to you. Look for signs of a good person and displays of family photos etc. Get a good inner feeling and sense of peace of mind. When satisfied move ahead comfortably.

"On a higher plane of hesitancy, it is pertinent to mention that brokering cars by Internet is not legal in all states. In some states it is viewed as a threat to local car dealers and state laws have been enacted to protect them from such competition. Dealers must be licensed by the State to protect consumers. Some states' politicians view Internet brokering as a way to circumvent the fees and associated rules of being a dealership. They also see the potential for local dealerships going out of business, thus losing sales tax revenue and income tax from their employees. A possible factor is that brokering a car could be viewed as prone to a **STRAW PURCHASE**."

Straw Purchase

"What's a **STRAW PURCHASE**, Dad?"

"A **STRAW PURCHASE** occurs when a person purchases something for another person (legally able to make the purchase themselves) in order to obtain better financing. If a person buys a car intended for that person (say an adult sibling) because he or she has a better credit rating and thus interest rate, it's a **STRAW PURCHASE**. A car **STRAW PURCHASE** is illegal in most states.

"Yes, the **CAR BROKER** who buys a car for a brokered resale is 'buying a car for another person'. But the **CAR BROKER** is not personally obtaining financing for the client. It is immediately sold to the client who must then obtain his or her own financing. The **CAR BROKER** doing a **STRAW PURCHASE** is not the issue. Rather, they must reject any client discovered to be engaging in a **STRAW PURCHASE**. If a **CAR BROKER** offers financing as a service, then he or she needs to avoid allowing a **STRAW PURCHASE**."

"As always, Dad you've helped me feel much more informed and less intimidated by something I have to do. In this case it's car buying through a **CAR BROKER**. I didn't even know they exist. I feel a lot better as the time to consider that option approaches. I see that if I decide to do it, I have to do it myself.

If I asked and you did it for me then it's a **STRAW PURCHASE** and I'd be getting you in big trouble."

"Nicole, that's great. And I would never do a **STRAW PURCHASE** for you. If I tried an honest **CAR BROKER** would reject it. I could purchase a car for you, brokered or not, if I just paid cash for it and no bank financing was involved. Now that you're older and independently supporting yourself, I very likely wouldn't do that either.

"And be aware, the **STRAW PURCHASE** law also applies to car purchases directly from a dealership or private individual. If the buyer is financing the purchase for someone else, the seller is not allowed to do the sale."

Helpful Resources

"I've mostly shared my general impressions and approaches to **CAR BROKERING**. There are websites you can access on this topic. For more philosophical and strategic advice I found www.edmunds.com/car-buying/using-a-car-broker-to-buy-your-next-vehicle.html. **Car-Buy-Her** offers **CAR BROKER** services. For a thorough walk through of the ins and outs and pros and cons, I found their website www.car-buy-her.com/auto-broker-services-article.html to be very informative. That article has details about how they do their car brokering. It also provides pertinent step wise advice about the general ways **CAR BROKERING** is done and how to be effective at doing it. Their overall site www.car-buy-her.com details all aspects of car buying.

"That covers everything I want to say about car buying in general. There are quite a lot of resources which I mentioned. It's probably best you look into them before we chat about the monetary aspects and costs involved in paying for a car. When you are ready to Skype again, just let me know."

"Ok, I'll do that Dad as time permits. When I'm ready to talk more, I'll let you know. Thanks again for your help."

ASIDE: *A straw purchase occurs when a person (an agent) agrees to acquire goods or service for someone who is either unable or unwilling to purchase the goods or service by them self. Straw purchases are legal except when the ultimate receiver of goods or services uses those goods or services to commit a crime with the prior knowledge of the straw purchaser or if the ultimate possessor is not legally able to purchase the goods/services. Purchasing a firearm at a federally licensed dealership for another person can be illegal, if improperly done. In most states, knowingly purchasing alcohol for an underage person is an illegal straw purchase. Financing a car loan for another person, who cannot do it himself or herself due to poor credit, is not allowed. If a dealer knows that is taking place, they will not sell you the car.*

Side Story

Some years ago, my daughter had a hurry-up need to purchase a car. Due to having much less than stellar creditworthiness at that time, she was offered a pretty steep loan interest rate, atop a somewhat high cash down payment requirement. She telephoned me from the dealership to inquire as to whether I would either co-sign the loan or do the loan in my name – knowing my superb creditworthiness would lead to the lowest annual rate of interest.

Unaware of the straw purchase restriction, I agreed to solely sign the auto loan. When she mentioned my intent to the salesperson, he advised her that it would be an illegal straw purchase. He could not and would not sell her the car that way. She called to inform me of the dilemma.

I could sense how the dealer had put my daughter in a bind and left her feeling she was at a dead end. I said to her, "Ask the dealer of he would accept cash." She said, "I don't have the cash needed." Gently, I replied, "Just go and ask him." She quickly came back on the phone and said the dealer had smiled and replied "Cash is always good!" I said, "Tell him you'll pay in cash, so please hold the car for you until tomorrow."

The next day I went to the dealership with her and paid cash for the car, purchasing it in both our names. In time, we worked out a fool proof way that she could and would repay me over time (which she did). We signed a short contract between us. I would not have done this had she had not long ago built up my confidence that she would pay me back. Part of me also wanted to "outsmart a car salesman." Above all, I wanted to illustrate to my daughter the necessity for and maneuverability of having cash at hand. There was something in the deal for me. I also added a bit extra interest to the debt; collected up front. Had the sole signed loan been possible, I would have acted the same way.

LESSON 6 Hitting the Road in My New Car Loan

"Good morning, Nicole. It's nice to see your virtual face once again. Do you see mine?"

"Hello Dad! You look great and it's equally nice to see yours again."

"After our last talk, I got kind of carried away in researching the topic of **CAR LOANS**. I have a lot to share. Did you look into it, too, Sweetie?"

"I wanted to, but I couldn't make the time. They sent me out into the field to cover a rural story and I was away in a motel for four days. I had to write it up each evening. Time flew by."

"That's very interesting. I'm sure you did a wonderful job. I can't wait to read your article."

"Thank you, Dad. I'll send it to you digitally. I'm ready to get started on the **CAR LOAN**S topic. I will only be buying a car I can afford and expect I will need to borrow some of the funds. I'd like your guidance on that aspect."

"You're on target there. Rarely is a car purchased without borrowing money to do so. Let's talk about that aspect – financing the purchase of a car."

Car Loans

"To begin, financing a **CAR LOAN** can occur via four primary avenues: the dealership selling you the car; banks; credit unions; or on-line lenders. In case of the dealership the financing may come either directly from that dealership or from the vendor for the car brand (e.g. Ford Motor Company for a Ford make and model) or via arrangements they have in place with particular banks or credit unions. In the latter mode, the actual lender is likely paying a fee to the dealership for passing the loan to that lender."

"Dad, are there any advantages or disadvantages to any of them?"

"Naturally, if you opt to finance directly with the dealership then you are at the mercy of the negotiation process with that dealership – one of the possible woes of purchasing a car. I mentioned that last time. If you have negotiated a price advantageous to you, then the dealership can and likely will try to offset it via the financing step. If so, then the dealership interest rates come into play and they can offer and maneuver you to unfavorable rates compared to banks and credit unions. If you turn them down the dealership might attempt to regain the financial advantage via offering extended warranty and car service plans unfavorable to you."

"That's good to know, Dad."

"There's another precaution. Regularly, when searching the car sale advertisements one finds captivating, bold print mention of very low or even 0.00% **APR** dealership financing being available."

"I have seen those, Dad. I never gave them much thought, other than wondering how they could do that."

"Unless you are near or at the upper limit of creditworthiness, don't get captivated. If you do, you will find that if you are not a 'well qualified' applicant for the auto loan, then those offers do not apply to you. Once you have walked through the doorway the objective has been achieved. You are an interested buyer and a salesperson will begin to try to sell you a car. Once you are shifted to the car selling process, it's harder to walk out the door than to enter. Should you end up negotiating a car purchase, a normal **APR** will come into play. You may not know that until after you have negotiated a price and the dealership financing step begins. Then the potential dealership financing maneuvering occurs."

"Hmm, that's another trick of their sleeve. How do I avoid it?"

"My personal advice is to arrange financing through a local bank or credit union and be pre-qualified before you begin looking for the car. Once you have a particular car honed in and are about to go to negotiate the final price, use that source. If a trade-in is involved, then be ready to negotiate that, too. Once the price and any trade-in values are verbally negotiated, inform the salesperson of that choice of lender. Here in our home town, most local and even some statewide dealerships have an agreement with the credit union Mom and I use. In that case there is no need to revisit the credit union. Via email or phone call, the dealership can and will quickly confirm you are pre-qualified and can obtain the needed financing."

"That sounds really handy, Dad. I'll look into it here."

"That's why I mentioned it. And you need to be alert to another thing. When you are about to sign the **SALES AGREEMENT** be sure to check that the correct source of financing is indicated in it. Some salespersons or dealership finance officers might take one last stab at you and intentionally indicate the dealership or the auto manufacturer as your source of the financing instead of the one you intend to use. If you sign the **SALES AGREEMENT**, then the financing will come via that source, not your other desired source."

"Wow! Can that really happen?"

"Indeed it can. It actually happened to me, once. Whether it was done by mistake or by intent of the dealership, I caught it before signing anything."

"What did you do? Cancel the sale?"

"No, it was corrected and I did not back out on the sale. I wanted the car and had gotten a negotiated cost that I liked. However, when I did leave driving my 2-year old **USED** car I was wondering if I had gotten the best deal. If the initial financing entry error was indeed intentional, then I probably did get a good deal and that may have provoked the end game subterfuge. At the very least, I made sure my long-time credit union had the loan commitment. Let's turn to the specifics of how bank and credit union financing work.

"To get a **CAR LOAN,** whether it's a bank or a credit union involved, two main components need to be achieved. The first is your creditworthiness must be satisfactory for approving the **LOAN AMOUNT** involved. The second is the **ANNUAL RATE OF INTEREST** (and **APR**) that you will be charged. The two components are actually linked. The specifics of how that's done are not overly involved; indeed, it's almost a rote process. Of course, the current value of the car enters the picture, too, but less so. It's imbedded in the linked components."

"Dad, I remember our first chat when you taught me about creditworthiness. That was way back in my high school days. Now, being a college grad and working, I keep an eye on it all the time. I've built up a pretty good **CREDIT RATING** and aim to keep it that way."

Smiling, Dad replies, "I sure do remember that and diverting you from that credit card you wanted to get when you were just sixteen years old. When you finally did get one in college, I knew you were well prepared for it.

"Nicole, for fun, why don't you sort of summarize what creditworthiness is all about? That way I can get to ask the questions and you can answer them, sort of reversed roles."

"You're on Dad. I'm sort of caught unexpectedly, but let the games begin."

"Ok, I'll start."

Credit Reports

"Nicole, what's a **CREDIT REPORT** and how do you get one?"

"For creditworthiness, banks and credit union lenders commonly depend on your **CREDIT REPORT** from one or more of the three major credit reporting agencies. They are Equifax, Experian and Transunion. The **CREDIT REPORTS** differ for each of the three agencies. That's because they collect and update data on different timings, have different inquiry occurrences, etc. The lender will request yours from one of them. If your creditworthiness is satisfactory, then it is unlikely the lender will check more than that one."

"What's in a **CREDIT REPORT**?"

"A **CREDIT REPORT** shows your debt and repayment history in detail over a long period of time. Your history includes very detailed information on the types of credit and debts you have and/or have had; how long you have had and/or had the credit or debt; how much of each debt you still owe; your repayment history such as were payments made on time, missed, gone into collection; any new credit applications; inquiries from lenders regarding loan and credit card applications; inquiries from promotional marketers; inquiries from potential employers, etc."

"Do you have to pay for a **CREDIT REPORT**?"

"You are entitled to a free **CREDIT REPORT** annually from each of the agencies. You can request them any time either via an Internet site or by phone. Of course, I don't have that information right at hand, Dad."

ASIDE: *You can obtain a* ***CREDIT REPORT*** *either via* www.annualcreditreport.com *or calling 1-877-322-8228. It is a good idea to request one every four months and rotate the requests to each agency. That will give you a periodic general sense of your situation. If you find questionable and/or erroneous information you can act to try to get it corrected. Should that happen, you should investigate at the credit reporting agency from which the report at hand came. Once clarified and acted on, you should check your reports at the other two agencies, even if you have to pay for the reports.*

FICO SCORES

"Nicole, can you tell me what a **FICO SCORE** is?"

"I sure can.

"Credit reporting agencies use the so-called **FICO SCORE** to indicate an overall **CREDIT RATING**. An individual's **FICO SCORE** is a number determined from the information in their **CREDIT REPORT**. It's calculated by the credit agency issuing that **CREDIT REPORT**."

"Ok, Peanut, what's the equation for calculating it?"

"Aha! You're trying to trick me. As I recall, there is actually a methodology and algorithm behind it, but it's secret. Only the agency that developed it knows how it's done."

"Who might that be?"

"Come on Dad. Trying to trick me again? Honestly, who can remember that? I think **FICO** is its initials."

"You're right. I can't remember the full name, either."

ASIDE*: The* ***FICO SCORE*** *process was developed by the* ***F****air,* ***I****saac* ***CO****rporation and, indeed, is proprietary.*

"How does one find out their **FICO SCORE**? Is it in their **CREDIT REPORT**?"

"Actually, it's not in any **CREDIT REPORT** you obtain for yourself. A lender will be given that information, but not you. You have to purchase one. There's a website for doing it, but I'd have to Google it to find it."

ASIDE: *Previously, it cost $15.95 to get a* ***FICO SCORE****, via* www.myfico.com. *Now, via that source, it costs $29.95 to obtain a* ***CREDIT REPORT*** *for each major credit bureau, on a quarterly cycle. It costs $39.95 to obtain them monthly. That source is marketing that your* ***FICO SCORE*** *varies by source and for auto loans, credit cards, and mortgage loans. Hence, they include 28* ***FICO*** *scores. The situation appears to be due to changing times. Avenues to get a free* ***FICO SCORE*** *are arising. They appear to be mostly from someone trying to sell you something or their services or offer you a loan. More important there are fraudulent or imposter websites out there, often using the word free to entice one. It might be worth the money to be sure you avoid accidentally using any of them. It also eliminates the need to regularly obtain free* ***CREDIT REPORTS****. Likely, when a lender decides on a loan, you can ask if your* ***FICO SCORE*** *was a factor. That lender might tell you your score and its effect on your* *outcome. The author's credit union offers free* ***FICO SCORES*** *unconditionally. It's seems to be a growing trend.*

"Nicole, can you recall the range of possible **FICO SCORES**? And how critical is your actual **FICO SCORE** to your creditworthiness?"

"Actually I can. The lowest **FICO SCORE** one can be given is 300. The highest **FICO SCORE** is 850. Your **FICO SCORE** is a critical aspect of your creditworthiness. It's a significant factor in a lender's decision on loan applications, particularly for **CAR LOANS**. The lower is your **FICO SCORE**, the higher will be the **ANNUAL RATE OF INTEREST** charged for a loan. Each lender has their own criteria for matching an **ANNUAL RATE OF INTEREST** to your **FICO SCORE**.

"A **FICO SCORE** in the range of 750-850 is excellent. As you drop toward 700 you are nearing an average **CREDIT RATING. FICO SCORES** below 600 might prevent you from obtaining the loan. If you do get one, it will be at a very high rate of interest."

"That's amazing, Smarty Pants. Even I cannot readily recall those numbers."

"Dad, I have a confession to make. A little while ago I wrote a news article about creditworthiness for my paper. It led to my reviewing the topic and recalling our past talk. I guess I sort of pulled the wool over your eyes. I actually knew that the **FICO SCORE** system was created by the Fair, Isaac Corporation. I knew my saying so would be very suspicious. I passed it by to keep you in the dark."

"Now that's a bright flashlight in my eyes. It's terrific to know what we chatted about became directly useful in your career. Just like that college paper you wrote about student loan brackets. Just mentioning it brings a few tears of joy to my eyes."

"That's why I gave myself away, Dad. I wanted to sort of relive that moment.

"In my article, I also covered some dos and don'ts. Generally, there are five factors that **FICO** considers. They are types of credit, total debt amount, length of credit history, payment history and new credit debts. You can find articles indicating about how much **FICO** considers each of them. As I said, finding their formulas for calculating your **FICO SCORE** is like trying to find out how the **Internal Revenue Service** decides to audit particular taxpayers. There are some general considerations.

"To build a high **FICO SCORE**, you need to develop a great credit history. That's done by paying all loan payments on time. It's not the only factor. The overall debt you are carrying is a factor, too. And it's good to have a mix of credit types, student loans, car loans, credit cards etc. It's not good to apply for too many loans and credit cards in a short amount of time.

"For credit cards and similar revolving debts, it's very important to keep the **OUTSTANDING BALANCE** as low as possible. Ideally it should be a small percentage of the credit limit on the card. The longer you keep doing that, the higher your **FICO SCORE** will become. It's also wise to limit the number of credit cards you have opened. It's advisable to not close any credit card accounts, even if you don't need them and they have a zero balance.

"You should limit the number of requests others make for your **CREDIT REPORT**. Of course, you don't directly control that. If you can get a lender to avoid requesting one unless you are going to be approved, it helps a lot. If you obtained a **CREDIT REPORT** yourself, then pose the situation to the lender. Ask if the loan would be approved once they confirm the facts. If so, then apply for the loan. If not, then don't.

"Failure to do these things causes your **FICO SCORE** to drop. It can happen fast, especially if you miss payments on loans and credit cards. One lapse hurts, a few is very harmful, and a steady diet knocks you out. It's especially bad if you get turned down on loan applications.

"I've never heard of anyone having a perfect **FICO SCORE** of 850. Those are the main things that lead to a very high one. It takes longevity to get there. It may be a negative to have too much debt early in your life. As time moves on, with a good credit history, things happen. You get higher credit limits, qualify for larger loans and pay off higher amounts consistently. Over time, the breadth of your credit history grows. As the bulk increases, if it is good stuff, then your **FICO SCORE** climbs."

"Ok Nicole, I'll give you an A+ for your great research on the job and recall concerning what a **FICO SCORE** is all about."

"Thank you, Dad. I really appreciate that."

"It's my pleasure!"

Effect of FICO SCORE on Car Loans

"Let's get back to you buying a car. I want to talk about how a **FICO SCORE** comes into play in getting a **CAR LOAN**. Since the time we last talked I research some of the details."

"That's fine, Dad. I promise I didn't research it and write a news article about it."

"That's good, as I don't want to have the wool pulled over my eyes again. I don't like saying 'baaah'. Feel free to look into it as well, if you have time and want to do so."

"I'll see how this talk goes first, Dad."

"Nicole, from my own experience, I knew banks and credit unions use three direct criteria for setting the **APR** for a **CAR LOAN**. At least it was so the last time I had to take out a **CAR LOAN**. The first criterion was the **AGE OF THE CAR**. The second criterion used was the length of the **TERM** of the requested loan. The third criterion was the **CREDIT RATING** of the borrower.

"The measure for the age of the car was simply whether it was either **NEW** or **USED**. I did a spot check at Bank of America via www.bankofamerica.com/AutoLoans for a **CAR LOAN** in Colorado. For a 60-month **TERM** indicated their rate was 2.49% for a **NEW** car and 2.74% for a **USED** car. That web site provides advertised rates for all states. Those rates applied for many other states as well. However, the fine print indicated they were based on an assumed excellent borrower credit history. For three local banks I checked the offered rates for that **TERM** and a **NEW CAR** were 4.00%, 4.85%, and 6.75%. For a 48-month **TERM** they were, 4.00%, 5.00% and 6.75%. The level of creditworthiness needed was not indicated. I took that to mean they would do the usual request for a **CREDIT REPORT** and make a judgement.

"It appears that the **FICO SCORE** is becoming the specific measure of creditworthiness for **CAR LOANS**. Some lenders offer interest rates based on the level of that score. They vary somewhat in the range of rates offered for different **FICO SCORE** limits. Here's a tabulation of national average **APR** values I found at one website."

	TERM IN MONTHS		
FICO SCORE	36	48	60
720-850	3.18%	3.20%	3.24%
690-719	4.53%	4.54%	4.59%
660-689	6.60%	6.62%	6.67%
620-659	9.71%	9.74%	9.84%
560-619	14.00%	14.00%	14.10%
500-589	15.42%	15.40%	15.50%

"The listed **TERMS** are selective; they can be other durations. What do you notice in the trends, Sweetie?"

"I see that as the **FICO SCORE** gets lower and lower the **APR** gets pretty high. Who would want to pay 14.00% to 15.50% on any loan? But it seems that the length of the **TERM** makes only a minor difference in **APR**."

"That's how I saw the results, too. That particular website did not distinguish between **NEW** and **USED** cars. Perhaps, that's because they are overall averages. For specific lenders we might find the interest rates are lower than shown for a **NEW CAR** and higher for a **USED CAR**. With poor creditworthiness, for a **USED CAR** it may be even worse than 14.00%-15.50%.

"**CAR LOANS** are done by **amortization**. I calculated **amortization schedules** to see the impact of those tabulated **APR** values on the loan costs. I assumed a **LOAN AMOUNT** of $30000.00 and took the **APR** as the **ANNUAL RATE OF INTEREST**. The following table lists the loan costs corresponding to each of the listed **APR** values."

LOAN AMOUNT = 30000.00	MONTHLY PAYMENT			CUMULATIVE INTEREST		
	TERM IN MONTHS			TERM IN MONTHS		
FICO SCORE	36	48	60	36	48	60
720-850	874.82	666.68	542.27	1493.95	2000.88	2535.97
690-719	892.81	684.65	560.52	2141.16	2862.96	3131.15
660-689	920.84	713.11	589.38	3150.10	4229.29	5362.57
620-659	963.94	757.14	635.05	4701.70	6342.58	8103.13
560-619	1025.33	819.79	699.60	6911.84	9350.13	11976.23
500-589	1046.14	841.02	721.60	7661.07	10368.86	13295.74

"This tabulation indicates that **FICO SCORE** brackets are very important in **CAR LOANS**. Consider the following trends.

"For each **TERM**, as the **FICO SCORE** decreases the **MONTHLY PAYMENT** gradually increases, but by just tens of dollars. However, the **CUMULATIVE INTEREST** increases rapidly. You can pay anywhere from about $1500.00 to about $13000.00 in **CUMULATIVE INTEREST** for the very same car! $13000.00 is about 43% of the **LOAN AMOUNT**.

"For each **TERM**, a **FICO SCORE** of 500-589 leads to about five times as much **CUMULATIVE INTEREST** as for a score of 720-850. Similar penalization probably occurs for any type of loan for which a **FICO SCORE** enters the financing picture, not just a **CAR LOAN**. The message is loud and clear. Do everything possible to achieve and maintain as high a **FICO SCORE** as possible."

"I'm getting that loud and clear, too, Dad. I never want to be in a credit situation where I pay about 43% of the **LOAN AMOUNT** in interest."

"There's more to note. For any **FICO SCORE**, by going from a 36-month **TERM** to a 48-month **TERM** to a 60-month **TERM**, the **MONTHLY PAYMENT** drops noticeably, by hundreds of dollars. The **CUMULATIVE INTEREST** increases much more noticeably, by 500 to 1000s of dollars.

"The vital observation is that the combined effect of lowering the **FICO SCORE** and increasing the **TERM** is almost devastating. For a **FICO SCORE** of 500-589 and **TERM** of 60 months, the **CUMULATIVE INTEREST** of $13295.14 is about nine times as much as the $1493.95 for a **FICO SCORE** of 720-850 and **TERM** of 36 months."

"That really tells a story, Dad. I can assure you my **FICO** score is not in that big worry zone."

"That's great, Peanut. What I just described is based on a simple **NEW CAR** vs. **USED CAR** characterization of the car. I found that, at some banks and credit unions, the age of the car is becoming characterized more distinctly. Internally, a tabulation that reflects both the age of the car by model year (not just **NEW** vs. **OLD**) and the **FICO SCORE** is done. For competitive reasons they do not advertise or publish the detailed values they use.

"My local credit union loan officer indicated they increase the **APR** for each of three factors; for longer terms, an older car, and lower **FICO SCORES**. She provided me some information at the extremes.

"For a car aged 2014-2017, for a **TERM** of 63 months or less, and a **FICO SCORE** of 800; the **APR** would be at 3.14%. That's for the newest cars. At the other end of the age spectrum, for a car aged 2006 or older, the **APR** would increase to 4.64%.

"At the low end of the **FICO SCORE** spectrum, for a **NEW** car aged 2014-2017, for a **TERM** of 63 months or less, and a **FICO SCORE** of 600; the **APR** would be 14.39%. (if less than 600, the credit rate would be 20.65%) For a car aged 2005 or older, the **APR** increases to 15.89%. (if less than 600,the credit rate would be 21.00%)

"She indicated that for 2007 and somewhat newer cars, a **FICO SCORE** of 640-719 credit score would put you the mid-range of **APR**, usually between 4.89% and 8.00%."

“Gee, Dad. It’s amazing they even consider charging anyone that an interest rate as high as 21.00%. That would be really disheartening to anyone facing that news.”

“Yes, it would. Surely they only do it because they see a high risk from the individual’s **CREDIT REPORT**. That’s why it’s important to have that in good order.

“Generally worded, for a given **FICO SCORE,** the older the car the higher is the **APR**. For a given **AGE OF CAR**, the lower the **FICO SCORE,** the higher is the **APR**. For any combination of **FICO SCORE** and **AGE OF THE CAR**, the longer the **TERM** of the loan, the higher is the **APR**.”

“Dad, why does the **APR** increases as the age of the car increases?”

“Again, it’s very likely related to perceived risk. The older the car becomes, the more likely its condition worsens. As its condition worsens, the maintenance and repair costs increase. If they become disproportionate to the value of the car then a borrower might just stop making payments and ‘junk the car’. That might be why lenders seem to prefer a ‘pay me now’ stance to a ‘pay me later’ stance. That is, they collect interest at higher rates in case the borrower stops paying. The same might be said of low **FICO SCORES**. The lower the **FICO** the more apparent it is that the borrower is a risky customer and at some point in time might skip some or all payments.”

“What I just covered is specific to my credit union. In general, for any given **TERM** the overall trend of the **APR** values for **FICO SCORE** and **AGE OF CAR** together are as shown in this table.”

LOAN TERM = T		**FICO SCORE**				
		Highest	• • •	•	• • •	**Lowest**
AGE OF THE CAR	**Newest**	**Lowest APR**	• • •	**Increasing APR**	• • •	**Higher APR**
	•	•		•		•
	•	•		•		•
	•	•		•		•
	•	**Increasing APR**	• • •	**Medium APR**	• • •	**Increasing APR**
	•	•		•		•
	•	•		•		•
	•	•		•		•
	Oldest	**Higher APR**	• • •	**Increasing APR**	• • •	**Highest APR**

“That’s great, Dad. Seeing it this way puts it all together for me.”

Car Base Loans and Scaling

"Nicole, do you remember back when we were looking at student loans I used **BASE LOANS** and a scaling approach to produce loan costs?"

"I do, Dad. You took the **LOAN AMOUNT** for the base loan as $1000.00. In reality, it would be various amounts. You scaled the **BASE LOAN** results for that **LOAN AMOUNT** to get them for other **LOAN AMOUNTS**. It involved a **SCALING FACTOR**. The results for the actual **LOAN AMOUNT** are obtained by multiplying the **BASE LOAN** results by the applicable **SCALING FACTOR**."

"What was the equation for the **SCALING FACTOR**, Nicole?"

"The **SCALING FACTOR** is equal to the actual **LOAN AMOUNT** divided by $1000.00."

"That's right. Mathematically that's given by this equation."

SCALING FACTOR = LOAN AMOUNT/$1000.00

CAR-BASE LOAN TABLE

"Nicole, do you remember me creating **BASE LOAN TABLES** for student loans and why I did that?"

"Yes, I do. Once you had them, it eliminated the need to directly calculate **AMORTIZATION SCHEDULES**."

"Very good, Sweetie!

"This past week I created one for **CAR LOANS**. I calculated **AMORTIZATION SCHEDULES** for various combinations of **ANNUAL RATE OF INTEREST** and **TERM**. I used the **BASE LOAN AMOUNT** of $1000.00. Here is a tabulation of the **MONTHLY PAYMENT** and **CUMULATIVE INTEREST** results. Let's refer to it as a **CAR–BASE LOAN TABLE**."

CAR-BASE LOAN TABLE						
LOAN AMOUNT = 1000.00	MONTHLY PAYMENT TERM IN MONTHS			CUMULATIVE INTEREST TERM IN MONTHS		
ANNUAL RATE OF INTEREST	36	48	60	36	48	60
2.00%	28.64	21.70	17.53	31.13	41.37	51.67
6.00%	30.42	23.49	19.33	95.19	127.28	159.97
10.00%	33.27	25.46	21.25	161.62	217.40	274.82
14.00%	34.18	27.33	23.27	230.39	311.67	396.10
18.00%	36.15	29.37	25.39	301.49	410.00	523.61
22.00%	38.19	31.51	27.62	374.86	512.29	657.13

"Nicole, if the **BASE LOAN** has an **ANNUAL RATE OF INTEREST** of 6.00% and a **TERM** of 48 months, then what are the loan costs?"

After a short glance at the **CAR–BASE LOAN TABLE**, Nicole replies, "The **MONTHLY PAYMENT** is $23.49 and the **CUMULATIVE INTEREST** is $127.28."

"That's correct. Now what do we do for any **LOAN AMOUNT** other than $1000.00?"

Using the CAR-BASE LOAN TABLE

"For other **LOAN AMOUNTS**, your **SCALING FACTOR** approach is used."

"Right again, Peanut.

"The last step is to combine the **LOAN AMOUNT** and the **CUMULATIVE INTEREST** to get the **TOTAL LOAN COST**. In math form that's,

TOTAL LOAN COST = LOAN AMOUNT + CUMULATIVE INTEREST

"That's straightforward, right?"

"Yes it is, Dad."

"Ok, let's try a hypothetical example."

<u>SITUATION 6</u>

"Randall is purchasing a 2009 car for $7500.00, including **SALES TAX**. He has a **FICO SCORE** of 675 and seeks a **CAR LOAN** for that **LOAN AMOUNT** with a **TERM** of 48 months. The best loan he can obtain is for an **ANNUAL RATE OF INTEREST** of 6.00%.

"Nicole, what's the **SCALING FACTOR** value?"

"The **SCALING FACTOR** = $7500.00/$1000.00 = 7.50."

"Good. What are his **MONTHLY INTEREST**, **CUMULATIVE INTEREST** and **TOTAL LOAN COST** amounts?"

"Let me take out my calculator.

"Both the **ANNUAL RATE OF INTEREST** of 6.00% and **TERM** of 48 months are directly listed. I just told you the **BASE LOAN RESULTS**. Scaling them, I get these results."

MONTHLY PAYMENT = 7.50 x $23.49 = $176.18

CUMULATIVE INTEREST = 7.50 x $127.28 = $954.60

PERCENT CUMULATIVE INTEREST = ($954.60/$7500.00) x 100 = 13% (rounded)

TOTAL LOAN COST = $7500.00 + $954.60 = $8454.60

SITUATION 6 – CONTINUED

"That's spot on, Sweetie!

"Those approximate results are extremely close to precise values. For an actual **AMORTIZATION SCHEDULE**, the **MONTHLY PAYMENT** = $176.14 and **CUMULATIVE INTEREST** = $954.61."

"Nicole, what if the **ANNUAL RATE OF INTEREST** is not one of the listed values?"

"I guess you would have to use interpolation."

"Interpolation? You remember that word? What's it mean?"

"Yes, I do. You told me about it when we covered student loans. Since then I learned about it in my senior year of high school. And I used it in some of my college classes, too. In this case, it's the process you use for finding results for **ANNUAL RATES OF INTEREST** that fall between any two listed values."

"I'm impressed.

"Nicole, I illustrated that way back when we worked on your student loan needs. That was about eight years ago, so let me do it again.

"For approximate and easiest use, you can round the actual **ANNUAL RATE OF INTEREST** value to the nearest listed value. Then you take the listed **CAR-BASE LOAN TABLE** results and scale them to the actual **LOAN AMOUNT**.

"For more accurate approximate results, you can interpolate between the two closest listed values of **ANNUAL RATE OF INTEREST**. For example, results for 3.00%, 4.00% and 5.00% are ¼, ½ and ¾ of the way between the values listed for 2.00% and 6.00%. Results for 7.00%, 8.00% and 9.00% are ¼, ½ and ¾ of the way between the values listed for 6.00% and 10.00%, and so on. For values other than those, you can round the actual **ANNUAL RATE OF INTEREST** to the closest intermediate whole value as well."

"Ok, now I remember you doing that for the various possible **ANNUAL RATES OF INTEREST** for my student loans. That was really clever."

"It's nice you think that."

"Why are the results only approximate, Dad?"

"Do you remember me showing you linear and nonlinear plots when I taught you about acceleration of a loan?"

"Yes, I do. That was neat, too."

"By using interpolation one assumes the relationships between the **CAR LOAN** costs and the **ANNUAL RATE OF INTEREST** are linear, that is each plots as a straight-line. The actual relationships between **CAR LOAN** costs and the loan **ANNUAL RATE OF INTEREST** are nonlinear. They come from the **AMORTIZATION EQUATION**, which is anything but linear. That's why a linear interpolation between two **ANNUAL RATES OF INTEREST** is approximate."

"Thanks, Dad. That makes sense."

"Let's look at using interpolation for a hypothetical case of a **CAR LOAN**."

SITUATION 7

"Randall of SITUATION 6 decides he cannot afford to purchase the car. A second party, Linda, was looking at it too and for the same price. Her **FICO** score is a much better 750. She is offered a **CAR LOAN** with a **TERM** of 48 months with an **ANNUAL RATE OF INTEREST** of 4.00%.

"The **ANNUAL RATE OF INTEREST** is 4.00% and is not directly listed. It is midway between the listed values of 2.00% and 6.00%."

"Nicole, what are the results for an **ANNUAL RATE OF INTEREST** = 2.00%?"

"The **BASE LOAN MONTHLY PAYMENT** = $21.70 and **BASE LOAN CUMULATIVE INTEREST** $41.37"

"And for 6.00%?"

"Actually, Dad, we already got that in SITUATION 6. The **BASE LOAN MONTHLY PAYMENT** = $23.49 and **BASE LOAN CUMULATIVE INTEREST** = $127.28."

"That's right. What's next?"

"For the **ANNUAL RATE OF INTEREST** of 4.00%, the approximate results are 1/2 of the way between those two results."

BASE MONTHLY PAYMENT = $21.70 + 1/2($23.49 – $21.70) = $21.70 + $0.90 = $22.60

BASE CUMULATIVE INTEREST = $41.37 + 1/2($127.28 – $41.37) = $41.37 + $42.96 = $84.33

MONTHLY PAYMENT = 7.5 x $22.60 = $169.50

CUMULATIVE INTEREST = 7.5 x $84.33 = $632.48

PERCENT CUMULATIVE INTEREST = ($632.48/$7500.00) x 100 = 8% (rounded)

TOTAL LOAN COST = $7500.00 + $632.48 = $8132.48

SITUATION 7 – CONTINUED

"Well, Nicole. Compared to Randall, Linda pays \$954.60 – \$632.48 = \$322.12 less **CUMULATIVE INTEREST**. That's 34% less. Of course, her **TOTAL LOAN COST** is less by that \$322.12, too. She is well rewarded for her higher **FICO** score."

"Indeed she is!"

"For an actual **AMORTIZATION SCHEDULE**, the results are **MONTHLY PAYMENT** = \$169.34 and **CUMULATIVE INTEREST** = \$628.46. The approximate amounts are very close to those values."

ASIDE: *If, and only if, the interpolated value is half way between two listed values, there is an alternative calculation. Calculating the average of those two values will give the same result. For SITUATION 7, we do the following.*

BASE LOAN MONTHLY PAYMENT = (\$21.70 + \$23.49)/2 = \$22.60

BASE LOAN CUMULATIVE INTEREST = (\$41.37 + \$127.28)/2 = \$84.33

"The two SITUATIONS I just showed you were for a **USED CAR**. I also took a look at a hypothetical case of a **NEW CAR**."

SITUATION 8

"Assume Carl is purchasing a 2016 car for \$32500.00, including **SALES TAX**. He has a **FICO SCORE** of 715 and seeks a **CAR LOAN** with **TERM** of 60 months. The best loan he can obtain is for an **ANNUAL RATE OF INTEREST** of 5.00%.

"The **SCALING FACTOR** = 32.5.

"The closest listed **ANNUAL RATE OF INTEREST** is 6.00%. For that value his approximate **BASE MONTHLY PAYMENT** = \$19.33 and **CUMULATIVE INTEREST** = \$159.97.

"For an **ANNUAL RATE OF INTEREST** = 2.00% his **MONTHLY PAYMENT** = \$17.53 = and **CUMULATIVE INTEREST** = \$51.67.

"For his **ANNUAL RATE OF INTEREST** of 5.00%, the approximate results are 3/4 of the way between those two results."

BASE MONTHLY PAYMENT = \$17.53+ 3/4(\$19.33 – \$17.53) = \$17.53 + \$1.35 = \$18.88

BASE CUMULATIVE INTEREST = \$51.67 + 3/4(\$159.97 – \$51.67) = \$51.67 + \$81.23

= \$132.90

MONTHLY PAYMENT = 32.5 x \$18.88 = \$613.60

CUMULATIVE INTEREST = 32.5 x $132.90 = $4319.25

PERCENT CUMULATIVE INTEREST = $4319.25/$32500.00) x 100 = 13% (rounded)

TOTAL LOAN COST = $32500.00 + $4319.25 = $36819.25

SITUATION 8 – CONTINUED

"For an actual **AMORTIZATION SCHEDULE**, the results are a **MONTHLY PAYMENT** = $613.32 and **CUMULATIVE INTEREST** = $4298.91. Those are pretty accurate results.

"What about the results for the 6.00%, Nicole? How do they compare?"

"Hmm, the **MONTHLY PAYMENT** is fairly close but the **CUMULATIVE INTEREST** is much farther off. It looks like the interpolation was necessary."

"Dad, I'm curious about results for someone with a very high **ANNUAL RATE OF INTEREST**."

"You read my mind again. I also looked at an example of that possibility."

SITUATION 9

"Lucy is purchasing a 2005 car for $3500.00, including **SALES TAX**. She has a **FICO SCORE** of 605 and seeks a **CAR LOAN** with a **TERM** of 48 months. The best loan she can obtain is for an **ANNUAL RATE OF INTEREST** of 20.50%.

"What's the **SCALING FACTOR**, Nicole?"

"It's 3.50."

"The closest listed **ANNUAL RATE OF INTEREST** is 22.00%. What are Lucy's results for that value?"

"Her approximate **BASE LOAN MONTHLY PAYMENT** = $31.51 and her approximate **BASE LOAN CUMULATIVE INTEREST** = $512.29."

"If you interpolate, what is the other closest listed **ANNUAL RATE OF INTEREST** you need to use?"

"It's 18.00%."

"And what are the results for that value?"

"Lucy's **BASE LOAN MONTHLY PAYMENT** = $29.37 and her **BASE LOAN CUMULATIVE INTEREST** = $410.00."

"Perfect, of course. Here's the next step.

"If Lucy rounds her **ANNUAL RATE OF INTEREST** to 21.00%, then the approximate results are 3/4 of the way between those two results."

BASE LOAN MONTHLY PAYMENT = $29.37 + 3/4($31.51– $29.37)
= $29.37 + $ 1.67 = $30.98

BASE LOAN CUMULATIVE INTEREST = $410.00 + 3/4($512.29 – $410.00)
= $410.00 + $76.72 = $486.72

MONTHLY PAYMENT = 3.50 x $30.98 = $108.43

CUMULATIVE INTEREST = 3.50 x $486.72 = $1703.52

PERCENT CUMULATIVE INTEREST = (1703.52/$3500) x 100 = 49% (rounded)

TOTAL LOAN COST = $3500.00 + $1703.52 = $5203.52

SITUATION 9 - CONTINUED

"How do these results look, Peanut?"

"I think paying that much interest is awful. I'll make sure to avoid it happening to me."

"Just for awareness, from the actual **AMORTIZATION SCHEDULE** for an **ANNUAL RATE OF INTEREST** = 20.50%, Lucy's precise results would be a **MONTHLY PAYMENT** = $107.44 and **CUMULATIVE INTEREST** = $1657.16."

"Hmm, it's a little bit lower, Dad. But it's still a pile of interest."

ASIDE: *For the interested reader, a more accurate approximation would be based on the 20.5% value. Those results are:*

BASE LOAN MONTHLY PAYMENT = $29.37 + 2.5/4($31.51 – $29.37)
= $29.37 + $1.34 = $30.71

BASE LOAN CUMULATIVE INTEREST = $410.00 + 2.5/4($512.29 – $410.00)
= $410.00 + $63.93 = $473.93

MONTHLY PAYMENT = 3.5 x $30.71 = $107.49

CUMULATIVE INTEREST = 3.5 x $473.93 = $1658.67

"Dad, I it's a similar process, but what if the **TERM** of the **CAR LOAN** is not one of the listed values?"

"Approximate results for **TERMS** of 42 months and 54 months can be obtained by taking the tabulated value halfway between the applicable two adjacent **TERMS**. For 42 months use the values halfway between 36 months and 48 months. For 54 months, use the values hallway between 48 months and 60 months. That pretty much covers the most common range of **TERMS** that are offered for **CAR LOANS**."

"Let's look at an example, Sweetie."

SITUATION 10

"Sebastian purchases a **USED** car for $10000.00, including **SALES TAX**. His **FICO SCORE** combined with the age of the car results in a **CAR LOAN** for a **TERM** of 54 months with an **ANNUAL RATE OF INTEREST** of 10.00%.

"The **SCALING FACTOR** = 10.00.

"His **ANNUAL RATE OF INTEREST** is a listed value. The **TERM** is midway between the listed 48 months and 60 months. That means we need to interpolate between the two of them.

"Here are the results for each of those **TERMS**."

For 10.00% and 48 months:

MONTHLY PAYMENT = 10.00 x $25.46 = $254.60

CUMULATIVE INTEREST = 10.00 x $217.40 = $2174.00

For 10.00% and 60 months:

MONTHLY PAYMENT = 10.00 x $21.25 = $212.50

CUMULATIVE INTEREST = 10.00 x $274.82 = $2748.20

SITUATION 10 - CONTINUED

"I did things a little differently here. In the previous SITUATIONS, I interpolated for the **BASE LOAN** values, and then scaled the results. Here, I scaled the **BASE LOAN** values first. Now, we interpolate for those results. Can you see that it works that way, too?"

After a pause, Nicole indicates, "That's right. I see you did that. My math recall tells me, if you interpolate those values, it is OK in the end."

"Ok, what comes next, Nicole?"

"I see it's straight-forward. We get the values half way between them."

"Ok. In this case, you can just average the two values, right?"

"Yes, that's right. Ok, I'll do that."

Calculator in hand, Nicole scratch notes her calculations. "Here's what I get, Dad."

MONTHLY PAYMENT = ($254.60 + $212.50)/2 = $233.55

CUMULATIVE INTEREST = ($2174.00 + $2748.20)/2 = $2466.10

PERCENT CUMULATIVE INTEREST = (2466.10/$10000) x 100 = 25% (rounded)

TOTAL LOAN COST = $10000.00 + $2466.10 = $12466.10

SITUATION 10 – CONTINUED

"Excellent, Nicole. As a check, can you do it the other way?"

"I think so." Again scratch noting, Nicole indicates the results. "Here's what I get that way."

BASE LOAN MONTHLY PAYMENT = ($25.46 + $21.25)/2 = $23.36

BASE LOAN CUMULATIVE INTEREST= $217.40 + $274.82)/2 = $246.61

SITUATION 10 – CONTINUED

"Multiplying by 10 gives the same results."

"Indeed it does, Peanut. The precise results from an **AMORTIZATION SCHEDULE** are **MONTHLY PAYMENT** = $230.72 and **CUMULATIVE INTEREST** = $2459.11."

"Nicole, why do you suppose the results of doing this interpolation are also only approximate?"

"Well, given what you said about the **ANNUAL RATE OF INTEREST**, I realize it's because using interpolation assumes the relationship between the loan costs and the loan **TERM** are linear. To mimic your words, the actual relationship between loan costs and the loan **TERM** are nonlinear. They come from the **AMORTIZATION EQUATION**, which is anything but linear. That's why a linear interpolation between two **TERMS** is approximate."

"Exactly! And now can you be a ventriloquist and impersonate my voice?"

"Oh, Dad! I'd never do that to you. You sure aren't a dummy."

"Ok, that's enough joking. Let's look at using interpolation for another hypothetical case. Let's modify

SITUATION 10."

SITUATION 11

"Assume Sebastian's **FICO SCORE** combined with the **AGE OF THE CAR** results in a **CAR LOAN** for a **TERM** of 54 months with an **ANNUAL RATE OF INTEREST** of 12.00%, instead of 10.00%.

"His **ANNUAL RATE OF INTEREST** is midway between the listed 10.00% and 14.00% values. His **TERM** is midway between the listed 48 months and 60 months. That means we need to interpolate for both of these. Because in each case the result is midway between them, we can just average the two listed values each time. Let's take them one at a time."

"That spins my head around, Dad. I'm anxious to see how that's done."

"Don't worry, I'll walk through it step by step.

"First, I interpolate to get the **BASE LOAN** results for the 12.00% using the **TERM** of 48 months. Then, I scale them to actual **LOAN AMOUNT**. The **SCALING FACTOR** = 10.00.

"For 10.00% and 48 months, from the **CAR-BASE LOAN TABLE** the **BASE MONTHLY PAYMENT** = $25.46 and **BASE CUMULATIVE INTEREST** = $217.40.

"For 14.00% and 48 months, the **BASE MONTHLY PAYMENT** = $27.33 and **BASE CUMULATIVE INTEREST** = $311.67."

For 12.00% and 48 months:

Interpolating,

BASE MONTHLY PAYMENT = ($25.46 + $27.33)/2 = $26.40 (rounded)

BASE CUMULATIVE INTEREST = ($217.40 + $311.67)/2 = $264.54.

For the actual LOAN AMOUNT,

MONTHLY PAYMENT = 10.00 x $26.40 = $264.00

CUMULATIVE INTEREST = 10.00 x $264.54 = $2645.40

SITUATION 11 – CONTINUED

"Are you following this, Nicole?"

"So far, I'm right with you, Dad."

"Great!

"For 10.00% and 60 months, from the **CAR-BASE LOAN TABLE** the **MONTHLY PAYMENT** = $21.25 and **CUMULATIVE INTEREST** = $274.82.

"For 14.00% and 60 months, the **MONTHLY PAYMENT** = $23.27 and **CUMULATIVE INTEREST** = $396.10.

"Here, I'll condense the next calculations."

For 12.00% and 60 months:

MONTHLY PAYMENT = SCALING FACTOR x BASE MONTHLY PAYMENT

= 10.00 x ($21.25 + $23.27)/2 = 10.00 x $22.26 = $222.60

CUMULATIVE INTEREST = SCALING FACTOR x BASE CUMULATIVE INTEREST

= 10.00 x ($274.82 + $396.10)/2 = 10.00 x $335.46 = $3354.60

SITUATION 11 – CONTINUED

"Do you follow that, Peanut?"

Squinting a bit, Nicole mentions, "It puzzled me a bit at first. Looking closer at the equations, I got it. I see you merged the two steps into one line for each calculation."

"Exactly, Nicole. Can you surmise how to handle the 54-month **TERM**?"

After some thought, she nervously replies, "For 12.00% and 54 months, the approximate results are 1/2 of the way between the above two results. That is, halfway between the 12% results for 48 months and 60 months."

"Perfect! Just go ahead and do it."

"Ok, Dad." After calculating away, "Here's what I get."

For 12.00% and 54 months:

MONTHLY PAYMENT = ($263.95 + $222.60)/2) = $243.28

CUMULATIVE INTEREST = ($2645.40 + $3354.60)/2 = $3000.00

PERCENT CUMULATIVE INTEREST = (3000.00/$10000) x 100 = 30%

TOTAL LOAN COST = $10000.00 + $3000.00 = $13000.00

SITUATION 11 – CONTINUED

"Ok, that's right, Sweetie. Doing it the other way, as a check, I got this.

BASE LOAN MONTHLY PAYMENT = ($26.395 + $22.26)/2 = $24.33 (rounded)

BASE LOAN CUMULATIVE INTEREST = ($264.54 + $335.46)/2 = $300.00

SITUATION 11 – CONTINUED

"Multiplying by 10 gives same results."

"Indeed it does, Dad. You did great!"

"Oh so funny you are, Peanut.

"I did the **AMORTIZATION SCHEDULE** for a **TERM** = 54 months and an **ANNUAL RATE OF INTEREST** = 12.00%. The precise results are a **MONTHLY PAYMENT** = $240.57 and **CUMULATIVE INTEREST** = $2990.55."

"Considering you did a bunch of interpolations, the approximate results are pretty close, Dad."

"Even though it's not likely to happen for anyone, what if I had a perfect **FICO SCORE**?"

"You read my mind. I was curious about that, too. I did look at it. I also made a slight change in the way to interpolate for both the **ANNUAL RATE OF INTEREST** and the **TERM** being unlisted values."

SITUATION 12

"Assume a third party, Danielle, is also interested in the $7500.00 car that Randall of SITUATION 9 turned down. Her **FICO** score is a perfect 850. She qualifies for a loan with an **ANNUAL RATE OF INTEREST** of 3.00% and a **TERM** of 42 months.

"The **ANNUAL RATE OF INTEREST** is 3.00% and is not directly listed. The **TERM** is not directly listed either. Nicole, let's check if you know the drill by walking along together.

"What are the loan cost results?"

"Ok, Dad. To start, the **ANNUAL RATE OF INTEREST** of 3.00% is ¼ the way between the listed 2.00% and 6.00%. The **TERM** of 42 months is ½ the way between the listed **TERMS** of 36 months and

48 months. That means we have to interpolate multiple times."

"That's right Nicole. What comes first?"

"I have to get the **BASE LOAN** results for 2.00% for each of those **TERMS**. Then interpolate between them for the 42 months."

"That's correct. But let's change things a bit. Before interpolating, let's scale the **BASE LOAN** results for each **TERM**.

"Using the **SCALING FACTOR** of 7.50, for an **ANNUAL RATE OF INTEREST** = 2.00% and a **TERM** of 36 months, what are the scaled **BASE LOAN** costs?"

"Well? Let me think it out."

After a two-minute pause, Nicole replies, "From the **CAR-BASE LOAN TABLE**, the **BASE MONTHLY PAYMENT** = $28.64 and the **BASE CUMULATIVE INTEREST** = $31.13.Scaling those, I get the following."

For 2.00% and 36 months:

MONTHLY PAYMENT = 7.50 x $28.64 = $214.80

CUMULATIVE INTEREST = 7.5 x $31.13 = $233.48

SITUATION 12 – CONTINUED

"Super, Nicole! And what are they for a **TERM** of 48 months?"

"Here's what I got, Dad."

For 2.00% and 42 months:

MONTHLY PAYMENT = 7.50 x $21.70 = $162.75

CUMULATIVE INTEREST = 7.5 x $41.37= $310.28

SITUATION 12 – CONTINUED

"Do you follow me, Dad?"

"Ha! Ha! I do see you condensed it. Very good, Smarty Pants!

"Then what are the results for 42 months, Sweetie?"

"They're halfway between the results for 36 months and 48 months. Let me calculate it."

After pausing a little longer to do so, Nicole indicates the following.

For 6.00% and 42 months:

MONTHLY PAYMENT = $214.80 + 1/2(162.75 – $214.80) = $214.80 –$26.03 = $188.77

CUMULATIVE INTEREST = $233.48 + 1/2 (310.28 – $233.48)
= $233.48 + $38.40 = $271.88

SITUATION 12 – CONTINUED

"Perfect, Nicole. What's next?"

"We do it again for 6.00% in place of 2.00%."

"Exactly! What are the results for a **TERM** of 36 months?"

"I just have to take the appropriate **CAR - BASE LOAN** results for 6.00% and 36 months and then scale them." Talking as she calculates, Nicole indicates, "Her **MONTHLY PAYMENT** = 7.50 x $30.42 = $228.15 and her **CUMULATIVE INTEREST** = 7.5 x $95.19 = $713.93."

"Great, Nicole. For a 6.00% and 48 months, we can look back at SITUATION 6. Looking back at it, her **MONTHLY PAYMENT** = $176.18 and **CUMULATIVE INTEREST** = $954.60. What's next?"

"Like before, the results for 42 months are halfway between those we got for 36 months and 48 months."

For 6.00% and 42 months:

MONTHLY PAYMENT = $228.15 + 1/2(176.18 – $228.15) = $202.17.

CUMULATIVE INTEREST = $713.93 + 1/2 ($954.60 – $713.93) = $834.27

SITUATION 12 – CONTINUED

"Perfect, again. Let's summarize all that."

For 2.00% and 42 months:

MONTHLY PAYMENT = $188.77 and CUMULATIVE INTEREST = $271.88

For 6.00% and 42 months:

MONTHLY PAYMENT = $202.17 and CUMULATIVE INTEREST = $834.27

SITUATION 12 – CONTINUED

"What's the last step, Nicole?"

"The approximate results for 3.00% are 1/4 of the way between those two results."

For 3.00% and 42 months:

MONTHLY PAYMENT = $188.78 + 1/4(202.17 – $188.78) = $192.13.

CUMULATIVE INTEREST = $271.88 + 1/4(834.27 – $271.88) = $412.48

SITUATION 12 – CONTINUED

"Perfect, Nicole. The precise results I got from an **AMORTIZATION SCHEDULE** are a **MONTHLY PAYMENT** = $188.33 and **CUMULATIVE INTEREST** = $410.00. The approximate results are pretty close and good enough."

"I agree, Dad."

"There are a couple side points I want to make.

"Compared to Linda, who had a **FICO SCORE** of 750, Danielle would pay $626.50 - $412.48 = $214.02 (34%) less **CUMULATIVE INTEREST**.

"Compared to Randall, who had a **FICO SCORE** of 675, Danielle would pay $954.60 - $412.48 = $542.12 (58%) less **CUMULATIVE INTEREST**.

"She is very well rewarded for her perfect **FICO** score, isn't she?"

"She sure is, Dad! I'd love to have a perfect **FICO SCORE**."

Exercise 7: *To confirm the results in SITUATION 12, redo it by first interpolating the* ***BASE LOAN*** *values all the way through. Then scale the results at the very end.*

Your results should be: *The complete solution is given in* ***APPENDIX I.***

ASIDE: *The loan* ***terms*** *for the various SITUATIONS for each* ***FICO SCORE*** *and* ***LOAN AMOUNT*** *are fictitious. What a specific lender would actually do in each circumstance is unknown. Based on the general tabulated trends given earlier for* ***CAR LOANS****, the author did set their relatives values to reflect the different degrees of creditworthiness presented in each SITUATION. Even if the loan* ***terms*** *are somewhat off in values of a specific lender, they are likely well within the ball park. On that basis the relative results do tell a sufficiently realistic story.*

"Sweetie, you've been your usual Smarty Pants. You did think it all through. It takes concentrated effort to do that, even for me. To help out, I created a road map for the process. Let's call it a 'cheat sheet'. I'll email it to you. By filling in the needed information and doing the calculations, you get the results all on one sheet of paper. All you need is a calculator.

"I'll also send you the completed cheat sheets for some of the SITUATIONS we just covered. That will help you figure out how to use it. I doubt it will take my Smarty Pants very long. Then you can use it as a guide to help you with creating that spreadsheet."

"That's awesome! Dad. I sure am glad you have that. With all that homework to try, I can't get it soon enough. If I get those all correctly done, then I might agree that my pants are pretty smart."

ASIDE: *Dad's cheat sheet is in* ***APPENDIX II****. It is also applicable to Lesson 7.*

Exercise 8: *Geraldine wishes to purchase a* ***NEW*** *car for $21000.00, including* ***SALES TAX****. Based on her* ***FICO SCORE*** *and the desired 36-month* ***TERM****, the best* ***CAR LOAN*** *she can obtain is for an* ***ANNUAL RATE OF INTEREST*** *of 10.00%. What are her approximate* ***MONTHLY PAYMENT, CUMULATIVE INTEREST, PERCENT CUMULATIVE INTEREST*** *and* ***TOTAL LOAN COST****?*

Your <u>partial</u> results should be: MONTHLY PAYMENT *= $698.67;* ***CUMULATIVE INTEREST*** *= $2970.24.*

Exercise 9: *Gordon obtained a* ***CAR LOAN*** *for $28700.00 including* ***SALES TAX****. The* ***TERM*** *is 60 months and an* ***ANNUAL RATE OF INTEREST*** *of 9.00%. What are his approximate* ***MONTHLY PAYMENT, CUMULATIVE INTEREST, PERCENT CUMULATIVE INTEREST*** *and* ***TOTAL LOAN COST****?*

Your <u>partial</u> results should be: CUMULATIVE INTEREST *= $33038.58.*

Exercise10: *Bobbi obtains a* ***CAR LOAN*** *for $20000.00 including* ***SALES TAX*** *with a* ***TERM*** *of 54 months at an* ***ANNUAL RATE OF INTEREST*** *of 6.00%. What are her approximate* ***MONTHLY PAYMENT, CUMULATIVE INTEREST, PERCENT CUMULATIVE INTEREST and TOTAL LOAN COST****?*

***Your results should be: MONTHLY PAYMENT** = $428.20; **CUMULATIVE INTEREST** = $2872.50.*

***Exercise 10A:** Bobbi obtains a **CAR LOAN** for $20000.00 including **SALES TAX** with a **TERM** of 42 months at an **ANNUAL RATE OF INTEREST** of 8.00%. What are his approximate **MONTHLY PAYMENT**, **CUMULATIVE INTEREST, PERCENT CUMULATIVE INTEREST** and **TOTAL LOAN COST**?*

***Your partial results should be: MONTHLY PAYMENT** = $563.20; **TOTAL LOAN COST** = $23007.45.*

LESSON 7 How Much Does That Car Really Cost?

"Nicole, so far we've talked about the process of how you go about purchasing and financing a car. The important monetary matter is how much the car actually costs when it comes time to pay for it. Knowing that you can determine the **LOAN AMOUNT** you need, if any, and the **TOTAL LOAN COSTS**. I bet you remember that if you are buying from a dealership there are all kinds of prices: **MSRP, FACTORY INVOICE**, etc."

"Dad, I sure do and with all the maneuvering that happens at a dealership I can understand how a customer can get confused. Isn't it the **SELLING PRICE + OPTIONS** what I pay for a car?"

Loan Amount

"Good recall on that terminology, Nicole. That's the price the dealership and you agree to after negotiations conclude. It is not what you actually pay. There will be a **SALES TAX** collected on those two costs. The amount depends on the **SALES TAX RATE** applicable to your locale. The **SALES TAX RATE** combines the state, county and local portions.

"If you get a **CASH REBATE**, then it is applied to that price. That reduces the cost to you."

"Dad, what happens with the **SALES TAX**?"

"Excellent question! I was just about to comment about it. You beat me to it."

ASIDE: *The following also applies to a* ***CASH BONUS****. For simplicity, the author will use the term* ***CASH REBATE*** *to mean either one.*

"What happens depends on the state where the sale transpires. Some states do tax the **CASH REBATE**. They apply the **SALES TAX RATE** to the full **SELLING PRICE + OPTIONS**. Some states do not tax a **CASH REBATE.** It is subtracted before applying the **SALES TAX RATE**. However, some states have no **SALES TAX** on cars, or anything else. That's the best case.

"A **CASH REBATE** is modest amount of money. In the big picture, the **SALES TAX** on it is pretty small. For our purposes, I am going to assume we pay **SALES TAX** on the full **SELLING PRICE + OPTIONS**. For a state where that is not the case, our cost calculation will give a result that is higher by a small amount."

"I don't know what the rule is here, Dad. That's probably best."

"Ok, you can check into that when the time comes to purchase a car.

"If it is a **USED CAR** commonly you buy it '**AS IS**'. If it is a **CERTIFED PRE-OWNED** car it normally comes with a modest warranty and you might negotiate some minor repairs at no cost. In either case, there are no **OPTIONS** in play and that cost is $0.00.

"Adding in the **SALES TAX**, you get the total amount owed.

"Having those amounts, you can decide how much **CASH DOWN** you want to pay out of pocket. Subtracting that gives you the **LOAN AMOUNT** you need to finance. That reduces the amount you owe, but not the cost of the car. You get no break on the **SALES TAX.**

"Are you following all this, Peanut?"

"It's a lot and pretty wordy, Dad. I'm losing you."

"I can see that in your facial expressions. Let me put onto math form. Here are the equations."

SALES TAX = (SALES TAX RATE/100) x (SELLING PRICE + OPTIONS)

LOAN AMOUNT = SELLING PRICE + OPTIONS + SALES TAX
– CASH REBATE – CASH DOWN

"Is it clearer this way, Nicole?"

"Actually, seeing it in math form clarifies it for me."

Total Cost to Purchase

"Ok, that's good. Knowing the **LOAN AMOUNT**, you can calculate the loan costs using the **CAR-BASE LOAN TABLE** and **SCALING.**"

"I understand, Dad. That **SCALING** procedure has really settled in for me."

"Great! Having the **MONTHLY PAYMENT,** you can multiply it by the **TERM** of the **CAR LOAN** in months to get **TOTAL COST OF THE LOAN**. Adding the **CASH DOWN**, you get **TOTAL COST TO PURCHASE**.

"Here are the math equations."

TOTAL LOAN COST = MONTHLY PAYMENT x TERM

TOTAL COST TO PURCHASE = CASH DOWN + TOTAL LOAN COST

"The resulting amounts include the **CUMULATIVE INTEREST**. Still following me, Sweetie?"

"I am, Dad. And that gives the amount of money it costs to purchase the car, right?"

"Exactly, Peanut!

"Ok. Let's try an example with numbers."

SITUATION 13 – OPTION P1

"Assume Sam, a successful photographer, is interested in purchasing a **NEW** car. The **MSRP** is $26000.00. The dealership offers Sam a **SELLING PRICE** of $23200.00 and he adds $1400.00 of **OPTIONS**. There is a **CASH REBATE** of $1300.00 available and the dealership will credit it to him. He has a **PRESENT CAR** but will neither sell it nor trade it in. Sam elects to pay an out of pocket **CASH DOWN** of $1600.00.

"Based on his **FICO SCORE** of 702, Sam's credit union will finance the car for a 60-month **TERM** at an **ANNUAL RATE OF INTEREST** of 4.00%. For his locale, the **SALES TAX RATE** is 7.00%.

"Here are my calculations for the **LOAN AMOUNT**."

SELLING PRICE + OPTIONS = $23200.00 + $1400.00 = $24600.00

SALES TAX = (SALES TAX RATE/100) x (SELLING PRICE + OPTIONS)
= (7.00/100) x ($24600.00)
= 0.07 x $24600.00 = $1722.00

LOAN AMOUNT = (SELLING PRICE + OPTIONS) + SALES TAX
– CASH REBATE – CASH DOWN
= ($24600.00) + 1722.00 – $1300.00
= $23422.00

SITUATION 13 – OPTION P1 – CONTINUED

"Do you agree with my calculations, Nicole?"

"I'm following you fine, Dad."

"That's good.

"If a **SALES TAX RATE** is not applied to the **CASH REBATE**, then the **LOAN AMOUNT** would be lower by 0.07 x $1300 = $91.00. It actually is an insignificant amount.
"Now, how do we calculate Sam's loan costs?"

"We use the **CAR-BASE LOAN TABLE** and **SCALE** the base results."

"Great, Sweetie. Do we have to interpolate?"

"Yes, we do. The **ANNUAL RATE IF INTEREST** of 4.00% is not listed. It's midway between the listed 2.00% and 6.00%"

"You're correct, Sweetie. Using the listed **BASE LOAN** amounts for each of those I calculated these interpolated values."

BASE MONTHLY PAYMENT = ($17.53 + $19.33)/2 = $18.43

BASE CUMULATIVE INTEREST = ($51.67 + $159.97)/2 = $105.82

SITUATION 13 – OPTION P1 – CONTINUED

"What's the **SCALING FACTOR**, Nicole?"

"It's the **LOAN AMOUNT** of $23422.00 divided by $1000.00, 23.422."

"Right. Using that value I calculated the actual loan costs."

SCALING FACTOR = 23.422

MONTHLY PAYMENT = 23.422 x $18.43 = $431.67

CUMULATIVE INTEREST = 23.422 x $105.82 = $2478.52

TERM = 60 months

TOTAL LOAN COST = 60 x $431.67= $25900.00 (rounded)

TOTAL COST TO PURCHASE = CASH DOWN + TOTAL LOAN COST
= $1600.00 + $25900.00 = $27500.00

SITUATION 13 – OPTION P1 – CONTINUED

"That $27500.00 is $2900.00 more than the **SELLING PRICE** + **OPTIONS** of $24600.00. Sam incurred that as an added cost because of his **CAR LOAN**. It's about 12% of the $24600, 2.4% per year. How's that look, Nicole?"

"Very fair Dad. It gives me some confidence before I actually have to buy a car."

"Yes, as long as you do your homework, and are well prepared to haggle and negotiate, it will turn out fine."

"Nicole, the cheat sheet I gave you last time also applies to this Lesson. I'll send you the completed one for **OPTION P1**. You can use it as a guide for doing the following Exercises."

"That's great Dad. I did see a note about that in the cheat sheet. Having seen that and **OPTION P1**, I'm pretty sure I understand how to apply the cheat sheet to it."

"I am sure you will, Sweetie."

***Exercise 11**: Repeat **SITUATION 13 – OPTION P1** for a **SELLING PRICE** of $19300.00, $0.00 in **OPTIONS**, a **CASH REBATE** of $0.00, **CASH DOWN** of $1200.00, **ANNUAL RATE OF INTEREST** of 8.00%, **TERM** of 36 months, and **SALES TAX RATE** of 6.00%.*

***Your partial answer should be**: **LOAN AMOUNT** = $19258.00, **CUMULATIVE INTEREST** = $2472.92, **TOTAL LOAN COST** =$22081.00, **TOTAL COST TO PURCHASE** = $23281.00.*

***Exercise 11A**: Repeat **SITUATION 13 – OPTION P1** for a **SELLING PRICE** of $29400.00, $550.00 in **OPTIONS**, a **CASH REBATE** of $1600.00, **CASH DOWN** of $2400.00, **ANNUAL RATE OF INTEREST** of 6.00%, **TERM** of 48 months, and **SALES TAX RATE** of 8.00%.*

***Your partial answer should be**: **LOAN AMOUNT** = $28346.00, **MONTHLY PAYMENT** = $3885.85, **TOTAL COST TO PURCHASE** = $34361.00.*

Trading In or Selling a Present Car

"Let's turn our attention to another the matter. SITUATION 13 assumes that Sam has no **PRESENT CAR** involved. If Sam has one and keeps it, then he has that car as an asset. It has no bearing on the cost of purchasing another one. While that can be the case for some buyers, many if not most buyers are at least considering doing a trade-in. And if you watch the TV ads, you see some of the dealership owners saying something like, 'I want your trade-in, no matter what shape it's in, even if you have to tow it in.' There's a reason for that statement. They can make money off it."

"Ok, Dad, I'm anxious to learn about the trade-in aspect and if I should trade in my **VW** or not. As you know it's a very, very **USED CAR** now. It's got almost 150,000 miles on it. From what you just said about TV ads, something tells me it's not a good thing to trade my car in."

"Actually, trading in a car has pros and cons. I'll cover both.

"If you do plan to trade in your **PRESENT CAR**, then it's a little involved to account for the monetary effect on the cost of purchasing another car. I'll try to simplify it."

"Great, you always seem to do that well, Dad."

"There is also the possibility of selling your **PRESENT CAR** privately and applying that money to the purchase. I'll cover that, too."

"That's good, Dad. I hadn't thought of that possibility."

- Book Value -

"The easiest way to explain both possibilities is to treat your **PRESENT CAR** as an existing asset. It's worth the monetary value you should get if you sell it on the open market; that is privately. Ideally, you would sell it for its **KELLY BLUE BOOK** value or some other measure or close to it. Whatever way it's derived, most people refer to it as the **BOOK VALUE**.

"If you sell the car privately, then you will have the amount you sold it for as a cash asset. You want to get at least its **BOOK VALUE**. If you opt to just keep the money, then it has no bearing on the cost of purchasing another car. Alternatively, you can use some or all of that money as a **CASH DOWN FROM SALE**. It adds to any **CASH DOWN** you plan to take from your savings. As another alternative, you can trade in the **PRESENT CAR** to the dealership. Let's call the amount they pay you for it the **CASH DOWN FROM TRADE-IN**. Let's cover the trade-in first."

- Trading In a Present Car -

"A trade-in involves two transactions. The first transaction is that the dealership purchases your **PRESENT CAR** from you. The dealership will pay you a certain amount of money for it. The second transaction is you use that money as **CASH DOWN FROM TRADE-IN**. Directly or indirectly, the paperwork you sign will indicate both transactions. You don't actually pass the money in two steps. The transactions are simultaneous and happen at the time both parties sign the **SALES AGREEMENT**."

"Well, Dad. It seems a lot easier to just trade in my car then to go about selling it privately."

"Sweetie, it might be. It's not necessarily the best choice. Almost invariably, selling to a private party will yield a noticeably higher value than for selling to a dealership."

"Why's that so, Dad?"

"One reason for the difference is the dealership will resell or auction off the car and builds in a margin to make a profit for doing so. For reselling it, the dealership might also need to make some repairs to the car, which costs the dealer money. Consequently, the dealership offers noticeably less for a trade-in the than the **BOOK VALUE**. By trading in the car you have lost the difference."

"Then why would anyone do a trade-in instead of selling it themselves?"

"You said it yourself just now, 'It seems a lot easier to just trade in my car then to go about selling it privately.' You're right. It takes a lot more time and effort to sell a car privately. And it costs a bit to advertise it for sale. Then, you have to meet with each potential buyer, let he or she try the car, wait to see if any potential buyer makes an offer, haggles etc. In effect, you become a car salesperson. Some people just don't want to bother doing it.

"Some people also see risks in having to meet with strangers and let them try the car out. There are lots of reasons to hesitate. If you do it, then there are some precautions to take. Meet in daylight in a populated area. Make sure the potential buyer is licensed and insured. Accept only cash or a certified check as payment. You have to consider those sorts of things.

"As alternative you can advertise via the internet on sites such as **Craig's list**. That seems the contemporary way of selling almost anything privately. You have to worry about transacting the exchange of goods for payment correctly and successfully. Sometimes the buyer and seller have to meet to do that. For selling a car it almost certainly will be needed. If so it carries the same risks as dealing with responders to printed ads and the like."

"I see the point, I'll have to think them over and decide the path I want to take."

"Ok. As the next step, here's the aspect of a trade-in shown in math equations."

LOAN AMOUNT = SELLING PRICE + OPTIONS + SALES TAX – CASH REBATE – CASH DOWN – CASH DOWN FROM TRADE-IN

TOTAL COST TO PURCHASE = CASH DOWN + TOTAL LOAN COST + BOOK VALUE

COST OF TRADE-IN = BOOK VALUE – CASH DOWN FROM TRADE-IN

"Do you see the logic behind these equations, Nicole?"

"I understand the first one. You've further reduced the **LOAN AMOUNT** by the amount of money the dealership gives me for my **PRESENT CAR**. I'm not seeing why you added the **BOOK VALUE** into the **TOTAL COST TO PURCHASE**. Don't I get the **CASH FROM THE TRADE-IN**? And I only spent the difference between the **BOOK VALUE** and that amount?"

"Terrific question Nicole! The answer to your dilemma is subtle.

"You are correct that you spent that difference. But it's in addition to what you spend if you do not trade-in. You gave the dealer your entire **PRESENT CAR**, not just part of it. In other words, you gave away its full **BOOK VALUE**. Presumably, you could have sold it for that amount. So the **TOTAL COST TO PURCHASE** must include that full amount. The only thing the **CASH FROM TRADE-IN** did was reduce the **LOAN AMOUNT**.

"Also, when you subtract the **CASH FROM TRADE-IN** from the **BOOK VALUE** the result is the **COST OF THE TRADE-IN**. If you get less than the full **BOOK VALUE**, then the **COST OF THE TRADE-IN** comes out a positive result. You lost some money. If you get exactly the **BOOK VALUE** it comes out $0.00. If you get more than the full **BOOK VALUE** it comes out a negative result. You gained some money. But, as I said, it unlikely you will get full **BOOK VALUE**, let alone more, from the dealership.

"Are you still following this, Sweetie?"

"Kind of, Dad. What's the benefit of doing the trade-in?"

"Two things happen.

"Because you reduce your **LOAN AMOUNT**, compared to not trading in, you reduce your **MONTHLY PAYMENT** and **CUMULATIVE INTEREST**. The result is a certain amount of **CUMULATIVE INTEREST SAVED.** That amount is the difference in **CUMULATIVE INTEREST** paid with no trade-in and **CUMULATIVE INTEREST** paid with a trade-in.

"Taking that into account, we get this equation."

NET COST OF TRADE-IN = COST OF TRADE-IN – CUMULATIVE INTEREST SAVED

"Does it make sense to you?"

"Ok, I see that Dad. Now the trade-in seems like it could be either a bad thing or a good thing?"

"Actually, you're correct. If you trade-in, then there can be a either a net gain of money or a net loss of money. When we look at some examples, you'll see the **TOTAL COST TO PURCHASE** can either increase or decrease compared to not trading in. That's why I wrote the equation for **NET COST OF TRADE-IN.** That's the amount the **TOTAL COST TO PURCHASE** will change due to trading in your **PRESENT CAR**. If it is positive, then it's more costly than keeping it. If it's negative, then it's less costly than keeping it.

"If you look the equation for the **COST OF THE TRADE-IN**, you should recognize it as calculating that difference you mentioned. The **COST OF THE TRADE-IN** by itself is, indeed, the **BOOK VALUE** minus the **CASH FROM THE TRADE-IN**. That amount is offset by any gain due to the reduced **CUMULATIVE INTEREST**. The **NET COST OF TRADE-IN** gives us the result of those offsetting effects."

"Gosh! Dad, that's not sinking in. I think it's time for those numbers to arrive."

"I can imagine it sounding pretty confusing. I intend to clear it up by doing some numbers. Before doing that, let's add in the aspect of selling the **PRESENT CAR** privately."

- Selling a Present Car -

"If you sell your **PRESENT CAR** privately, then there is no trade-in. There is no **CASH FROM TRADE-IN**. Instead, there is amount of **CASH DOWN FROM SALE** that you can use from that sale. To allow for that difference, I've modified the math equation for the **LOAN AMOUNT**."

LOAN AMOUNT = SELLING PRICE + OPTIONS + SALES TAX – CASH REBATE – CASH DOWN – CASH DOWN FROM SALE

"That makes sense to me, Dad."

"Of course, since the **CASH DOWN FROM SALE** reduces the **LOAN AMOUNT** relative to the base of not involving your **PRESENT CAR** in the new purchase, the **CUMULATIVE INTEREST** is lowered too.

ASIDE: *Technically, a person who has two **PRESENT CARS** could trade in one and sell the other privately. In that circumstance, the term **CASH DOWN FROM TRADE-IN** is also needed. It's unlikely that would occur because the person would end up with replacing two cars with one car. But, who knows?*

"Once you have the **LOAN AMOUNT**, the rest of the calculation procedure is when you trade your **PRESENT CAR**. Except for the use of **CASH DOWN FROM SALE** instead of **CASH DOWN FROM TRADE-IN**, the math is the same."

TOTAL COST TO PURCHASE = CASH DOWN + TOTAL LOAN COST + BOOK VALUE

COST OF SALE = BOOK VALUE – CASH DOWN FROM SALE

NET COST OF SALE = COST OF SALE – CUMULATIVE INTEREST SAVED

"Whether you use **CASH DOWN FROM TRADE-IN** or **CASH DOWN FROM SALE**, if the amount is the same, then the **LOAN AMOUNT** and resulting costs will be the same. Does that make sense, Peanut?"

"I get it, Dad. It makes no difference where the extra cash down came from. Either way it leads to the same outcome?"

"Right! To abbreviate, we can show it this way."

TOTAL COST TO PURCHASE = CASH DOWN + TOTAL LOAN COST + BOOK VALUE

COST OF TRADE-IN (or SALE) = BOOK VALUE – CASH DOWN FROM TRADE-IN (or SALE)

NET COST OF TRADE-IN (or SALE) = COST OF TRADE-IN (or SALE) – CUMULATIVE INTEREST SAVED

"Yeah, I like the shorthand form of it. Depending on what is done with the **PRESENT CAR**, we use either **CASH DOWN TRADE-IN** or **CASH DOWN FROM SALE**."

"Terrific! Nicole. Now we're ready to look at the numbers for Sam's case."

Examples

-Trading in a Present Car -

SITUATION 13 – OPTION P2

"Sam's fully paid off **PRESENT CAR** has a **BOOK VALUE** of $6500.00. He does a **TRADE-IN** for $4500.00. Here are the calculations."

LOAN AMOUNT = SELLING PRICE + OPTIONS + SALES TAX – CASH REBATE – CASH DOWN – CASH DOWN FROM TRADE-IN
= $23200.00 + $1400.00 + $1722.00 – $1300.00 – $1600.00 – $4500.00
= $18922.00

SITUATION 13 – OPTION P2 – CONTINUED

"Do you agree with my numbers so far, Peanut?"

"I'm right with you, Dad."

"Ok. Compared to **OPTION P1** the trade-in reduces the **LOAN AMOUNT** to $18922.00. How do we re-calculate Sam's loan costs?"

"It's the same as before, but we use a **SCALING FACTOR** of $18.922.."

"Right again. Using that value, I calculated these scaled results."

SCALING FACTOR = 18.922

MONTHLY PAYMENT = 18.922 x $18.43 = $348.73

CUMULATIVE INTEREST = 18.922 x $105.82 = $2002.33

TERM = 60 months

TOTAL LOAN COST = 60 x $348.73 = $20924.00 (rounded)

TOTAL COST TO PURCHASE = CASH DOWN + TOTAL LOAN COST + BOOK VALUE

= **\$1600.00 + \$20924.00 + \$6500.00**
= **\$29024.00**

SITUATION 13 – OPTION P2 – CONTINUED

"Nicole, as you can see, the **MONTHLY PAYMENT** is \$348.73. Compared to the previous \$431.67, it's \$82.94 less. The **CUMULATIVE INTEREST** is \$2002.33, compared to the previous \$2478.52."

CUMULATIVE INTEREST SAVED = \$2478.52 - \$2002.33 = \$476.19

SITUATION 13 – OPTION P2 – CONTINUED

"Why did that happen, Sweetie?"

"As you said earlier, trading in reduces the **LOAN AMOUNT**. In Sam's case it's \$4500.00 lower."

"That's right, Nicole. We can also get that result by scaling the **BASE CUMULATIVE INTEREST** by the amount by which the **LOAN AMOUNT** was decreased."

SCALING FACTOR = \$4500.00/\$1000.00 = 4.50

CUMULATIVE INTEREST SAVED = 4.50 x \$105.82 = \$476.19.

SITUATION 13 – OPTION P2 – CONTINUED

"That's interesting and simpler, Dad?"

"Yes it is. Now, how about the **TOTAL COST TO PURCHASE?"**

"The **TOTAL COST TO PURCHASE** did increase. It's \$29024.00. Compared to \$27500.00 without the trade-in, it's higher by \$1524.00."

"Right again. Let's show that in calculations."

COST OF TRADE-IN = BOOK VALUE – CASH DOWN FROM TRADE-IN
= \$6500.00 - \$4500.00 = \$2000.00

NET COST OF TRADE-IN = COST OF TRADE-IN – CUMULATIVE INTEREST SAVED

= $2000.00 – $476.19 = $1523.81 = $1524.00 rounded

SITUATION 13 – OPTION P2 – CONTINUED

"Do you follow the calculations, Sweetie?"

"Well, I see the **CASH DOWN FROM TRADE-IN** is $4500.00. That's because Sam did not get full **BOOK VALUE**. Because of the trade-in, he no longer has his **PRESENT CAR** which was worth $6500.00. In effect he spent $2000.00. He lost money. That's the **COST OF TRADE-IN**.

"I see the **CUMULATIVE INTEREST** went down, as well. Apparently, it didn't go down enough to offset the $2000.00 that the trade-in cost him. That's why his **NET COST OF TRADE-IN** was $1524.00."

"Outstanding! Nicole.

"Notice that's the same amount as the $1524.00 increase in the **TOTAL COST TO PURCHASE** due to the trade-in. They should be and are the same amount.

"What's your conclusion from this, Smarter Pants?"

"Apparently, and as you indicated it could, it actually costs Sam more money to trade-in **his PRESENT CAR** than to keep it. The positive result for **NET COST OF TRADE-IN** indicates that."

"Exactly!

"For the aspect of trading in or not, it comes down to Sam having to decide one thing? Does he keep his **PRESENT CAR** or does he trade it in to reduce his **MONTHLY PAYMENT** and **CUMULATIVE INTEREST**. Again, in this case the **NET COST OF TRADE-IN** indicates it costs $1524.00 more to do the latter."

"Yeah, Dad, that is the bottom line. Thank you for demonstrating that dilemma."

"I'm glad you understand, Sweetie. And what if Sam sells his car privately?"

"If he sells it for $4500.00, then we use the **CASH DOWN FROM SALE** term instead of the **CASH DOWN FROM TRADE-IN**. All the calculated numbers and results would be the same."

"Great, Nicole."

***Exercise 12**: Repeat **SITUATION 13 – OPTION P2** for a **SELLING PRICE** of $19300.00, $0.00 in **OPTIONS**, a **CASH REBATE** of $0.00, **CASH DOWN** of $1200.00, **BOOK VALUE** of $4500.00,*

***CASH DOWN FROM TRADE-IN** of $3000.00, **ANNUAL RATE OF INTEREST** of 8.00%, **TERM** of 36 months, and **SALES TAX RATE** of 6.00%.*

***Your <u>partial</u> answer should be:** **LOAN AMOUNT** = $20458.00, **CUMULATIVE INTEREST** = $2087.69, **TOTAL LOAN COST** =$16482.00, **TOTAL COST TO PURCHASE** = $24342.00, **NET COST OF TRADE-IN** =$1114.77.*

***Exercise 12A**: Repeat **SITUATION 13 – OPTION P2** for a **SELLING PRICE** of $29400.00, $550.00 in **OPTIONS**, a **CASH REBATE** of $1600.00, **CASH DOWN** of $2400.00, **BOOK VALUE** of $11000.00, **CASH DOWN FROM TRADE-IN** of $8000.00, **ANNUAL RATE OF INTEREST** of 6.00%, **TERM** of 48 months, and **SALES TAX RATE** of 8.00%.*

***Your <u>partial</u> answer should be:** **LOAN AMOUNT** = $19346.00, **MONTHLY PAYMENT** = $454.44, **TOTAL COST TO PURCHASE** = $35213.00, **NET COST OF TRADE-IN** = $854.48.*

- Selling a Present Car -

"Nicole, remember for other **CASH DOWN FROM TRADE-IN** or **CASH DOWN FROM SALE** amounts the outcome can be a benefit. Let's see what happens if Sam sells his **PRESENT CAR** for its full **BOOK VALUE** and uses the money toward the purchase of the **NEW CAR**."

<u>SITUATION 13 – OPTION P3</u>

"As before, Sam's fully paid off **PRESENT CAR** has a **BOOK VALUE** of $6500.00. He sells it privately for that amount and uses that amount as **CASH DOWN FROM SALE**. Let's recalculate the outcome."

LOAN AMOUNT = SELLING PRICE + OPTIONS + SALES TAX – CASH REBATE
– CASH DOWN – CASH DOWN FROM SALE
= $23200.00 + $1400.00 + $1722.00 — $1300.00 — $1600.00 — $6500.00
= $16922.00

<u>SITUATION 13 – OPTION P3 – CONTINUED</u>

"What's different here, Peanut? And what's next?"

"It's just the **CASH DOWN FROM SALE** being $2000.00 higher than for the **CASH DOWN FROM TRADE-IN** used in **OPTION P2** we just looked at. It drops the **LOAN AMOUNT** further, to $16922.00. Now, we repeat all the calculations using a **SCALING FACTOR** of 16.922."

"Perfect. Here's what I calculated."

SCALING FACTOR = 16.922

MONTHLY PAYMENT = 16.922 x $18.43 = $311.87

CUMULATIVE INTEREST = 16.922 x $105.82 = $1790.69

TERM = 60 months

TOTAL LOAN COST = 60 x $311.87 = $18712.00 (rounded)

TOTAL COST TO PURCHASE = CASH DOWN + BOOK VALUE
+ TOTAL LOAN COST
= $1600.00 + $6500.00 + $18712 = $26812.00

<u>SITUATION 13 – OPTION P3 – CONTINUED</u>

"Nicole, as you can see the **MONTHLY PAYMENT** is $311.87 compared to $348.73 in **OPTION P2**, $36.87 less. Sam's **CUMULATIVE INTEREST** is $1790.69 compared to $2002.33 in **OPTION P2**, $211.64 less. That's the benefit of reducing the **LOAN AMOUNT** by $2000.00 more than for the trade-in.

"Compared to $431.67 in **OPTION P1** without the trade-in, the **MONTHLY PAYMENT** is $119.80 less.

"Compared to the $2478.52 in **OPTION P1**, the **CUMULATIVE INTEREST** is $687.83 less. Here are the calculations for that."

CUMULATIVE INTEREST SAVED = $2478.52 — $1790.69 = $687.83 ($688.00 rounded)

Alternatively, SCALING FACTOR = $6500.00/$1000.00 = 6.50

CUMULATIVE INTEREST SAVED = 6.50 x $105.82 = $687.83

<u>SITUATION 13 – OPTION P3 – CONTINUED</u>

"Do the results of these comparisons make sense to you, Sweetie?"

"They do, Dad. It's logical that the more you get for a trade-in or sale, the lower the loan costs will be."

"Ok, how about the **TOTAL COST TO PURCHASE** compared to **OPTION P2**?"

"I see it's a whole lot lower than the $29024.00 in **OPTION P2**. It's $2212.00 less for doing the trade-in."

"And why is that the outcome, Sweetie?"

"I suppose that's due to getting $2000.00 more for the trade-in plus saving a little on **CUMULATIVE INTEREST**."

"That's it exactly. We saw that Sam's **CUMULATIVE INTEREST** was indeed $211.64 less than for **OPTION P2**. Rounded, that's $212.00.

"And how does the **TOTAL COST TO PURCHASE** result compare to **OPTION P1**?"

"I see it's also lower than for **OPTION P1**, $26812.00 compared to $27500.00. That's $688.00 less for doing the private sale. It's the same amount as the **CUMULATIVE INTEREST SAVED**. Why does that happen, Dad?"

"To answer that, I need to finish the calculations."

COST OF SALE = BOOK VALUE – CASH DOWN FROM SALE
= $6500.00 - $6500.00 = $0.00

NET COST OF SALE = COST OF SALE – CUMULATIVE INTEREST SAVED
= $0.00 – $687.83 = -$687.83 = -$688.00 rounded

SITUATION 13 – OPTION P3 – CONTINUED

"Ok, Smarty Pants. Why don't you give it a try at what these results tell us compared to **OPTION P2**? What about the **COST OF THE SALE**?"

"Yeah, I noticed the **COST OF THE SALE** is $0.00. I was scratching my head a bit on that one. When the dealership paid Sam $4500.00 for trading in, Sam lost $2000.00. Here somebody else paid the **BOOK VALUE** of $6500.00 and he used it as **CASH DOWN FROM SALE**. As a result of that, he neither made money nor paid money so the **COST OF THE SALE** to him was $0.00. That's due to the extra $2000.00."

"That's right. Keep going, Sweetie. What about the **NET COST OF THE SALE**?"

"Let me think out loud a bit.

"With that $0.00 value for the **COST OF SALE**, the equation becomes **NET COST OF SALE** = $0.00 – **CUMULATIVE INTEREST SAVED.**

"That means **NET COST OF SALE** = – **CUMULATIVE INTEREST** = – ($688.00) = –$688.00. The negative result tells us Sam gains $688.00. It is $688.00 less expensive for Sam to sell his **PRESENT CAR** than to purchase the **NEW CAR** outright."

"You're doing great. Keep going."

"It seems the main reason for the lower **TOTAL COST TO PURCHASE** is the change from **CASH DOWN FROM SALE** of $4500.00 to $6500.00. By getting full **BOOK VALUE** it swung the results $2000.00 toward the favorable side; from a **NET COST OF SALE** of $1524.00 for the trade-in to a **NET COST OF SALE** of -$688.00 for the private sale.

"Gee, Dad, I just realized that's why that -$688.00 **NET COST OF SALE** is the same as the $688 decrease in the **TOTAL COST TO PURCHASE.** At least I'm pretty sure I do."

"Bravo! That's exactly the right explanation, Smartest Pants."

"Thanks, Dad. That makes me feel great."

"You asked me why the **NET COST OF THE SALE** is the same as the **CUMULATIVE INTEREST SAVED**. Think on it, again. Overall, what do conclude about that?"

After a few minutes,

"Dad, I think it means the only benefit of putting either **CASH DOWN FROM TRADE-IN** or **CASH DOWN FROM THE SALE** is the drop in **CUMULATIVE INTEREST**. I mean, when I don't put it anything down, my **TOTAL COST TO PURCHASE** is $27500.00. And when I do put down $6500.00 it's not much less, it's $26812.00. That's a $688.00 difference."

"BINGO! Nicole, that's perfect. Maybe I should begin to call you a genius."

"I'm not that Dad, but sometimes I think you are."

"Nope, I'm just dear old Dad with more experience in these sorts of things."

"Now all of this is beginning to make more and more common sense, Dad. I had to dig a little in my mind and ask your help to see some things. Now, I really understand a whole lot about the actual cost purchasing a car than I did yesterday.

"Most of all what I see is that in this case Sam can sell his **PRESENT CAR**, reduce his **MONTHLY PAYMENT** and save $688.00 in **CUMULATIVE INTEREST**. He wins on all scores. You were correct, Dad. Selling privately can be a benefit. But, of course, you're right. You always are."

"I do err now and then, but not in this case."

"I'll be waiting for the day to come when you do err, Dad. I still want to outsmart you some day, too."

"Fair enough. Let's wait and see which happens first."

***Exercise 13**: Repeat **SITUATION 13 – OPTION P3** for a **SELLING PRICE** of $19300.00, $0.00 in **OPTIONS**, a **CASH REBATE** of $0.00, **CASH DOWN** of $1200.00, **BOOK VALUE** of $4500, **CASH DOWN FROM TRADE-IN** of $4500.00, **ANNUAL RATE OF INTEREST** of 8.00%, **TERM** of 36 months, and **SALES TAX RATE** of 6.00%.*

***Your <u>partial</u> answer should be**: **LOAN AMOUNT** = $20458.00, **CUMULATIVE INTEREST** = $2087.69, **TOTAL LOAN COST** =$16482.00, **TOTAL COST TO PURCHASE** = $24342.00, **NET COST OF TRADE-IN** =$1114.77.*

***Exercise 13A**: Repeat **SITUATION 13 – OPTION P3** for a **SELLING PRICE** of $29400.00, $550.00 in **OPTIONS**, a **CASH REBATE** of $1600.00, **CASH DOWN** of $2400.00, **BOOK VALUE** of $11000.00, **CASH DOWN FROM SALE** of $11000.00, **ANNUAL RATE OF INTEREST** of 6.00%, **TERM** of 48 months, and **SALES TAX RATE** of 8.00%.*

***Your <u>partial</u> answer should be**: **LOAN AMOUNT** = $19346.00, **MONTHLY PAYMENT** = $454.44, **TOTAL COST TO PURCHASE** = $35213.00, **NET COST OF SALE** = $854.48.*

"Dad, from what you just showed it looks like trading in actually is a losing scenario?"

"That's right. It usually is. Again, that's because it's highly unlikely any dealership will give you **BOOK VALUE** for Sam's **PRESENT CAR**. If they did, they would try to offset it somewhere in the buying process. Of course, Sam might not get full **BOOK VALUE** for selling his **PRESENT CAR** either. However, almost certainly, it would sell for more than $4500.00.

"That leads me to a subtle observation about Sam trading in or selling his **PRESENT CAR**. If Sam neither trades in nor sells his **PRESENT CAR**, then his **TOTAL COST TO PURCHASE** = $27500.00. If he either trades it in or sells it for $4500.00, then his **TOTAL COST TO PURCHASE** = $29024.00. It's $2212.00 <u>less</u> to purchase a new car outright than to do a trade-in. If Sam either trades in or sells it for $6500.00, then his **TOTAL COST TO PURCHASE** = $26812.00. It's $688.00 <u>more</u> to purchase a new car outright than to do a trade-in.

"Nicole, what strikes you in these comparisons?"

"Well, Dad, what I see is just what you said to me. A trade-in or sale can either lead to more cost or to less cost in the **TOTAL COST TO PURCHASE**. I'm not seeing anything else."

"That's Ok, Sweetie. It's why I said it was a subtle observation.

"When Sam trades-in or sells for full **BOOK VALUE** of $6500.00, he gets a net benefit. When he trades in or sells for $4500.00 he gets a net loss. There must be an amount for **CASH FROM TRADE-IN** or **CASH DOWN FROM SALE** for which the outcome is a tie, that is the **NET COST OF TRADE-IN OR SALE** = $0.00. Does that seem logical to you, Sweetie?"

"Now that you mention it, it sure seems so. Why is it useful to know that amount?"

"If Sam gets more than that amount, then the resulting cost is lower if he trades in his **PRESENT CAR**. Otherwise, it's better to purchase the **NEW CAR** outright."

"Oh, I see that now. And how do you determine that amount?"

"Actually there is no direct way to get it. We have to get it by trial and error. Here's how we do that.

"We can deduce that it is an amount between $4500.00 and $6500.00. For $6500.00 we get a positive value for the **NET COST OF TRADE-IN** (or **SALE**). By incrementally reducing the **CASH DOWN FROM TRADE-IN** (or **SALE**) from $6500.00 and doing the numbers, we will get a series of results for the **NET COST OF TRADE-IN** (or **SALE**).

"Eventually we'll get a negative result. Then we keep refining the **CASH DOWN FROM TRADE-IN** (or **SALE**) value more closely until we get $0.00. Maybe start with $6200.00, then $5900.00, then $5600.00 and so on. We can choose any decreasing string of values we want. Once we get a negative result, we go in the other direction until we get a positive result. Then reverse direction again until we get a negative result. Eventually we hone in."

"Wouldn't that would take a lot of time, Dad?"

"With a spreadsheet like the one I use, we can readily do it. I'm going to give you mine, so you can try that for homework. I'll also give you the correct needed **CASH DOWN FROM TRADE-IN** amount for the $0.00 result to happen. But do try to hone in on it as well."

"Ok, Dad. That's one homework assignment I find interesting to try."

***Exercise 14**: Repeat **SITUATION 13 – OPTION P2** for **CASH DOWN FROM SALE** amounts of $6200.00, $5900.00 and $5600.00. Then hone in on the needed amount.*

***Your <u>partial</u> answer should be**: For **CASH DOWN FROM SALE** amounts of $6200.00, $5900.00 and $5600.00 the corresponding **COST OF SALE** results are -$356.09, -$24.34 and +307.40. The -$24.34 results indicates the needed amount is a little less than $5900.00.*

*Needed **CASH DOWN FROM SALE**= $5878.00. For that value, **LOAN AMOUNT** = $17544.00, **MONTHLY PAYMENT** = $323.34, **CUMULATIVE INTEREST** = $1856.51, **TOTAL LOAN COST** =$19400.00, **TOTAL COST TO PURCHASE** = $27500.00, **NET COST OF SALE** =$0.00.*

"Nicole, there is an important general observation to make. Whenever you have cash in hand, you can either keep it there or use it toward the purchase of a car. That includes **CASH DOWN** from savings and **CASH DOWN FROM SALE**. If you keep all the money, then you still have it. However, you pay higher car loan costs. If you put all the money down, then you don't have it any more. However, you reduce your loan costs. It's a matter of individual personal financial circumstances as to which choice to make. And, you can always go in-between and not use all of it for **CASH DOWN** and/or **CASH DOWN FROM SALE**."

"I'm seeing that clearly, Dad."

"That's great, Nicole. Let's continue.

"In **OPTION P3**, Sam sold his **PRESENT CAR** for its **BOOK VALUE**. In reality, he might actually get more than or less than that amount. For example, he might only get $4500.00. In that case we know the outcome is the same as **OPTION P2** when he traded in for that amount. Let's look at the other possibility; he sells it for more than **BOOK VALUE**."

SITUATION 13 – OPTION P4

"Assume Sam sells his car privately for $7500.00 and uses that money as **CASH DOWN FROM SALE**. Here are the calculations."

LOAN AMOUNT = SELLING PRICE + OPTIONS + SALES TAX – CASH REBATE
– CASH DOWN – CASH DOWN FROM SALE
= $23200.00 + $1400.00 +1722.00 – $1300.00 - $1600.00 – $7500.00
= $15922.00

SCALING FACTOR = 15.922

MONTHLY PAYMENT = 15.922 x $18.43 = $293.44

CUMULATIVE INTEREST = 15.922 x $105.82 = $1684.87

TOTAL LOAN COST = 60 x $293.44 = $17606.00 (rounded)

TOTAL COST TO PURCHASE = CASH DOWN + BOOK VALUE
+ TOTAL LOAN COST
= $1600.00 + $6500.00 + $17606.00
= $25706.00

COST OF SALE = BOOK VALUE – CASH DOWN FROM SALE
= $6500.00 - $7500.00 = –$1000.00

SITUATION 13 – OPTION P4 – CONTINUED

"The **CUMULATIVE INTEREST** of $1684.87 is less than the $2478.52 paid in **OPTION P1**. That leads to the following."

CUMULATIVE INTEREST SAVED = $2478.52 - $1684.87 = $793.65

Alternatively, SCALING FACTOR = $7500.00/$1000.00 = 7.50

CUMULATIVE INTEREST SAVED = 7.50 x $105.82 = $793.65

NET COST OF SALE = COST OF SALE - CUMULATIVE INTEREST SAVED
= -$1000.00 – $793.65 = -$1793.65

SITUATION 13 – OPTION P4 – CONTINUED

"Do you follow this one, Nicole?"

"I see it's basically a repeat of **OPTION P3**, but with a different amount of **CASH DOWN FROM SALE**. Because it's $1000.00 higher, the **MONTHLY PAYMENT** and **CUMULATIVE INTEREST** are lower than for when Sam sells the car for $6500.00. That's because the **LOAN AMOUNT** is lowered by $1000.00.

"As a result, the **TOTAL LOAN COST** is lower as well, $17606.00 compared to $18712.00. The lower **TOTAL LOAN COST** results in a lower **TOTAL COST TO PURCHASE**, $25706.00 compared to $26812.00."

"That sure was rapid fire, Peanut. You're spot on. How do these results compare to those for not trading in or selling the **PRESENT CAR**?"

"The **CUMULATIVE INTEREST SAVED** is that $793.65. The **NET COST OF SALE** is a negative amount, -$1793.95. That means it costs Sam $1793.65 less, overall, to sell his **PRESENT CAR** than to trade it in."

"And what about that -$1000.00 value for the **COST OF SALE**? What does that indicate?"

"I was waiting for you to ask that, Dad. I skipped commenting to see if you would ask. The negative sign means Sam made $1000.00 above the **BOOK VALUE**. He got $7500.00, $1000.00 more than $6500.00."

"Peanut, you got me there. Great observation!"

"I guess I outsmarted you?"

"Nope, not yet, Sweetie. You only tricked me a bit."

***Exercise 15**: Repeat **SITUATION 13 – OPTION P4** for a **SELLING PRICE** of $19300.00, $0.00 in **OPTIONS**, a **CASH REBATE** of $0.00, **CASH DOWN** of $1200.00, **BOOK VALUE** of **PRESENT CAR** of $4500.00, **PRESENT CAR** sold privately for $5500.00, **CASH DOWN FROM SALE** of $5500.00, **ANNUAL RATE OF INTEREST** of 8.00%, **TERM** of 36 months, and **SALES TAX RATE** of 6.00%.*

***Your <u>partial</u> answer should be**: **LOAN AMOUNT** = $13758.00, **CUMULATIVE INTEREST** = $1766.66, **TOTAL LOAN COST** =$15775.00, **TOTAL COST TO PURCHASE** = $21475.00, **NET COST OF SALE** = -$1000.00, **NET COST OF SALE** = -$1706.26.*

***Exercise 16**: Repeat **SITUATION 13 – OPTION P4** for a **SELLING PRICE** of $29400, $550.00 in **OPTIONS**, a **CASH REBATE** of $1600.00, **CASH DOWN** of $2400.00, **BOOK VALUE** of **PRESENT CAR** of $11000, **PRESENT CAR** sold privately for $13000.00. **CASH DOWN FROM SALE** of $13000.00, **ANNUAL RATE OF INTEREST** of 6.00%, **TERM** of 48 months, and **SALES TAX RATE** of 8.00%.*

***Your <u>partial</u> answer should be**: **LOAN AMOUNT** = $15346.00, **MONTHLY PAYMENT** = $360.48, **TOTAL LOAN COST** = $17303.00, **TOTAL COST TO PURCHASE** = $30703.00, **COST OF SALE** = -$2000.00, **NET COST OF SALE** = -$3654.64.*

"Ok, Sweetie. I mentioned that Sam can take an in between step of selling his **PRESENT CAR** but not using all the money as **CASH DOWN FROM SALE**. Let's take a look at how that's calculated."

<u>SITUATION 13 – OPTION P5</u>

"Assume Sam sells his car for $7500.00 but only uses $4500.00 as **CASH DOWN FROM SALE**. How do we get the loan costs, Nicole?"

"Well, we used that amount in **OPTION P2**. The results we got there should apply here."

"Perfect.

"Ok, how about this point? The extra $3000.00 for the sale of Sam's **PRESENT CAR** didn't enter into those calculations. How is that handled?"

"Hmm! You've got me there. I know he has that extra money. I just don't see how to take it into account."

"Well, another subtlety arises. It's a matter of a decision by Sam. If he keeps the $3000.00, then he has it in his bank account. The calculations for the transaction of purchasing the car are correct because he gains that $3000.00 asset.

"On the other hand, he could use the money to accelerate the payments on the **CAR LOAN**. If he does that, then his **TOTAL COST TO PURCHASE** decreases by that $3000.00 compared to **OPTION P2**."

TOTAL COST TO PURCHASE = $29024.00 - $3000.00 = $26024.00

SITUATION 13 – OPTION P5 – CONTINUED

"Hmm, that seems odd Dad. Didn't he just spend another $3000.00? Shouldn't the $3000.00 be added to the **TOTAL COST TO PURCHASE**?"

"Nice observation. Unfortunately, it's incorrect. The $3000.00 was accounted for already; in it not being applied to reduce the **LOAN AMOUNT**. By not doing that, Sam paid more **CUMULATIVE INTEREST** than if he did. Let's examine that.

"In **OPTION P4,** Sam sold his **PRESENT CAR** for $7500.00 and used it all as **CASH DOWN FROM SALE**. His resulting **CUMULATIVE INTEREST** was $1684.87. His **TOTAL COST TO PURCHASE** was $25706.00.

"In this **OPTION P5,** his **CUMULATIVE INTEREST** is $2002.33. That's a difference of $2002.33 - $1684.87 = $317.46. It's indeed higher than for using the entire $7500.00. And the **TOTAL COST TO PURCHASE** is $26024.00. It's $26024.00 - $25706.00 = $318.00 higher. That's essentially the same amount as the increase in **CUMULATIVE INTEREST**. With precise calculations they would be the same value. We know that should happen.

"Nicole, you can also look at it this way. If we were to add in the $3000.00, then Sam's **TOTAL COST TO PURCHASE** would become $29024.00 + $3000.00 = $32024.00. That's $32024.00 - $25706.00 = $6318.00 higher than for **OPTION P4**. That suggests the following. By selling his **PRESENT CAR** for $7500.00, Sam's **TOTAL COST TO PURCHASE** is $6318.00 higher for spending $3000.00 of it on making **MONTHLY PAYMENTS** than for using all of it as **CASH DOWN FROM SALE**. How could $3000.00 cause a $6318.00 effect? That's makes no sense. It's nonsense. Correct?"

"Yeah, it sure seems like an illogical result. I guess my observation was incorrect. It's kind of tricky to understand your explanation. I'll have to think about it more. Maybe, I'll just trust you on it."

"Those were all great examples, Dad. They show me how to calculate and compare realistic choices. And they're the ones that seem most logical."

Summary of Results

"Nicole, we covered a lot of ground and details of how to calculate and compare **OPTIONS**. It will take time for you to put the procedures in your memory bank. As to the outcomes, I put them into this table."

OPTION	ACTION	CASH DOWN FROM TRADE or SELL	LOAN AMT*	MP	CI	TOTAL COST LOAN	TOTAL COST PURCHASE
P1	PURCHASE OUTRIGHT	0	23422	431.67	2478.52	25900	27500
P2	TRADE or SELL	4500	18922	348.73	2002.33	20924	29024
P3	TRADE or SELL	6500	16922	311.87	1790.69	18712	26812
P4	TRADE or SELL	7500	15922	293.44	1684.87	17606	25706
P5	SELL for $7500	4500	18922	348.73	2002.33	20924	26024
TIE	TRADE or SELL	5878	17544	323.34	1856.51	19400	27500

*NOTE: TERM OF LOAN = 60 MONTHS ** RESULTS TAKEN FROM EXERCISE 14

"Maybe you can summarize what they tell us Sweetie?"

"OK, Dad. I'll give it a whirl. Here's what I see.

"The most important thing is that whether you trade in or sell the car privately, if the entire proceeds are used as **CASH DOWN** on the purchase of a **NEW CAR**, then the calculations and outcomes are the same. Some names of terminology change, but not the numbers.

"Another is that, the higher is the **CASH DOWN** from the trade-in or private sale, the lower is the **LOAN AMOUNT**, **TOTAL COST OF THE LOAN**, and **TOTAL COST TO PURCHASE**.

"Also, depending on the amount of the money gotten for the trade-in or sale, those resulting costs can be either lower, or the same, or higher, than the costs for purchasing the **NEW CAR** outright. In this case, they come out the same when the amount is $5878.00. If Sam gets more than that amount, then the resulting cost is lower if he trades in his **PRESENT CAR**. Otherwise it better to purchase the **NEW CAR** outright.

"Those are the main things I learned."

"That's super, Sweetie. And of course, if we change the numbers for any or all of the given information, then we get different results. Maybe the relative outcomes of the various **OPTIONS** will change. If you have my spreadsheet you can play around with all of them to see the effects. That way, if you have a particular car in mind you can do that to compare things before you even approach a salesperson."

"I guess that's why you gave me so much homework on this topic. I'll do as much of it as I'll do as much as I can manage within the time constraints of my job. I'll even create my own spreadsheet."

"That's entirely up to you, Peanut.

"Nicole, you can use my cheat sheet for the possibility of either the trade-in or sale of a **PRESENT CAR**. The only new numerical entries needed are the **BOOK VALUE** and the **CASH DOWN FROM TRADE-IN (or SALE)**. I'll also send one that has all the numbers and results for some of the

OPTIONS filled in. You can try it for the other ones."

"That's terrific, Dad. I'll at least give your cheat sheet a try for this Lesson. If I need your help, I'll ask."

"Ok. I'm done on this topic. Is there anything else on your curious mind?"

"Actually, I could use a refresher on car insurance. I purchase it on my own now. That's for my old VW. When I buy a brand new car, I want to be sure I handle that well. There may be some differences."

"I'm glad to do that with you. Does Skype time next Saturday work for you?"

"That morning works fine."

"Ok. Where on for now."

ASIDE: *While not considered in this book, there are some additional costs for purchasing a car. They are the* ***TITLE FEES****,* ***REGISTRATION FEES*** *and any other* ***SPECIAL FEES*** *paid to acquire license plates for the car. For example, in Colorado one is charged a* ***SPECIAL FEE*** *related to funding bridge repairs. These can amount to several hundred to a thousand dollars or so. As the car ages, some or all of these costs decline. Ownership of a car also involves fuel costs and paying to maintain the car and fix any repairs.*

ASIDE: *If you have an existing* ***CAR LOAN****, then it is best to pay it off before buying another car. Otherwise selling the first car is a bit involved. Until the* ***CAR LOAN*** *is paid off, the* ***TITLE*** *for ownership of the car is held by the lender. You must sell the car for enough money to pay off the existing* ***CAR LOAN*** *and still be able to finance the purchase of the next car. If you are trading in a car as part of the purchase, then it gets more involved. Reputable dealerships will assist and do the transaction for you as part of the paperwork of the contract you sign. However, be wary of possible unscrupulous dealers who could fail to pay off your former loan, leaving you with four huge flat tires.*

LESSON 8 Car Insurance and Minding the Gap

Nicole and her Dad have returned to the Skype world. Let's look and listen as they cover the topic of car insurance.

"Hi! Dad. I'm looking forward to your guidance about insuring a **NEW CAR**."

"Hi! Sweetie. It's nice to see you again. Let's get started.

"Now that you are independent and have insured your car on your own, maybe we can begin with you telling me what you know about **STANDARD CAR INSURANCE**."

"I actually looked it over as prep for today."

Standard Car Insurance

"By state law, a car owner or driver is required to have a **STANDARD CAR INSURANCE** policy. While each state has some different requirements, they all include **LIABILITY COVERAGE**."

"And what does that mean, Nicole?"

"If you are involved in a car accident which you caused, then you are legally responsible for the cost of damages and injury to other persons that result from it. Damages include those to the vehicle you hit and to the property of everyone hit in it. Injury means physical injury to those persons."

"And how much coverage must you have?"

"The amounts vary from state to state. For my car, the amounts I have are $250000 per person for bodily injury, $500000 for total bodily injuries for everyone in the vehicle, and $100000 for property damage. The state requirements are a lot lower, but you always carried more when you were paying for my VW coverage. I did the same."

"That's right, Sweetie. In insurance lingo, that's called a 250/500/100 standard policy. Those amounts are much higher than what our state requires as minimum of coverage protection. I did that as an added margin of protection. The persons you are liable to can sue you personally for costs of damages and injury that exceed your coverage. The 250/500/100 is what my insurance agent recommended as reasonable protection to avoid that from happening.

"What about damage to your car and injuries to yourself?"

"Well, Dad, that's where **COMPREHENSIVE INSURANCE** and **COLLISION DAMAGE INSURANCE** comes into play. At that time, I looked it up in my policy and on the web. I jotted down some notes.

"**COMPREHENSIVE INSURANCE** covers my car if it is stolen (and not found, or found but is damaged) and for other sources of damage other than collision. Examples are: damage from theft; vandalism; being hit by moving objects; hitting or being hit by animals; and natural disaster such as flood, fire, and storms. I believe it also covers damage that occurs during riots. It has a **COMPREHENSIVE DEDUCTIBLE** involved. That means the insurer will deduct a specified amount of money from the actual cost of the loss or repairs. I get to choose the amount, but the lower is the amount, the higher is the cost. The net amount they pay you is called the **COMPREHENSIVE PAYOUT**.

"**COLLISION AND DAMAGE INSURANCE** is coverage for damage to my car from hitting another car or an object; or an object hitting it; or damage from things like a roll-over. This coverage has a **COLLISION AND DAMAGE DEDUCTIBLE** involved. The net they pay you is called the **COLLISION AND DAMAGE PAYOUT**."

ASIDE: *For brevity and ease of reading, the author will use the terminology **C&CD INSURANCE** in place of **COMPREHENSIVE INSURANCE** and **COLLISION DAMAGE INSURANCE**. **C** and **CD** will be used for the respective separate prefixes. **C or CD** will be used to indicate "whichever one is applicable".*

ASIDE: *For a car individually owned, some owners opt to cancel **CD INSURANCE** once their car gets older. That tends to occur when the **BOOK VALUE** is low relative to the **MONTHLY PREMIUM** and **DEDUCTIBLE** for that coverage. Some people don't purchase it at all. If you are still paying on a **CAR LOAN**, then the lender will require you to continue the coverage.*

"Terrific, Nicole. You sure did your homework on it."

"And you didn't even ask me to do it."

"Indeed, Peanut. You likely know **C and CD** coverages are optional?"

"I sure do. I guess they don't care if you don't care to cover your own car, as long as you are covered for damage to those of others in accidents you cause."

"That's how I see it, too.

"Maybe that's enough of quizzing you, Peanut. Let me mention a few other coverages. You may or may not be aware of them. In our state and most others, they are optional. In some other states, some of them are required."

"You can purchase **UNINSURED MOTORIST PROPERTY DAMAGE INSURANCE** to protect you if you are hit by an uninsured or underinsured driver. That can happen either if the driver ignored purchasing **C&CD INSURANCE**, albeit illegal, or is from a state that does not require the coverage. Typically, the coverage is the same as it is for your own coverage. If you have a 250/500/100 standard policy, the amounts will be the same for coverage of an uninsured motorist. It doesn't include coverage for medical expenses of either you or your passengers. If your own health insurance policy does not cover yours, then you can purchase **PERSONAL INJURY PROTECTION** coverage for it. You can purchase **MEDICAL PAYMENTS INSURANCE** to cover passengers in your car. Some of these coverages might have a **DEDUCTIBLE** in play.

"Insurers will also offer you coverage for **EMERGENCY ROAD SERVICE** and **CAR RENTAL & TRAVEL EXPENSE**. The former serves to provide for getting your car up and running if, for example, your battery goes dead. It also includes the cost of towing your car to a repair shop. The latter provides partial coverage for renting a car while your car is being repaired and for costs of meals, lodging, and transportation home because of damage that occurs more than a specified number of miles from home. A return trip to pick up your car is also covered. It might pay for a portion or all the deductible if you have an accident in the rental car."

"I am aware of them from my insurance agent. I purchased all of them."

"That's wonderful, Sweetie! How much did your policy cost?"

"I pay about $50.00 per month for all of it."

"That's great. I pay almost double that for my much newer car."

- Total Loss -

"Nicole, if a car is heavily damaged in an accident, then it's possible the insurance company will declare the car to be a 'total loss', or, more simply, to be 'totaled'." Do you know what that means?"

"I understand it means the car cannot be repaired, right?"

"That's one way a total loss happens. Another way is that the car could be repaired but it would cost more to repair it than the **DEPRECIATED VALUE** of the car prior to the damage. From the moment a car is purchased, it begins to lessen in market value. At any particular time into the **TERM** of a **CAR LOAN**, it is worth its **DEPRECIATED VALUE**.

"The insurance company will use the **DEPRECIATED VALUE** to determine, as applicable, either the **C or CD PAYOUT** to the insured owner. Some insurance companies will deem the car a total loss even if the repair costs are somewhat lower than the **DEPRECIATED VALUE**. In those cases, they require that the cost of repairs only be above a certain high percentage of the **DEPRECIATED VALUE**."

"Dad, I know that, at any time after buying it, my car will be worth less than when I bought it. How can I get its **DEPRECIATED VALUE**? Even if I don't have an accident, I'd like to know that when I either sell it or trade it in."

- Depreciated Value -

"It's hard to determine actual depreciation. Depreciation lowers the market value rapidly for some cars, less so for others. No matter, cars depreciate more in the early years than in the ensuing years. It's a well know cliché that the moment a car leaves the lot it is worth noticeably less than before.

"I looked at the website www.edmunds.com/car-buying/how-fast-does-my-new-car-lose-value-infographic.html. It includes an example of a **NEW CAR** (Nissan 370z) with a claimed average **INITIAL VALUE** of $29873.00. At the moment it leaves the lot it has lost 9% of value to $27314.00. Thereafter, it depreciates as shown in their table."

Years	Depreciated Value	Yearly Depreciation	Cumulative Depreciation	% Cumulative Depreciation	% of Initial Value
Initial	29873				
0+	27314	2559	2559	9	91
1	24186	3128	5687	19	81

2	20579	3607	9294	31	69
3	17406	3173	12467	42	58
4	14593	2813	15280	51	49
5	12069	2524	17804	60	40

Exercise 17: *Calculate the missing entries in the following table.*

Years	*Depreciated Value*	*Yearly Depreciation*	*Cumulative Depreciation*	*% Cumulative Depreciation*	*% of Initial Value*
Initial	*29873*				
0+	*28073*	*1800*	*1800*	*6.0*	*94.0*
1	*25773*	*2300*	*4100*	*13.7*	*86.3*
2	*23073*	*2700*	*?*	*22.7*	*77.3*
3	*20673*	*2400*	*9200*	*?*	*?*
4	*18573*	*2100*	*?*	*37.8*	
5	*16773*	*1800*	*?*	*?*	*?*

Your partial results should be:

5	*16773*	*1800*	*13100*	*43.9*	*56.1*

"The listed percentages are rounded to whole numbers. For example, to get the **DEPRECIATED VALUE** of $24186.00, the precise **% CUMULATIVE DEPRECIATION** is 19.036%. The **DEPRECIATED VALUE** drops about 9% to 12% each year. After five years it has lost 60% of its initial value to $12069.00. That makes the **DEPRECIATED VALUE** 40% of the **INITIAL VALUE.** Searching some other websites, I get the sense the listed percentages are significantly exaggerated. And they vary a lot from one car make and model to another. Even if it's only 5% per year, that's a lot."

"Hmm. That's very interesting Dad. I didn't know a car loses value so fast. Mine must be worth next to nothing now."

"Maybe so."

- Salvage Value -

"Another factor is the **SALVAGE VALUE** of the damaged car. **SALVAGE VALUE** is the amount the insurer estimates the damaged car and its usable parts etc. could be sold for to a salvage company. The insurer's **C or CD PAYOUT** is based on the **DEPRECIATED VALUE** of the car minus the **SALVAGE VALUE.**"

"How do they determine that the extent of the damage is sufficiently high to total the car?"

"An **INSURANCE APPRAISER** will inspect the damaged car and estimate the cost of repairs etc. and take the **SALVAGE VALUE** into consideration. Including that, the **DEPRECIATED VALUE** likely will be somewhat less than **BOOK VALUE** of the car before the accident. It's worth trying to negotiate at least full **BOOK VALUE**."

- Insurance Payout -

"Then the insurer applies the applicable deductible amount in the coverage. It's subtracted from the **DEPRECIATED VALUE**. If the resulting amount exceeds the cost of repairs, the car will be deemed totaled. The resulting amount is the **C or CD PAYOUT**, whichever is applicable. Typically, the insurance company will offer the option to settle the claim in either of two ways.

"Without taking the **SALVAGE VALUE** into consideration, the **SETTLEMENT AMOUNT** will be offered. It reflects their appraisal of the market value of the car before the accident. If taken, the insurance company will pay the amount offered and take possession of the car and salvage it themselves.

"As an alternative offer, the **SETTLEMENT AMOUNT** minus the **SALVAGE VALUE** will be offered. If taken, the owner gets the reduced amount and keeps the car. In some jurisdictions, the totaled car must be re-registered as a **SALVAGE VEHICLE**. My read on that is it serves to let a potential future buyer know it is a salvaged car. It is also likely some insurances companies will only insure a salvaged car for its salvage value.

"For example, the **SETTLEMENT OFFER** is $6000.00 and the **SALVAGE VALUE** is $2000.00. The owner can either forfeit the car and accept $6000.00 or keep the car and accept $4000.00.

ASIDE: *If you have made any recent major upgrades to the car, make sure you inform the insurance company when you file the claim. Examples are a new or rebuilt engine or transmission. They will be taken into consideration and result in a higher* ***SETTLEMENT AMOUNT****. Their higher value might also prevent the totaling of the car.*

ASIDE: *Typically, the insurance company obtains its settlement* ***SALVAGE VALUE*** *by bids obtained from reputable salvage companies. Because insurance companies can supply many vehicles, theirs bids will likely be higher than the owner would get if he or she keeps the totaled car and tries to salvage it. However, if new engine and/or transmission or other major part is involved, the owner might make more by trying to sell the car for those parts.*

ASIDE: *If the car is totaled only due to body damage (e.g. from a hailstorm) keeping the totaled car could be wise. People simply looking for a low-cost car for transportation need might pay more than the insurance company's salvage value. Examples would be a parent purchasing a first-time car for a high school kid or a college student in need of a relatively inexpensive car to buy.*

Gap Insurance

"Nicole, with a **CAR LOAN** in play for a **NEW CAR**, there's also a need to consider purchasing what is termed **GAP INSURANCE**."

"What in the world is a **GAP** and why do I have to insure it?"

- What It Covers -

"Funny thing, Sweetie. The word **GAP** always makes me think of getting on and off a car in the subway, which they call the 'tube', in London. A recorded voice calls out, 'Mind the Gap!' We would say, 'Watch Your Step!' It means watch out as you step over the gap between the platform and the car. I suppose now I could say, 'Mind the Gap Insurance'."

"The actual name for **GAP INSURANCE** is **G**uaranteed **A**uto **P**rotection Insurance. While not required by law, it is important to consider having it. It provides for a particular risk involved while you are repaying a **CAR LOAN**. If the car is either stolen or 'totaled' in an accident, then having **GAP INSURANCE** could be valuable."

"Why is that so, Dad?"

"It's a kind of involved. Let's start by assuming you are making payments on a **CAR LOAN** and have a major accident. Thankfully, you survived relatively unscathed physically. The car is heavily damaged and the insurance company deems it to be totaled. You are still responsible to pay the **OUTSTANDING PRINCIPAL** of the **CAR LOAN**. The same is true if the car is stolen. If the **OUTSTANDING PRINCIPAL** exceeds the **DEPRECIATED VALUE** determined by the insurance company, then you will owe the difference out of pocket. That difference is called the **GAP AMOUNT**. Here's the equation for it."

GAP AMOUNT = OUTSTANDING PRINCIPAL – DEPRECIATED VALUE

"Typically, **CAR LOAN** repayment occurs at a slower pace than the rate of depreciation. If you total a car early in the lease, it's almost certainly going to have less **DEPRECIATED VALUE** than the **OUTSTANDING PRINCIPAL**. The resulting **GAP AMOUNT** can be a substantial amount of money, even several thousand dollars. Without **GAP INSURANCE** you would owe that amount to the lessor."

"Yikes! That sounds awful."

"That's why having **GAP INSURANCE** coverage to help pay it is something to consider.

"If your **CD INSURANCE** is in play, then the **CD DEDUCTIBLE** is applicable**.** The amount you receive is the **CD PAYOUT**. Here's the calculation."

CD PAYOUT = DEPRECIATED VALUE – CD DEDUCTIBLE

"The difference between the **OUTSTANDING PRINCIPA**L and the **CD PAYOUT** is what you still owe the lender."

AMOUNT STILL OWED = OUTSTANDING PRINCIPAL – CD PAYOUT

"That all makes sense and is straightforward to calculate, Dad. What if the car is stolen?"

"For any event for which the **C INSURANCE** comes into play, the **C DEDUCTIBLE** applies."

C PAYOUT = DEPRECIATED VALUE – C DEDUCTIBLE

AMOUNT STILL OWED = OUTSTANDING PRINCIPAL – C PAYOUT

"If you have **GAP INSURANCE**, then the amount you receive is the **GAP PAYOUT.** That payout reduces your **OUTSTANDING BALANCE.**"

NEW OUTSTANDING BALANCE = AMOUNT STILL OWED – GAP PAYOUT

"If the **GAP INSURANCE** includes coverage for the **C or CD DEDUCTIBLE**, then the **GAP PAYOUT** equals the **AMOUNT STILL OWED**. Your **NEW OUTSTANDING BALANCE** will be $0.00. Otherwise, the **GAP PAYOUT** is reduced by the amount of the **C or CD DEDUCTIBLE**. And, you will have an **NEW OUTSTANDING BALANCE** equal to the **C or CD DEDUCTIBLE.**"

"That makes sense, too, Dad."

- Cost of Gap Insurance -

"Dad, it sounds like **GAP INSURANCE** must cost a lot?"

"Actually, it's a fixed annual amount and is inexpensive. The cost is a small percentage of your **C&CD INSURANCE** premium. That implies you would purchase the **GAP INSURANCE** from the same insurance carrier. It is usually charged annually, at an **ANNUAL GAP INSURANCE RATE**. If the policy covers the **C or CD DEDUCTIBLE**, then it likely has higher cost. The amount depends on the make, model and features of the car you lease. It is about $50.00 to $75.00 per year. For the 3-year **TERM** of the **CAR LEASE** that would be $150.00 to $225.00 per year.

"Commonly, **GAP INSURANCE** is paid monthly using a **MONTHLY GAP INSURANCE RATE**. Here it is in math form."

MONTHLY GAP INSURANCE RATE = ANNUAL GAP INSURANCE RATE/12

TOTAL COST OF GAP INSURANCE = MONTHLY GAP INSURANCE RATE x TERM

"If the car is totaled, then you only pay for the **GAP INSURANCE** for the **MONTHS** up to that time."

COST OF GAP INSURANCE = MONTHLY GAP INSURANCE RATE x MONTHS

"Gee, that sounds like a lot, but I guess if it only about $5.00 a month. That's basically a cup of fancy coffee, which isn't that expensive."

"That's how I see it, too, Sweetie.

"Some insurance companies automatically offer **GAP INSURANCE** in their **STANDARD CAR INSURANCE** policy or will add it to an existing one. And, not all insurance companies offer **GAP INSURANCE**. If they don't, then the company usually has similar coverage available, with the same effect."

- Example -

"OK, it's time for some numbers. Let's use the Nissan example to do that."

SITUATION 14

"Alison purchased the Nissan 370z for that $29873.00. She took out a **CAR LOAN** for the full amount. Because of her modest **FICO SCORE**, the **ANNUAL RATE OF INTEREST** is 6.50% for a 5-year **TERM**. The **MONTHLY PAYMENT** is $584.50. Her **STANDARD CAR INSURANCE** has **CD DEDUCTIBLE** of $1000.00.

"She purchases **GAP INSURANCE** at a cost of $5.00 per month. It <u>does not include</u> coverage of her **CD DEDUCTIBLE**.

"One year later, the car is totaled in an accident. It has depreciated 19% (19.036% precisely) to a **DEPRECIATED VALUE** of $24186.00. I did the **AMORTIZATION SCHEDULE** and her **OUTSTANDING PRINCIPAL** is $24647.00.

"Can you do the calculations I just described for the insurance events?"

"It seems pretty straightforward. Let me give it a try."

Nicole writes the calculations on scratch paper. "Here's what I get, Dad."

COST OF GAP INSURANCE = MONTHLY GAP INSURANCE RATE x MONTHS
= $5.00 x 12 = $60.00

GAP AMOUNT = OUTSTANDING PRINCIPAL – DEPRECIATED VALUE
= $24647.00 – $24186 = $461.00

CD PAYOUT = DEPRECIATED VALUE – CD DEDUCTIBLE
= $24186.00 – $1000.00 = $23186.00

AMOUNT STILL OWED = OUTSTANDING PRINCIPAL – CD PAYOUT
= $24647.00 – $23186.00 = $1461.00

GAP PAYOUT = AMOUNT STILL DUE – CD DEDUCTIBLE
= $1461.00 – $1000.00 = $461.00

NEW OUTSTANDING BALANCE = AMOUNT STILL OWED – GAP PAYOUT
= $1461.00 – $461.00 = $1000.00

SITUATION 14 – CONTINUED

"Terrific! That's all correct, Peanut."

"The **GAP PAYOUT** is only $461.00. That's not a lot of money, Dad?"

"Maybe so. However, Alison only paid $60.00 to get coverage for $461.00. That coverage is almost 700% more than she paid for it.

"If her **GAP INSURANCE** does cover the **CD DEDUCTIBLE**, then here's what changes?"

GAP PAYOUT = AMOUNT STILL OWED = $1461.00

NEW OUTSTANDING BALANCE = AMOUNT STILL OWED – GAP PAYOUT
= $1461.00 - $1461.00 = $0.00

SITUATION 14 – CONTINUED

"Ok, Dad. I see that her **GAP PAYOUT** covered the entire **AMOUNT STILL OWED** and her **CAR LOAN** is paid off."

"And how much was the benefit amount?"

After a pause, Nicole replies. "Because the **CD DEDUCTIBLE** was paid, Alison paid $60.00 for a benefit of $1461.00. The benefit is about 2400% of what she paid. That's colossal."

"Yes, it is. Without **GAP INSURANCE** Alison would have to pay the entire **AMOUNT STILL OWED.** Because she wouldn't pay the $60.00, the net she pays is $1461.00 - $60.00 = $1401.00. It's still a significant amount out of pocket."

"To really see the pros and cons, we have to examine the trend over the **TERM** of the loan. I did **AMORTIZATION SCHEDULE** for this loan. I then added on columns to track the **GAP INSURANCE** results on a monthly basis. Here's a table with partial results."

Principal	29873								
Term in Years	**Annual Rate of Interest**	**Month**	**Outstanding Principal**	**Cumulative Interest**	**Depreciated Value in %**	**Depreciated Value**	**Gap Amount**	**CD Payout**	**Amount Owed**
5	6.5	0	29873	0	93.97	27314	2559	26314	3559
		1	29450	162	93.36	27053	2397	26053	3397
		-	-	-	-	-	-	-	-
		4	28168	633	91.43	26271	1897	25271	2897
		-	-	-	-	-	-	-	-
		8	26427	1230	88.87	25229	1198	24229	2198
		-	-	-	-	-	-	-	-
		12	24647	1788	86.30	24186	461	23186	1461
		13	24196	1921	85.54	23925	271	22925	1271

"I took out some of the usual columns and added the three at the right end. They track the effects of the **GAP INSURANCE**.

"What do you notice about the trends in the **GAP AMOUNT** and the **AMOUNT OWED**?"

Staring at the results, Nicole observes, "I see that, the sooner the accident occurs the larger are the **GAP AMOUNT** and the **AMOUNT OWED**."

"Exactly! If we say it in reverse, then the longer into the **LOAN TERM** the smaller are the **GAP AMOUNT** and the **AMOUNT OWED**.

"That means that, as time passes, the benefit of **GAP INSURANCE** decreases. Indeed, in Month 13 the **GAP AMOUNT** is negative. That indicates you no longer need the **GAP INSURANCE**. If the car has not been totaled by that time, you can cancel the **GAP INSURANCE** and save a little money. Of course, you don't want to total the car at all. You never know if and when it will occur. If it is going to happen, then the sooner it does, the more you save by having **GAP INSURANCE**.

"Did you notice the line I added for a Month 0?"

"I do now, Dad. What's that line for?"

"I put it in to illustrate the outcome if the car is totaled the moment you drive it off the lot. That's a horrible outcome. You owe the full **LOAN AMOUNT**. Without **GAP INSURANCE**, you would have an **AMOUNT OWED** = $3559.00 out of pocket. With **GAP INSURANCE**, if your **CD DEDUCTBL**E is not covered, then all you pay is $1000 **CD DEDUCTIBLE**. If it is covered, then you pay nothing. And you would have paid only one month of **GAP INSURANCE**, $5.00."

"Dad, that's incredible! It really is a no-brainer. I certainly will add **GAP INSURANCE** when I buy my **NEW CAR**."

"And wise you will be, to do so."

***Exercise 17A**: As a continuation of Exercise 17, calculate the missing entries in the table.*

Principal	*29873*

Term in Years	*Annual Rate of Interest*	*Month*	*Outstanding Principal*	*Cumulative Interest*	*Depreciated Value in %*	*Depreciated Value*	*Gap Amount*	*CD Payout*	*Amount Owed*
5	6.5	0	29873	0	93.97	27314	2559	26314	3559
		1	29450	162	93.36	27053	2397	26053	3397
		2	29025	321	92.72	26793	2233	-	-
		3	28598	479	92.08	26532	2066	25532	3066
		4	28168	633	91.43	26271	1897	25271	2897
		5	27737	786	90.79	26011	-	25011	-
		6	27302	936	90.15	25750	-	-	-
		7	26866	1084	89.51	25489	1376	24489	2376
		9	25985	1373	88.23	24968	1017	-	-
		10	25542	1514	87.58	24707	-	23707	1834
		11	25095	1652	86.94	24447	649	-	1649
		9	25985	1373	88.23	24968	1017	23968	2017

***Your partial results should be**:*

6	27302	936	90.15	25750	1552	24750	2552
10	25542	1514	87.58	24707	834	23707	1834

Loan/Lease Insurance

"Nicole, I need to mention an option to **GAP INSURANCE**. It's called **LOAN/LEASE INSURANCE**."

"What does that do?"

- What It Covers -

"In the event of a total loss or theft of your car, **LOAN/LEASE INSURANCE** pays out in the same manner as the **GAP INSURANCE**. The difference is **LOAN/LEASE PAYOUT (L/L PAYOUT**, for short) amount is capped up to a certain percentage of the **DEPRECIATED VALUE**. Researching it I always found mention of 25% as the **LOAN/LEASE INSURANCE CAP (L/L CAP**, for short)."

- Example -

"Let's apply **LOAN/LEASE INSURANCE** to SITUATION 14."

SITUATION 14A

"Alison of SITUATION 14 has, instead, purchased **LOAN/LEASE INSURANCE**. It pays up to 25.00% of the **DEPRECIATED VALUE**, but does not cover her **CD DEDUCTIBLE**. It costs $60.00 per year, the same as for the **GAP INSURANCE**.

"Some information is carried-over. The **DEPRECIATED VALUE** = $24186.00, **OUTSTANDING PRINCIPAL** = $24647.00, **GAP AMOUNT** = $461.00, **CD PAYOUT** = $23186.00, **AMOUNT STILL OWED** = $1461.00.

"Because the **DEPRECIATED VALUE** exceeds the **OUTSTANDING PRINCIPAL**, Alison's **LOAN/LEASE INSURANCE** applies. The **L/L CAP** = 0.25 x $24186.00 = $6047.00 (rounded). That exceeds the **AMOUNT STILL OWED** of $1461.00."

L/L PAYOUT = AMOUNT STILL OWED – CD CDEDUCTIBLE
= $1461.00 – $1000.00 = $461.00

SITUATION 14A - CONTINUED

"Alison's bank is paid $23186.00 + $461.00 = $23647.00. Her **OUTSTANDING BALANCE** would be $1000.00.

"If her **CD DEDUCTIBLE** was covered, then she would receive an **L/L PAYOUT** = $1461.00 – $0.00 = $1461.00 and her **OUTSTANDING BALANCE** would be $0.00."

"Did you follow this example, Nicole?"

"I did. Except for the **L/L CAP** aspect, the calculation process looks the same as for **GAP INSURANCE**. What am I missing?"

"You're correct about the process. That's why I did the example. There's also a vital observation to make.

"If you check and compare, the monetary amounts that result are exactly the same as for **GAP INSURANCE**. That suggests it makes no difference whether you have **GAP INSURANCE** versus **LOAN/LEASE INSURANCE**. Why do you suppose it doesn't?"

"As you went through the calculations, I was noticing that too, Dad. I was thinking about it in the back of my head. I believe the outcomes are the same because all the given information is the same in both cases. And because the calculation process is the same, you get the same answers."

"That's correct. But there is one difference in the process. What's that?"

After a serious-looking stare at the results, Nicole answers, "It seems the only thing different is using that **L/L CAP**. The **L/L PAYOUT** was less than the **L/L CAP**. Maybe that had something to do with it?

Like, since it was not exceeded, it did not actually come into play."

"Fantastic, Peanut! The Smarty Pants part of your head is really smart."

"Ha! Ha! Thanks, Dad."

"It is the important thing. Let me go into it some more."

- Reaching the Loan/Lease Cap -

"Sweetie, There was something I was curious about. To look into it, I played around with changing the **% CUMULATIVE DEPRECIATION** value. Let's look at a particular value."

> **<u>SITUATION 15</u>**
>
> "Repeating SITUATION 14A, I made the **% CUMULATIVE DEPRECIATION** = 33.99%, here are the numbers."

<u>For % CUMULATIVE DEPRECIATION of 33.99%</u>

DEPRECIATED VALUE = (1 - 0.3399) x $29873.00 = $19716.00

GAP AMOUNT = OUTSTANDING BALANCE - DEPRECIATED VALUE
= $24647.00 - $19716.00 = $4931.00

CD PAYOUT = DEPRECIATED VALUE – CD DEDUCTIBLE
= $19716.00 - $1000.00 = $18716.00

AMOUNT STILL OWED = OUTSTANDING PRINCIPAL – CD PAYOUT
= $24647.00 - $18716.00 = $5931.00

<u>GAP INSURANCE</u>:

GAP PAYOUT = AMOUNT STILL OWED – CD DEDUCTIBLE
= $5931.00 - $1000.00 = $4931.00

<u>LOAN/LEASE INSURANCE</u>:

L/L CAP = 0.25 x $19716.00 = $4929.00 < AMOUNT STILL OWED

L/L PAYOUT = L/L CAP = $4929.00 (essentially $4931.00)

GAP INSURANCE and LOAN LEASE INSURANCE provide the same coverage

NEW BALANCE = AMOUNT STILL OWED – GAP (= L/L) PAYOUT
= $5931.00 - $4931.00 = $1000.00

SITUATION 15 – CONTINUED

"The **L/L CAP** is essentially equal to the **GAP AMOUNT**. If used more precision for the percentage, they would be the same."

"Do you follow my calculations and the comparison, Nicole?"

"I do. But, what's the point of this particular **% CUMULATIVE DEPRECIATION**?"

"Sweetie, I wondered if the **GAP INSURANCE** and **LOAN/LEASE INSURANCE** would always give the same results. Then, I realized there must be a maximum **% CUMULATIVE DEPRECIATION** value for which the **LOAN/LEASE INSURANCE** leads to a **GAP AMOUNT** that is equal to the **L/L CAP**. In this case it turned out to be 33.99%"

"Why is that important, Dad?"

"Above that maximum, the **L/L CAP** will come into play. The **GAP AMOUNT** will exceed the **L/L CAP**. As a result, the **L/L PAYOUT** will be the **L/L CAP** amount. That is, it will be lower than the **GAP AMOUNT**.

"By comparison, for **GAP INSURANCE** the **GAP PAYOUT** will be the actual **GAP AMOUNT**. In other words, **GAP INSURANCE** provides more coverage.

"At or below that maximum **% CUMULATIVE DEPRECIATION** value, the two options provide the same coverage.

"Does that make sense to you, Sweetie?"

"I do see that in this example, **L/L CAP** does equal the **GAP AMOUNT**. I also see that, when that happens, the two insurances pay out the same amount. I have to think on the other part."

"Nicole, to make the **GAP AMOUNT** equal to the **L/L CAP** would we have to increase or decrease the **% CUMULATIVE DEPRECIATION** compared to the 19.00% value we used in SITUATIONS 14 and 14A?"

Pausing to scratch the back of her head, Nicole then replies. "Well, it seems logical to me that we need to make the **GAP AMOUNT** larger. To do that, we need to have a lower the **CD PAYOUT**. That means we have to depreciate the car faster by increasing the **% CUMULATIVE DEPRECIATION**."

"That's perfect. That's why my trial and error results ended up at 33.99%. Now that head of yours is really churning away.

"If you were to use a slightly higher **% CUMULATIVE DEPRECIATION** of 35.00%, what would happen? And if you were to use a slightly lower **% CUMULATIVE DEPRECIATION** of 33.00%, what would happen?"

"Hmm. My brain was working real hard as I follow your words before. Let me think a bit."

After a pause Nicole replies, "If I followed you correctly, Dad, then for 35.00% the **GAP PAYOUT** should be more than the **L/L PAYOUT**. And for 33.00%, the two insurances should end up paying out the same amount. It would be like what happened in SITUATIONS 14 and 14A. I sort of trust you on it, though."

"You're exactly right, Peanut. As to trusting me, you can confirm things by doing the calculations. For homework, you can try these exercises. Just repeat my calculations using the different **% CUMULATIVE DEPRECIATION** values. I'll give you the correct answers, too."

Exercise 18: *Repeat SITUATION 15 for a **% CUMULATIVE DEPRECIATION** of 35.00%.*

Your results should be: ***GAP PAYOUT*** *= $5230.0,* ***L/L PAYOUT*** *= $4854.00.* ***GAP INSURANCE*** *provides <u>more</u> coverage than* ***LOAN/LEASE INSURANCE!*** *See* ***APPENDIX III*** *for the complete solution.*

Exercise 18A: *Repeat SITUATION 15 for a **% CUMULATIVE DEPRECIATION** of 33.00%.*

Your results should be: ***GAP PAYOUT*** *=* ***L/L PAYOUT*** *= $4632.00.* *See* ***APPENDIX III*** *for the complete solution.*

"Ok, it actually looks easy, Dad. I'll try them later."

"Nicole, the **% CUMULATIVE DEPRECIATION** of 33.99% being needed is sky high. It's 14.99% higher than the 19% Nissan value. If I use a more realistic **% CUMULATIVE DEPRECIATION** of 75% of the Nissan value, that's 14.25%. The **L/L CAP** is 19.74% % higher. What's that tell you?"

"It tells me this circumstance cannot happen in reality. At least it can't for the leased car being totaled at one year."

"Perfect, Sweetie!"

"By trial and error, I checked some other timings of the accident. I tabulated the results."

Years Into Lease	Needed % Cumulative Depreciation (Cap)	% Cumulative Depreciation (Nissan Example)	% Cumulative Depreciation (Realistic)
0	20.00	9	6.75
1	33.99	19	14.25
2	48.39	31	23.25
3	64.86	42	30.75

"The needed **% CUMULATIVE DEPRECIATION** is sky high for all of them. What's that suggest to you, Sweetie?"

"It seems like the **L/L CAP** will never be reached."

"Exactly! It makes no difference whether you have **GAP INSURANCE** versus **LOAN/LEASE INSURANCE**. The **GAP PAYOUT** will be the same for both. And the cost is so low that, even if there was a small difference, it would be an insignificant factor.

"Of course, we can only know that for SITUATION 14. However, it's hard to imagine it not always being true. Knowing that, we can safely surmise that there is no need for separate calculations. Whatever realistic examples we look at, the results we get for **GAP INSURANCE** also apply if it was **LOAN/LEASE INSURANCE**."

"Perfect, Dad. I was waiting for you to figure that out."

"Ha! Ha! Ha! Ha!"

"Yeah, I was just kidding. I was actually trying to distract you, so you wouldn't ask if I wanted to see how you figured out all the others."

"Well, actually, you read my mind, Nicole. If you want to try, you can verify that all the needed percentages in my table are correct. Just repeat my calculations using different times for the totaling of the car. You being so nice to me, it's optional. I really don't expect you do to them all. It would be good of you tried any one of them."

"Again, it actually looks easy, Dad. I may try one of them. For the others, I'll trust your findings."

"Dad, again you've showed me something very interesting and which I would not have thought about on my own. Thank you."

"It's nice to hear that."

"Sweetie, I'm done on this topic. Is there anything else on your curious mind?"

"Actually, there is. Remember I mentioned that some of my colleagues told me that they actually leased a car instead of buying one. It would be great if you would explain that process to me."

"Sure. Sweetie! Anytime. I'll need some time to prepare. If you have time next week, then you might research it a bit as well. If you find useful websites, just forward them to me. You don't have to delve into the nitty gritty, as I will do that. I'll send you links to those I already found. Then we can Skype next Saturday. Does that work for you?"

"I would like to so that. I don't foresee any post work assignment distractions in play this week, so I can give it a try."

"Ok, we have a Dad-Daughter date. Knowing you, you might know more than me by that time. Maybe I'll learn a few things from you, too. And then I can call you Smartest Pants more often."

ASIDE: *The cost of* ***STANDARD CAR INSURANCE*** *was not included in the SITUATIONS.*
Roughly, it ranges from $75.00 to $150.00 per month for typical cars. For luxury cars, it can cost much more. Insurers have much higher rates if an individual less than 25 years old will be a driver of the car. All these costs vary widely according to the specific car purchased and your residence for the car ownership. The reader would need to investigate these costs for his/her actual locale

LESSON 9 Hitting the Road in My New Car Lease

Leasing a car is an alternative to purchasing one. Indeed, it seems that ads for leasing dominate in vast number over those for selling a car. Whether in newspaper print or online dealer websites, numerous car dealership ads indicate available terms for leasing specific cars. For example, 2015 Dodge Dart, SXT MSRP $21140, Stock #3260, $149/mo. 3-yr lease, $2229 down, and with an accompanying photo. What does that all mean? If you're experienced in leasing a car, you know. Otherwise, it's likely you are left to surmising.

In passing, our Nicole had seen many such ads in the Evening Gazette. With car leasing absent from her radar, she was in that surmising cubicle. Now that it has shown up there, her curiosity is much more motivated. As always, her Dad tuned into her request for advice. By teaming to search the web about car leasing, they found a pile of websites for Dad to research. Let's peek in on what transpires as Nicole and her Dad Skype to assess the findings.

"Good morning Dad! I'm looking forward to learning more about leasing a car. Actually, I shouldn't say 'more' as a week ago I knew virtually nothing about them. From your replies, I see you got the website links I have been passing on to you this week. In perusing them myself for applicability, I sort of picked up a lot of general things on the fly. Nothing in depth; mostly I glanced at overviews about the process and saw a lot of strange terminology flashing by on my monitor."

"Good morning, Nicole. I did look into many of your links, in depth. I also sent you others that I investigated closely. Did you get them?"

"Yeah, Dad, I saw lots of incoming stuff and glanced through some of it. I suspected you would dig into them as you always do. Basically, you can assume I have a beginner's viewpoint. My eyes and mind are pretty wide open to absorb what you found."

"Where do you want to start, Nicole?"

"Since I know little to nothing about it, what exactly is a **CAR LEASE**?"

Car Lease

"A **CAR LEASE** is a way to sort of rent a car for a long period of time, typically three years. That's a simplistic answer as there is a lot more to it."

"Dad, over the years, you've shown me a lot about borrowing money wisely. From scanning a few websites, leasing a car seems like a very different animal. It does not involve borrowing money."

"I understand that perception. While borrowing money is not likely involved in leasing, you are still borrowing something – the car itself. There are costs involved in doing that, which you will be financing and repaying over time. If you do lease a car, then you will be taking on debt. While being a bird of a different feather in looks, the extent of the costs is substantial.

"Nicole, in your passing look-see, did you notice anything about how you agree to lease a car?"

"Yes, I saw that the signing of an **LEASE AGREEMENT** or **CONTRACT** is a very involved decision. I don't know the details."

"Well, loosely, that agreement is called a **CAR LEASE**. By signing one, you mainly agree to incur the indicated **MONTHLY PAYMENT**. You also agree to the amounts of several up-front costs and end of lease charges. Before doing so, it's important to be knowledgeable about how car leasing works compared to purchasing one. You need to understand the typical details of such an agreement and the financial implications. You're right about one thing. For anyone unfamiliar with car leasing, there's a lot of terminology to absorb. From what I know and read, when considering a **CAR LEASE**, it is vital to understand all of it and be alert to its implications."

"Dad, what are the up-front costs and end of lease charges?"

"Those are charges such as an up-front **ACQUISITION FEE** and a **DISPOSITION FEE** that comes at the end of the lease. The various charges and all the different steps involved in leasing a car can bring the same angst about going through the process as does the purchasing one. If you have never investigated the possibility of leasing a car, then you have that foreign territory to navigate atop many of the usual time, effort and worries involved in purchasing one."

***ASIDE**: Just the above paragraphs likely created a bit of puzzlement and worry to readers unfamiliar with car leasing. The author's aim is to familiarize the reader with all the primary cost aspects of leasing a car. That should allow you to determine (calculate) the immediate costs, ongoing monthly costs and other costs that result from taking on car leasing debt. Sufficient detail is provided to enable you to do that as well as to compare those costs with those of the alternative of purchasing the car.*

***ASIDE:** As with purchasing a car, it is not the aim of this Lesson to present aspects of any psychology or strategy regarding car leasing. One can find an exhaustive amount of information online and guidance on what the car leasing process involves and how to work through it knowledgably and effectively. Some helpful websites are cited herein. Let's see what Nicole and her Dad found out about the monetary process.*

"Yeah, Dad, I certainly feel that way. Some of the websites you mentioned when we discussed online purchasing of a car, also provide leasing services. Some of those offer guidance on how to go about the leasing process. I mentioned that when I sent the links to you."

"That's right, Peanut. I was aware of that. Your mentioning them prompted me to review some of them again for content on leasing a car. For example, www.edmunds.com/car-leasing/10-steps-to-leasing-a-new-car.html summarizes the steps involved in leasing. I jotted down some notes.

"The content begins with Step 1: Get Acquainted with Leasing, Step 2: Design Your Lease Deal: Years, Miles and Insurance and so on. It ends with Step 10: Review and Sign the Paperwork. The written content for each step is cursory, but does describe each aspect in the order they occur.

"There are sub-links to more detailed content, such as a 'leasing glossary', 'pros and cons of leasing', 'calculate your own lease payment' and others. The sub-link 'Quick Guide to Leasing a New Car' provides a few more specific bits of information. A sub-link to 'Edmunds Price Promise ® Lease Offers' takes you to their own car leasing page. It walks you through how to use their on-line service. Once we cover things this morning, you should be able to read that content effectively and quickly."

"That's sounds great Dad. I'll surely do that."

"I also went to the link www.carbuyingtips.com/lease2.html that you sent me. It offers exhaustive guidance on car leasing and the 'ins-and outs' of getting a fair and honest outcome from leasing dealerships. If you are worried about possible dishonesty or scamming in the details of leasing a car, this site seems to very much have your back covered.

"The website guides one through the specifics of car leasing and with a very pessimistic viewpoint. Their main page covers 'How to Lease a New Car and Avoid Dealer Scams'. Their 'Auto Lease Glossary' defines all the main terminology and buttresses them with alerts beginning with 'Don't…' or 'Never…' If you're yearning to be ready to 'duke it out' with a leasing dealership, then this site provides the tools to do so. If you soak in the information, then it will be 'ready, set, and go!'"

"Wow, Dad! Now I am feeling that angst and worry that you mentioned newbies have about car leasing. My knees are feeling wobbly, too."

"There are many involved aspects to actually getting acquainted with car leasing. It's only a wobbly, negative process if you let it be. The negative concerns extensively covered at that www.carbuyingtips.com/lease2.html website can and do occur, either in part or entirely, in some instances. Nonetheless, many people lease cars. Most do work with a trustworthy salesperson. With that assurance and armed with knowledge and preparation, you can maneuver to a leasing deal with costs you understand and accept."

"That's nice to hear, Dad."

"At a quick glance, when you lease a car it is similar to renting a car. At closer look there are significant differences.

"Unlike renting a car from Alamo, Enterprise or the like, in leasing you will not have the car for only a few days to a week or two. In leasing, you agree to rent a car for a long period of time, pay for its usage, be properly insured for potential accidents etc., pay for fuel used and return it at the end of **TERM** of the **CAR LEASE**. Although it can be a shorter or longer period of time, typically car leasing involves a 3-year period of time. That's because, almost invariably, the car being leased is a **NEW CAR** and the **MANUFACTURER'S WARRANTY** is in place for that period of time."

***ASIDE**: While one can find lessors offering **USED CARS** for lease, leased cars are predominantly **NEW CARS**. For leasing a **USED CAR**, you have to be aware of the likely shortened or expired **MANUFACTURER'S WARRANTY**. If so, be careful about wording in the leasing agreement concerning maintenance and be clear who pays for usual maintenance needs. For major things you either will have to pay for them or agree to a dealership maintenance agreement. For repair or replacement of major things such as a failed transmission or engine problems you will be responsible* *for them. For this Lesson, it is assumed the reader is seeking a **NEW CAR** to lease. For **USED CARS**, it is essentially no different except you will have to navigate the same condition and value concerns you face when purchasing one.*

"Although some car rental companies advertise that 'you can choose any car on the lot', in most cases you cannot. Most vendor sites indicate various cars choices in the wording, e.g., 'a Ford Fusion or similar make and model'. They cannot guarantee specifically what cars will be on their lot on the day and at the time you arrive. When you arrive, the vendor has assigned you a car they chose to satisfy their flexible descriptor. If you do get to choose, then it is from whatever cars are on the grounds at the time you arrive that fit the size, type and pricing you reserved. It might be just a few. Unlike renting a car for a short term, when leasing a car, you pick the exact car you like from those available at dealer locations you are considering."

"Well, Dad, I sure like that aspect a lot. On occasion, I've rented cars at work for doing assignments away from home territory. Sometimes, I got a souped-up sporty car when I just wanted a simple small sedan."

Monthly Payment

"Dad, since leasing a car is not a loan of money, how is the **MONTHLY PAYMENT** determined?"

"That's where leasing a car gets rather involved. There's a whole lot of important terminology to explain. To begin, the **MONTHLY PAYMENT** is comprised of three parts: 1) the **MONTHLY DEPRECIATION FEE**, 2) the **MONTHLY FINANCE CHARGE** and 3) the **MONTHLY SALES TAX**. And each of those requires my explaining some terminology."

- Monthly Depreciation Fee -

"During the **TERM** of the **CAR LEASE**, a **MONTHLY DEPRECIATION FEE** is imposed. It accounts for two things: 1) **NORMAL WEAR AND TEAR** on the car and 2) the change in market value simply because the car is older."

"What do they consider as **NORMAL WEAR AND TEAR**, Dad?"

"Basically, you are required to return the leased car in the same condition as you received it, minus **NORMAL WEAR AND TEAR**. Over the **TERM** of the lease, there will be some usual and understandable degradation of its condition. An example is the upholstery will have worn somewhat. It's hard to be specific about what **NORMAL WEAR AND TEAR** includes because it varies with companies. And it may not be well defined up-front. Whatever occurs beyond 'normal' will cost you money.

"If there is any **EXCESS WEAR AND TEAR** in the car at the end of the **CAR LEASE**, then an **EXCESS WEAR AND TEAR CHARGE** will be incurred. That's for anything deemed as 'not usual'. An example is a major tear in the upholstery. The lessor may see your returned vehicle in a different light than you. Even when the leased car is returned in what you deem as 'good condition', be prepared for possible extra charges and a dispute. Before signing a **CAR LEASE**, be sure to ask for written criteria about both **NORMAL WEAR AND TEAR** and **EXCESS WEAR AND TEAR**.

"It is also your responsibility to make, and pay, for repairs needed for any damage incurred. For certain types of damage, you also are required to report the damage to the lessor at the time it takes place. At the end of the **CAR LEASE**, you will be charged for any existing **RESIDUAL DAMAGE**."

"What's **RESIDUAL DAMAGE**? And how is that determined? It sounds a lot like a putting down a security deposit when you rent an apartment. If you don't cause any damage, then you get it back."

"That's a perfect analogy, Nicole. **RESIDUAL DAMAGE** is anything that did not exist when you leased the car and has not been repaired. If you fail to repair things fully, then you are at the possible mercy of the lessor. Some of the websites mentioned some things to be particularly wary about. One is having even a minor ping in a window. You might be paying for a new window. Another is to rotate the tires or you might be replacing unevenly worn tires.

"And like your analogy to an apartment, some car lessors might ask for an up-front **SECURITY DEPOSIT** for possible **EXCESS WEAR AND TEAR** and/or **RESIDUAL DAMAGE**. From what I read, it should be rejected, if possible. Otherwise, you have prepaid for possible disputable charges and will have little or no monetary leverage. You probably wish you could do that with your landlord, too?"

"I sure do, Dad. Even so, this car leasing business is beginning to sound kind of intimidating."

"It can be. The way to tame it is to be armed with knowledge about all the aspects. And there's a lot more still to be explained."

***NOTE**: In effect, the leased car is the **COLLATERAL** on the **CAR LEASE** (just as a purchased car is in a **CAR LOAN**). The lessor has lent you the **COLLATERAL**. When the **CAR LEASE** ends, the **COLLATERAL** is returned to the lessor. If it has **EXCESS WEAR AND TEAR** and/or **RESIDUAL DAMAGE**, then the **COLLATERAL** has lessened in value. You have to pay for that unanticipated loss.*

- ## Capitalized Cost

"As I mentioned earlier, agreeing to a **CAR LEASE** does not have the appearance of taking out a **CAR LOAN**. However, it is a loan. If the dealer were to sell the car, then it would have a **SELLING PRICE**. For a **NEW CAR**, the buyer might add **OPTIONS** which are added to the **SELLING PRICE**. In leasing terminology, the resulting total cost (initial market value) is referred to as the **CAPITALIZED COST** of the **CAR LEASE**. Here's the equation for it."

CAPITALIZED COST = SELLING PRICE + OPTIONS

- ## Net Capitalized Cost

"When you lease a car, the dealer is lending it to you with that initial market value. However, several things either will or can occur to reduce the **CAPITALIZED COST** to what is termed the **NET CAPITALIZED COST**.

"In the transacting the **CAR LEASE,** you might either be required or elect to make a **DOWN**

PAYMENT. In leasing terminology, it is called either **CASH DOWN** or, more formally, **CAPITAL COST REDUCTION**. That's because it reduces the **CAPITALIZED COST** of the car.

"For a **NEW CAR**, a factory **CASH REBATE** might be in play and owed to you. It will be credited as a further reduction of the **CAPITALIZED COST.**

"Just as in purchasing a car, you can trade-in a **PRESENT CAR** as part of a **CAR LEASE**. If so, then the **CASH DOWN FROM TRADE-IN** further reduces the **CAPITALIZED COST**. If you sell a **PRESENT CAR** privately, then the **CASH DOWN FROM SALE** further reduces the **CAPITALIZED COST.**"

"Is there a tornado going on, Dad? My head is really spinning."

"I know it's a lot to absorb. It's just part of the terminology turf. Let's put it together in math terms."

"All the preceding stuff leads to establishing what is termed the **NET CAPITALIZED COST.** Here it is in equation form."

NET CAPITALIZED COST = CAPITALIZED COST – CASH REBATE
– CASH DOWN – CASH DOWN FROM
TRADE-IN (or SALE)

= (SELLING PRICE + OPTIONS)
– CASH REBATE – CASH DOWN
– CASH DOWN FROM TRADE-IN (or SALE)

"Just as in purchasing a car, either the **CASH DOWN FROM TRADE-IN** or the **CASH DOWN FROM SALE** applies, not both.

"The **NET CAPITALIZED COST** is what you agree to as the borrowed value when you sign the **CAR LEASE**.

"Does that make it clearer for you, Peanut?"

"The equation helps a lot, Dad. Now, I understand the difference between the **CAPITALIZED COST** and the **NET CAPITALIZED COST**."

"Peanut, if we added in a term for **SALES TAX**, then the equation for **NET CAPITALIZED COST** would be the same as the equation for the **LOAN AMOUNT** for purchasing the car. There is a **SALES TAX** involved. However, it's not included in the equation. That's because you haven't actually purchased the car. For a leased car, it's calculated separately and paid in a different way."

"Gosh, seems like there's always some twist to things."

"Yes, there is. There's even more to it."

"I figured the terminology trek was not yet over, Dad. Hit me with it."

- **Net Value**

"The initial market value of the leased car will **DEPRECIATE** over that time. At the end of the **TERM**, the car will have a reduced market value, called the **RESIDUAL VALUE**. The difference between the **NET CAPITALIZED COST** and the **RESIDUAL VALUE** is, in effect, how much money you borrowed when you signed the **CAR LEASE**. That difference is called the **NET VALUE**. That's expressed by the following equation."

NET VALUE = NET CAPITALIZED COST – RESIDUAL VALUE

"The resulting **NET VALUE** is what you borrow and pay back over time as <u>part</u> of the **MONTHLY PAYMENT**. That part is referred to as the **MONTHLY DEPRECIATION FEE** and is calculated by this equation."

MONTHLY DEPRECIATION FEE = NET VALUE/TERM

"The **TERM** of the **CAR LEASE** is in months."

"I'll try to store that one in my memory, too, Dad."

"Ok, but leave room for a lot more, Sweetie."

"Really?"

"Sadly, yes. Before covering more, let's illustrate the calculations for this part."

- **Example**

<u>SITUATION 16</u>

"Assume Ichabod plans to lease a **NEW CAR** for a 3-year **TERM**. He negotiates a **SELLING PRICE** of $27500.00 and adds several options worth $2500.00. He plans to pay $4000.00 up-front and will also receive a **CASH REBATE** = $1000.00. Ichabod has no **TRADE-IN** to offer. The **LEASE AGREEMENT** indicates the **MONTHLY DEPRECIATION FEE** = $250.00. Here's how that was calculated."

CAPITALIZED COST = SELLING PRICE + OPTIONS
= $27500.00 + $2500.00 = $30000.00

NET CAPITALIZED COST = (SELLING PRICE + OPTIONS)

– CASH REBATE – CASH DOWN
– CASH DOWN FROM TRADE-IN (or SALE)
= $30000.00 – $1000.00 – $4000.00 – $0.00
= $25000.00

NET VALUE = NET CAPITALIZED COST – RESIDUAL VALUE
= $25000.00 - $16000.00 = $9000.00

MONTHLY DEPRECIATION FEE = NET VALUE/TERM
= $9000.00/36 = $250.00

"Seeing the numbers really helps, Dad. Remembering the terminology will take some time."

"That's Ok. Anyhow, now we move on. Are you ready?"

"Hit me again, Dad."

"In some leases, the **MONTHLY DEPRECIATION FEE** is termed the **BASE MONTHLY PAYMENT**. That's because two other monthly charges are added to it. They are the **MONTHLY FINANCE CHARGE** and **MONTHLY SALES TAX**."

- Finance Charge -

"If the lessor had not leased the car to you, then it could have been sold. The profit would be available and could earn interest if deposited in a bank. By leasing the car to you that lost profit is obtained as part of establishing the **SELLING PRICE**. To offset that loss of interest and recover it, the lessor imposes a **TOTAL FINANCE CHARGE**."

"I guess it's like paying interest when a bank lends you money, except it's for the value of the car not money. Am I right, Dad?"

"That's exactly what they're doing, Smarty."

"If there's no actual money involved, then how is the interest calculated?"

"Unlike a **CAR LOAN,** by which money is borrowed, the repayment and interest for a **CAR LEASE** are not determined by the **AMORTIZATION PROCESS**. If they were, then the **MONTHLY INTEREST** amount would be declining as the months pass. Instead, the interest is calculated as what is commonly called **SIMPLE INTEREST**. The **MONTHLY INTEREST** amount is the same each month. In **CAR LEASE** terminology the **MONTHLY INTEREST** is called the **MONTHLY FINANCE CHARGE.**"

- **Total Financed Amount**

"During the **TERM** of the lease you are being charged interest based on what's termed the **TOTAL FINANCED AMOUNT**. The **TOTAL FINANCED AMOUNT** is the sum of the **NET CAPITALIZED COST** you borrowed in the **CAR LEASE** plus the projected **RESIDUAL VALUE** of the car.

"In math terms it's obtained by this equation."

TOTAL FINANCED AMOUNT = NET CAPITALIZED COST + RESIDUAL VALUE

- ### Monthly Finance Charge

"An **ANNUAL RATE OF INTEREST** is applied to the **TOTAL FINANCED AMOUNT**. The **ANNUAL RATE OF INTEREST** isn't used directly. Instead, to calculate the **MONTHLY FINANCE CHARGE**, you have to multiply the **TOTAL FINANCED AMOUNT** by a **MONEY FACTOR**."

"What in the world is a **MONEY FACTOR**, Dad? It sounds like a TV game show."

"I understand your puzzlement. As I read about it, I wondered if they were trying to confuse me or disguise something. It sure seems like it."

"Before I get to where it comes from, here's the math equation for how the **MONEY FACTOR** is used."

MONTHLY FINANCE CHARGE = MONEY FACTOR x TOTAL FINANCED AMOUNT

- ### Total Finance Charge

"Nicole, you only pay the **MONTHLY FINANCE CHARGE** for the length of time the car is in your possession. The **TOTAL FINANCE CHARGE** paid over the entire **TERM** of the lease is calculated as follows."

TOTAL FINANCE CHARGE = MONTHLY FINANCE CHARGE x TERM

"At the end of the **TERM**, the lessor recovers the car and, thus, its **RESIDUAL VALUE**. Your **MONTHLY PAYMENT** ends. In effect, if you return the car undamaged, then you only paid the **NET CAPITALIZED COST** plus the **TOTAL FINANCE CHARGE** applicable to that period of time."

- ### Money Factor

"Amidst the overwhelming terminology, it's tough to notice a subtlety in this equation. Notice, to get the **TOTAL FINANCED AMOUNT**, the **RESIDUAL VALUE** is <u>added</u> to (as opposed to <u>subtracted</u> from) the **NET CAPITALIZED COST**. In a glancing thought, one might think it should be a subtraction. After all, it was so in calculating the **NET VALUE**."

"Whew! Dad. Some serious head spinning is happening again. The logic of this is beyond me. For Ichabod's car, doesn't the **TOTAL FINANCED AMOUNT** come out $25000.00 + $16000.00 = $41000.00? That's way more than the **SELLING PRICE + OPTIONS** of $30000.00"

"I commiserate with you on that one. The calculation of the **TOTAL FINANCED AMOUNT** and the use of the **MONEY FACTOR** seem odd. I couldn't see the logic either. Being unsettling, I investigated it. At www.carbuyingtips.com/lease2.html, I found out that the **MONEY FACTOR** is just a number they use to simplify the calculation of the **MONTHLY FINANCE CHARGE**. Apparently, by using the **MONEY FACTOR**, they get the result they want for the amount of monthly interest. On this one, your Dad had to use a bit of a leap of faith to accept the method."

"It still seems illogical. I'll do like you and take it on faith."

"Ok!"

"Dad, how do we get the **MONEY FACTOR**? Don't be shocked by my asking, but can you show me in an equation for that?"

"Wow! I feel an earthquake.

"Usually, the **MONEY FACTOR** value is stated in the **CAR LEASE**. The underlying equation is hard to find. I continued to dig into it. Here's how we can calculate it."

"At some websites, it was mentioned that the **MONEY FACTOR** is obtained from this equation."

MONEY FACTOR = APR/2400

"Given that, the magnitude of the **MONEY FACTOR** reflects the **APR** you are being charged. As I explored various websites, I found nothing about the source of that relationship."

- ### Monthly Financed Amount

"On several websites, I also saw mention of the following equations without any explanation of their source."

MONTHLY FINANCED AMOUNT = TOTAL FINANCED AMOUNT/200

MONTHLY FINANCE CHARGE = MONTHLY FINANCED AMOUNT x APR/12

"In the second equation, the **APR** is in %. That's odd. It seemed it should be divided by 100 to get it as **RATIO**. However, it's actually correct. I got curious and figured out where all these equations came from. At first it stumped your dear old Dad. My curiosity and persistence won out. It's hard for me to use anything I don't understand. I kept trying, until if figured it out. Maybe you have that trait as well."

"I don't have your math wizardry, Dad. I do have the same determination when it comes to my journalism tasks. I guess I got it from watching you."

"Maybe so, Peanut. It's more important that you have it than where it may have come from."

"Dad, I have to say I'm shocked anything stumped you, especially here. Compared to other equations, these look much simpler."

"Often, the simple looking things are harder to understand, I could show you what I figured out. I'm guessing you might not want to have me plow into all of that?"

"Well, Dad. My mind is flashing a big red and white inner STOP sign to me. But, I hesitate to disappoint you. You can plow ahead if you want to and I'll try to keep up."

"Well, Nicole. My mind is flashing a big red valentine saying 'To Nicole, Let's STOP. Love, Dad'. I'll take that as mine confirming yours and will pass on the math antics."

With a relaxing inner sigh of relief Nicole reacts. "Now my mind has the same red valentine but with the names reversed. I'll take that the same way you just did. Maybe I'll try to figure it out on my own for optional homework."

"Sounds fine to me."

ASIDE: *Readers interested in Dad's math antics can find them in* ***APPENDIX IV***

"Dad, before you move on, something keeps confusing me."

"What's that, Peanut?"

"There is a **TOTAL FINANCED <u>AMOUNT</u>** and a **TOTAL FINANCE <u>CHARGE</u>**. And there is a **MONTHLY FINANCED <u>AMOUNT</u>** and a **MONTHLY FINANCE <u>CHARGE</u>**. It's hard to keep them straight. I lose track of difference in meanings of '**AMOUNT**' and '**CHARGE**'. It is confusingly similar terminology. I tend to see them as the same words and scratch my head."

"That's Ok, Peanut. The word **<u>AMOUNT</u>** means the amount of money that is subjected to interest. The word **<u>CHARGE</u>** is the amount of interest that has been paid on it. Does that help?"

"It does, Dad. I'll have to keep repeating that in my mind for a while.

"Ok, let's show all of this process with actual numbers."

- **Example**

<u>SITUATION 16 – CONTINUED</u>

"The **CAR LEASE** states that the **RESIDUAL VALUE** will be $16000.00. As he independently confirmed it as a fair estimate of the depreciated value of the car at the time the lease ends, Ichabod accepts it. The **CAR LEASE** indicates the **TOTAL FINANCED AMOUNT** is $41000.00 and **MONTHLY FINANCE CHARGE** is $102.50and the **TOTAL FINANCE CHARGE** is $3690.00 . It states that the **MONEY FACTOR** is 0.0025. Here are the confirming calculations."

TOTAL FINANCED AMOUNT = NET CAPITALIZED COST + RESIDUAL VALUE
= $25000.00 + $16000.00 = $41000.00

MONTHLY FINANCE CHARGE = MONEY FACTOR x TOTAL FINANCED AMOUNT
= 0.0025 x $41000.00 = $102.50

TOTAL FINANCE CHARGE = MONTHLY FINANCE CHARGE x TERM
= $102.50 x 36 = $3690.00

SITUATION 16 – CONTINUED

"How're you following this, Nicole?"

"I see the calculations all right, but the terminology and equations still have to sink in. And I'm still just 'trusting you' on the use of a **MONEY FACTOR**."

"I'm sure they will sink in over time. Now, here's an alternate way of calculating the **MONTHLY FINANCE CHARGE**."

MONTHLY FINANCED AMOUNT = TOTAL FINANCED AMOUNT/200
= $41000.00/200 = $205.00

MONTHLY FINANCE CHARGE = MONTHLY FINANCED AMOUNT x APR/12
= $205.00 x 6.00/12 = $102.50

- ## Handling an Unstated APR

"There's one more twist to add to this trek. It's possible, even likely, that the **CAR LEASE** will omit mention of the numerical value of the **MONEY FACTOR** and the implied **APR**, only indicating the **MONTHLY FINANCE CHARGE**."

"That sure seems murky. Is there a way to get them, Smarty Dad?"

"Well, Smarty Pants, I did deduce one.

"The **LEASE AGREEMENT** will indicate the **TOTAL FINANCED AMOUNT** and **MONTHLY FINANCE CHARGE**. We can use them to calculate the embedded **MONEY FACTOR**.

"We know the following."

MONTHLY FINANCE CHARGE = MONEY FACTOR x TOTAL FINANCED AMOUNT

"Rearranging the equation, we get the following,"

MONEY FACTOR = MONTHLY FINANCE CHARGE/ TOTAL FINANCED AMOUNT

"Well, Dad. Once you have shown it, then it seems pretty obvious."

"That's good, Nicole. Now consider this step."

MONEY FACTOR = APR/2400

"Reversing it, you get this."

APR/2400 = MONEY FACTOR

"Rearranging it, you get the **APR**."

APR = MONEY FACTOR x 2400

"Using the result, you can check with your bank to see if the implied **APR** is consistent with what they give you as an **APR** for a **LOAN AMOUNT** equal to the **CAPITALIZED COST** of and for the car you are looking to lease."

"Awesome! Dad. This part seems pretty clever and straightforward."

"Great, Nicole. Seems you followed it pretty well. Let's look at a quick example."

"Thanks, Dad. I'm ready, so fire away."

SITUATION 16 – CONTINUED

"For Ichabod, the value of the **MONEY FACTOR** implies the following **APR** value."

APR = MONEY FACTOR x 2400 = 0.0025 x 2400 = 6.00%

SITUATION 16 – CONTINUED

"Ichabod confirms by asking his credit union loan officer what rate he would get if he applied for a **CAR LOAN** for a $30000.00 **NEW CAR**. Based on Ichabod's **FICO SCORE**, the loan officer indicates it would be 6.15%. That satisfies Ichabod that the **MONEY FACTOR** value is reasonable.

"If the **MONEY FACTOR** had not been stated in the **CAR LEASE**, then Ichabod could get it as follows."

MONEY FACTOR = MONTHLY FINANCE CHARGE/TOTAL FINANCED AMOUNT = $102.50/$41000.00 = 0.0025

SITUATION 16 – CONTINUED

"That's easy enough, Dad."

ASIDE: *Ichabod's* ***TOTAL FINANCE CHARGE*** *constitutes ($3690.00/$25000.00) x100 = 14.76% of the* ***NET CAPITALIZED COST*** *for the* ***TERM*** *of the lease. That's an average interest percentage of 14.76%/3 years = 4.92% per year. That's consistent with the* ***APR*** *of 6%, which is effectively charged on a declining balance basis.*

"Ok. Let's move on to the next piece."

"What's that, Dad?"

"You can't escape the **SALES TAX** monster."

- Sales Tax -

"Unfortunately, but true, a **SALES TAX** is charged on the lease transaction. Typically, it is charged on a monthly basis using the **SALES TAX RATE** for the jurisdiction where you reside. That's taken as the delivered location of the car. Typically, the lessee resides in the state where he/she leased the car. That's what I'll assume. Otherwise, he or she needs to locally investigate the legalities and complications of trying to lease a car across state lines."

"Dad, that's interesting. I can see the issue if I leased a car where you live and took it to where I now live. That's conceivable, but it's not very likely I would do it.

"I agree with you. There's another possible twist. You might lease a car where you live now but move to another state before the lease ends. You would need to look into the implications of that step.

"In some states, the entire **SALES TAX** will be collected at the outset of the **CAR LEASE**. They do that by applying the **SALES TAX RATE** to the **NET CAPITALIZED COST** plus the **TOTAL FINANCE CHARGE**.

"In some states, the **CASH REBATE** is added back in and taxed. Even worse, some states tax the entire **CAPITALIZED COST = SELLING PRICE + OPTIONS**. In other words, all **CASH DOWN** is ignored. More significantly, it means you pay **SALES TAX** on its full value of the car, as if you had purchased it. The **TOTAL FINANCE CHARGE** might be added to that value, and charged **SALES TAX**. What happens depends on the rules in the state where the sale transpires."

"That's incredible, Dad. It seems some states treat you very unfairly. I hope mine is not one of them."

"I hope so, too. If it is one, then it will be a factor to consider. For our need, we will assume it is not one of those states, either. That way it's consistent with how we calculated the **MONTHLY**

DEPRECIATION FEE and **MONTHLY FINANCE CHARGE.**

"The **MONTHLY SALES TAX** and the **TOTAL SALES TAX** paid over the full **TERM** will be calculated as follows."

MONTHLY TAXABLE AMOUNT = MONTHLY DEPRECIATION FEE
+ MONTHLY FINANCE CHARGE

MONTHLY SALES TAX = (SALES TAX RATE/100) x MONTHLY TAXABLE AMOUNT

TOTAL SALES TAX = MONTHLY SALES TAX x TERM

"Whew, Dad. That's another mind boggler."

"Let me try to 'unboggle' your mind. I'm not sure that's an actual word, but you know what I mean."

"Unboggle away!"

"Actually, it's pretty straightforward. The **MONTHLY DEPRECIATION FEE** and **MONTHLY FINANCE CHARGE** are payments you are making associated with the leased car. You're paying those costs for its ongoing use, but it's still for a car. You are charged **MONTHLY SALES TAX** on the two costs you are paying out monthly during the time the leased car is in your possession."

"You're right, Dad. It's obvious now."

"That's good."

SITUATION 16 – CONTINUED

"Now, Nicole, can you give it a try with Ichabod's numbers? Assuming the **SALES TAX RATE** in Ichabod's location is 8.00% what is the **MONTHLY SALES TAX**?"

"Let me write it out. Ok, using your equations I get the following."

MONTHLY TAXABLE AMOUNT = (MONTHLY DEPRECIATION FEE
+ MONTHLY FINANCE CHARGE)
= ($250.00 + $102.50) = $352.50

MONTHLY SALES TAX = (SALES TAX RATE/100) x MONTHLY TAXABLE AMOUNT
= 0.08 x $352.50 = $28.20

TOTAL SALES TAX = MONTHLY SALES TAX x TERM
= $28.20 x 36 = $1015.20

SITUATION 16 – CONTINUED

"That's right, Nicole. If Ichabod had to pay **SALES TAX** up-front on the full value of the car, then he would pay the following."

TOTAL SALES TAX = SALES TAX RATE x CAPITALIZED COST
= SALES TAX RATE x (SELLING PRICE + OPTIONS)
= 0.08 x ($27500.00 + $2500.00) = $2400.00

SITUATION 16 – CONTINUED

"Gosh, Dad. That's more than twice as much. I sure will look into the rules for my state."

"That's why I showed it to you, Peanut. And if the **TOTAL FINANCE CHARGE** is included, that's another 0.08 x $3690.00 = $295.20."

"Let's put it all together."

- Totaling the Monthly Payment -

"As I indicated at the outset, the **MONTHLY PAYMENT** is the sum of the three parts I just described. Here it is as an equation."

MONTHLY PAYMENT = MONTHLY DEPRECIATION FEE + MONTHLY FINANCE CHARGE + MONTHLY SALES TAX

"Does that make sense, Sweetie?"

"Yes it does, once you put it all together, Dad."

"Ok. When the **CAR LEASE** ends, you will have paid the **MONTHLY PAYMENT** for its entire **TERM**. Here's the math equation for the **TOTAL PAYMENTS**."

TOTAL PAYMENTS = MONTHLY PAYMENT x TERM

"That's obvious to me, Dad."

SITUATION 16 – CONTINUED

"Ok, Nicole, what are Ichabod's **MONTHLY PAYMENT** and **TOTAL PAYMENTS**?"

"That's the easiest question you've ever asked me. Here they are."

MONTHLY PAYMENT = MONTHLY DEPRECIATION FEE + MONTHLY FINANCE CHARGE + MONTHLY SALES TAX
= $250.00 + $102.50 + $28.20 = $380.70

TOTAL PAYMENTS = MONTHLY PAYMENT x TERM
= $380.70 x 36 = $13705.20

ASIDE: *For comparison, assume the $41000.00 is a **CAR LOAN** amortized at 6.00% for 36 months. Omitting the calculations, Ichabod's **CUMULATIVE INTEREST** = $3902.78. The result is a similar amount, but a bit higher than the **TOTAL FINANCE CHARGE** of $3690.00 for the **CAR LEASE**. His **MONTHLY PAYMENT** = $1247.30; 3.27 times as much as the **MONTHLY PAYMENT** for leasing. But he owns the car outright. If Ichabod finances the purchase for a 5-year (60-month) **TERM**, then his **MONTHLY PAYMENT** is $792.64. That's still much higher than (about double) the amount for leasing. And his **CUMULATIVE INTEREST** increases to $6558.69; about 78% more than for leasing. The interested reader can confirm the results using the **CAR LOAN – BASE LOAN TABLE** and **SCALING** the values.*

Exercise 19: *Repeat **SITUATION 16** for a **SELLING PRICE** of $19300.00, $0.00 in **OPTIONS**, a **CASH REBATE** of $0.00, and **CASH DOWN** of $1200.00. The lessor and he agree to a **RESIDUAL VALUE** of $12500.00. The **LEASE AGREEMENT** indicates a **MONEY FACTOR** of 0.0022, **TERM** of 36 months, and **SALES TAX RATE** of 6.00%.*

***Your partial answer should be**: **NET CAPITALIZED COST** =$18100.00, **MONTHLY DEPRECIATION FEE** =$155.56, **MONTHLY FINANCED AMOUNT**=$153.00, **MONTHLY PAYMENT** =$236.25, **TOTAL PAYMENTS** =$8505.00 and **TOTAL FINANCE CHARGE** =$2423.52.*

***Exercise 20**: Repeat **SITUATION 16** for a **SELLING PRICE** of $29400.00, $550.00 in **OPTIONS**, a **CASH REBATE** of $1600.00, and **CASH DOWN** of $2400.00. The lessor and he agree to a **RESIDUAL VALUE** of $17500.00. The **LEASE AGREEMENT** indicates a **MONEY FACTOR** of 0.0028, **TERM** of 36 months, and **SALES TAX RATE** of 7.20%.*

***Your partial answer should be**: **NET VALUE** =$8450.00, **MONTHLY DEPRECIATION FEE** = $234.72, **TOTAL FINANCED AMOUNT** =$43450.00, **MONTHLY SALES TAX** =$25.60, **TOTAL PAYMENTS** = $13753.40 and **TOTAL FINANCE CHARGE** =4379.56.*

"All this is pretty intimidating, Dad. It's overwhelming to remember the flow of the calculations, especially atop all the terminology. I realize how important it is to work at fully understanding the cost involved in car leasing. I'm just going to have to keep reviewing it until my brain has soaked it all in. Until then, I guess I can scratch down a cheat sheet to follow. Maybe you have one, though?"

"Well, Peanut, you assumed correctly. I actually have to use a cheat sheet myself. I'll email mine to you. Using it, you can actually fill in needed information and do the calculations in the same order as done in

SITUATION 16. All you need is a calculator. I'll also send one that has all the numbers and results from SITUATION 16 filled in."

"Dad, you never stop amazing me. Just in time, again. It will really help. And maybe I'll try another spreadsheet, sometime down the road."

"That's exactly my intent, Nicole."

ASIDE: *Dad's cheat sheet is in **APPENDIX V**.*

Significance of the Residual Value

"Nicole, the **RESIDUAL VALUE** is a very important piece in the terms of a **CAR LEASE**. The amount set in the contract has two opposing considerations. The higher the amount, the lower will be your **MONTHLY PAYMENT**. But, the higher will be your cost to purchase the car at the end of the lease. Conversely, the lower the amount, the higher will be your **MONTHLY PAYMENT**. But, the lower will be your cost to purchase the leased car. You need to take your future plans into consideration and try to negotiate the **RESIDUAL VALUE** accordingly."

"I see the dueling aspect in play. I'm glad you pointed it out, Dad."

ASIDE: *Usually the lease provisions also allow you to sell the leased car privately at the end of the lease. You have to first purchase it from the dealership and pay the lessor the stated **RESIDUAL VALUE** plus **SALES TAX.** When you resell the car yourself at a **SELLING PRICE** above the **RESIDUAL AMOUNT**, then you pocket the difference. A lower **RESIDUAL VALUE** makes that more feasible. You have to arrange that **SALES TAX** is collected on the full amount of your **SELLING PRICE**, and paid to the local and state taxing agencies. Typically, you can work out a dual process with the dealership.*

Usage Charges

"In renting a car, you are 'paying for usage'. That involves several costs. A daily, weekend, weekly or other rate is charged for use of the car (hourly charges occur if the time period extends hours into a partial day). Atop that are other fees, which depend on the location. For example, for pick-up/return at Denver International Airport, a daily facility use fee, concession recoup fee, road safety program fee and sales tax are incurred. These can add 30%-40% to the base cost. Leasing usage is charged much differently."

"I saw a lot about that in my search of websites Dad, so I'm ready and waiting."

- Fuel Charge -

"With a rental car, if you refuel on your own then there is no fuel charge. Otherwise, you pay the vendor rate for any fuel top off necessary upon return. Over the duration of a **CAR LEASE** you simply pay for fuel on the go. Returning it with a filled tank at the end is a minor cost."

"That's easy and makes sense, Dad."

"It is Nicole. The next piece has more terminology to spin around."

- Excess Mileage Charge -

"For various reasons, **CAR LEASES** limit the lessee to a certain number of total miles per year. From websites I looked at, commonly it is 12,000 to 15,000 miles per year. Miles beyond that limit constitute **EXCESS MILEAGE**. You incur an **EXCESS MILEAGE CHARGE** for those miles. It's based on an **EXCESS MILEAGE RATE**. Commonly, it's about $0.10 to $0.20 per excess mile."

"That doesn't sound like a lot. My company reimburses a lot more when I use my car for job related travel."

"At face value, it isn't. There's a guessing game involved. In the **LEASE AGREEMENT** you will have to agree to a **MILEAGE LIMIT**."

"Dad, what's a **MILEAGE LIMIT** and what's the guessing involved?"

"It's the maximum number of miles per year for which there is no **EXCESS MILEAGE** charge. You and the lessor agree to the number of miles. Beyond that number of miles, you pay the **EXCESS MILEAGE CHARGE**.

"For example, assume Ichabod's **MILEAGE LIMIT** is 10000 miles. At the end of the **CAR LEASE**, he has 34000 total miles used. His **EXCESS MILEAGE** is 4000 miles. For an **EXCESS MILEAGE RATE** of $0.20 per mile, the **EXCESS MILEAGE CHARGE** = $0.20 x 4000 = $800.00.

"You also have to be wary of accepting a low **MILEAGE LIMIT** and/or high **EXCESS MILEAGE RATE** in your **CAR LEASE**. Before agreeing to them, carefully and rationally project the likely mileage you expect to incur plus some added leeway. Some websites also warned against accepting a lessor's offer for you to pay for projected extra miles up front, if it is not refundable. The risk involved is that you might not drive that many excess miles.

"Make the potential cost of likely **EXCESS MILEAGE** a factor in your leasing decision. And once you lease the car, you need to be very attentive to your mileage usage. That's because you pay the **EXCESS MILEAGE CHARGE** at the end of the **CAR LEASE**. If you haphazardly go about driving, you could be in for a big unpleasant surprise at that time."

"I can see the concern and need to accurately estimate the potential miles I would use the car. Then I need to be very attentive to the miles as I am accumulating them."

- Maintenance -

"What about the cost of maintaining the car? Paying for things such as oil changes and the like, and repairs?"

"Great questions, Peanut!

"For usual maintenance costs, your lease should specify who is responsible for those. In some cases, the lessor will require maintenance be done on a schedule, at their location, and they will pay for it. If not, then you will be responsible for that maintenance and its cost. In that circumstance, your lessor may try to sell you services in a maintenance plan. Some websites warn about possible inflated prices being charged."

***ASIDE**: If maintenance is not the lessor responsibility, then for a **USED CAR** you are especially vulnerable to the possible cost of major repairs during any part of the lease **TERM** that the car is not on the **MANUFACTURER'S WARRANTY**. Unless you want to risk paying those costs, don't lease a **USED CAR**.*

"Unless they are accident-related, with a 3-year lease for a **NEW CAR,** the **MANUFACTURER'S WARRANTY** will cover the major unexpected repairs. For damage caused in an accident the **STANDARD CAR INSURANCE**, which you must buy, covers them. Just as for a purchased car you must decide what coverage amounts to buy."

Additional Fees

"Dad, is there anything else to know, besides calculating all these things you showed?"

"It would be nice if that was all that was involved. The **MONTHLY PAYMENT** and the other monetary considerations leading to it are not the entirety of the **CAR LEASE** costs. There are some speed bumps ahead, before you drive that leased car off the lot. Unfortunately, some additional costs can be incurred as fees applied to the transaction. If you unaware they exist, you might be flabbergasted when you encounter them in the lease agreement.

"There are a lot of fees to cover. It's a pretty big jump you made just to this point. I think it would be best to meet again later today or tomorrow to cover that. What do you prefer, Nicole?"

"Surprise! Surprise! You're so thorough all the time. That's what I love about you, Dad. I have errands to do today. And, I need to let what we just covered sink in. I also want to study your cheat sheet. Let's do it later tomorrow afternoon."

"Ok, agreed. I'll send you my cheat sheet right now. See you about 3 PM tomorrow?"

"More or less, Dad. I'll Skype you around that time."

LESSON 10 Getting over the Fees Bumps in My New Car Lease

"Hi Dad! I've been reviewing what you discussed yesterday. Your cheat sheet really helped. I'm pretty clear now on how the **MONTHLY PAYMENT** is determined. It will still take some therapy to get used to the terminology. **NET CAPITALIZED COST**, **NET VALUE** and the like are still spinning like a tornado around my head. Otherwise, I'm ready to take on those speed bumps you mentioned. At least they sound like something you have to go over slowly."

"Good afternoon, Peanut! That's really great. I'm ready, too. As to that whirlwind of terminology, we'll be using it again today. It eventually settles in. Until then, we each have the cheat sheet to rely on. Unfortunately, we'll be adding to the terminology today."

"I figured so. I'm ready to continue through the word maze."

"Ok, let's get started."

Total Fees

"Those speed bumps are actually fee bumps. Some you have to cross at the front end of the leasing deal, when you finalize the **LEASE AGREEMENT**. Others you have to cross at the back end, when the lease **TERM** ends. They can amount to a lot of money.

"At the start of the lease **TERM**, an **ACQUISITION FEE** of several hundred dollars might be charged upfront for processing the lease. Sometimes it is added to your **TOTAL FINANCED AMOUNT**, increasing your **MONTHLY FINANCED AMOUNT** and **MONTHLY PAYMENT**. Sometimes a nebulous **BANK FEE** and a **DEALER SERVICE FEE** are included as well. Each is a modest cost.

"At the end of the lease **TERM,** a **DISPOSITION FEE** might be charged for preparing it for resale.

"If you want to terminate a lease before the end of its **TERM**, then an **EARLY TERMINATION FEE** might be charged. It can be several thousand dollars.

"Combining all of them, these are the **TOTAL FEES**."

TOTAL FEES = ACQUISITION FEE + BANK FEE + DEALER SERVICE FEE
+ DISPOSITION FEE + EARLY TERMINATION FEE
+ PURCHASE OPTION FEE

Sarcastically, Nicole remarks, "Wonderful."

"It does kind of sound like petty larceny, Nicole. You can and should try to negotiate some of them out of the **CAR LEASE**."

"It doesn't end there, though. Remember, when you return the leased car, you might also have to pay for **EXCESS MILEAGE** and/or **EXCESS WEAR AND TEAR**.

Excess Mileage Charge

"Here are the math equations for calculating the **EXCESS MILEAGE CHARGE**."

EXCESS MILEAGE = ACTUAL MILEAGE – MILEAGE LIMIT x TERM/12

EXCESS MILEAGE CHARGE = EXCESS MILEAGE RATE x EXCESS MILEAGE

Total Cost to Lease

"Including the **TOTAL FEES** involved, this is the equation for calculating the **TOTAL COST TO LEASE**."

TOTAL COST TO LEASE = CASH DOWN + TOTAL COST OF GAP INSURANCE
+ TOTAL PAYMENTS + TOTAL FEES
+ EXCESS MILEAGE CHARGE
+ EXCESS WEAR AND TEAR CHARGE

Where

TOTAL PAYMENTS = MONTHLY PAYMENT x TERM

"I also added a term for **TOTAL COST OF GAP INSURANCE**. It can be purchased for a leased car. I'll be covering that, too."

Sarcastically, Nicole sighs, "I can hardly wait for that topic."

"Usually, an **ANNUAL GAP INSURANCE COST** is used, but it is charged monthly at a **MONTHLY GAP INSURANCE COST**. The total cost over the **TERM** (in months) of the lease is calculated by this equation."

TOTAL COST OF GAP INSURANCE = MONTHLY GAP INSURANCE COST x TERM

Total Cost to Lease/Purchase

"At the end of the lease **TERM**, you have the option to purchase the car for the **RESIDUAL VALUE**. If you do so, then a **PURCHASE OPTION FEE** might also be charged to you. Some websites say you should try to eliminate it. You'll have to pay **ADDITIONAL SALES TAX** on the **RESIDUAL VALUE** for transacting the sale.

"Adding those costs into the picture, the **TOTAL COST TO LEASE/PURCHASE** is given by this equation."

TOTAL COST TO LEASE/PURCHASE = TOTAL COST TO LEASE + PURCHASE OPTION FEE + RESIDUAL VALUE + ADDITIONAL SALES TAX

"They sure do pile on a lot of things, Dad. It sounds like leasing a car is going to be costly."

"It would seem so. However, leasing a car can be very affordable. The main factor is whether you just do a **CAR LEASE** or do a **LEASE/PURCHASE**.

"Now, let's look at example of a **CAR LEASE** with all these added complexities included.

Example

<u>SITUATION 17 – OPTION L1</u>

"Sam of SITUATION 13 – **OPTION P1** (of LESSON 7) considers the alternative of leasing the same car for 36 months. Let's make all the given conditions identical.

"The **SELLING PRICE + OPTIONS** amount is $24600.00. Sam neither sells nor trades-in his **PRESENT CAR**. The dealership will credit a **CASH REBATE** of $1300.00. They ask for **CASH DOWN** of $2200.00. Sam negotiates it downward to $1600.00. The stated **RESIDUAL VALUE** is $13000.00. Because he knows he will not purchase the car at the end of the lease, Sam negotiates that upward to $14000.00. He will have to pay for required maintenance and any repairs.

"The stated **EXCESS MILEAGE RATE** is $0.15 per mile. The annual **MILEAGE LIMIT** is 15000 miles. Sam estimates he will drive the car for 17000 miles, per year.

"The stated **MONEY FACTOR** is 0.0020. That constitutes an **APR** = 2400 x 0.0020 = 4.80%, Sam negotiates it downward to 0.001667 (**APR** = 4.00%).

"Sam's insurance agent quotes him **ANNUAL GAP INSURANCE COST** of $60.00 which is a **MONTHLY GAP INSURANCE COST** of $5.00.

"Are you following this so far, Nicole?"

"It's hard to keep in mind all the numbers, but I do follow the given information. It'll be good to see how this all comes into play with all the speed bumps."

"Ok. Now let's add on some of those fee bumps.

"The dealer steadfastly requires an **ACQUISITION FEE** of $350.00. Sam steadfastly fends off a **BANK FEE** of $100.00 and a **DISPOSITION FEE** of $250.00, but must pay a **DEALER SERVICE**

FEE of $250.00.

"Should Sam purchase the car later, he will pay a **PURCHASE OPTION FEE** of $350.00. The **EARLY TERMINATION FEE** is $2200.00. That's the last of the fees."

Unsarcastically, Nicole says, "Finally."

"I agree. Along the way, you'll be seeing all the previous leasing terminology as a refresher."

"I did sort of suggest I needed that, anyway."

"All right. Let's do the refresher part first. It's coming all at once, so don't blink."

CAPITALIZED COST = SELLING PRICE + OPTIONS
= $23200.00 + $1400.00= $24600.00

NET CAPITALIZED COST = (SELLING PRICE + OPTIONS) – CASH REBATE
– CASH DOWN – CASH DOWN FROM TRADE-IN
(or SALE)
= ($24600.00) – $1300.00 – $1600.00 = $21700.00

NET VALUE = NET CAPITALIZED COST – RESIDUAL VALUE
= $21700.00 – $14000.00 = $7700.00

MONTHLY DEPRECIATION FEE = NET VALUE/TERM = $7700.00/36 = $213.89

TOTAL FINANCED AMOUNT = NET CAPITALIZED COST + RESIDUAL VALUE
= $21700.00 + $14000.00 = $35700.00

MONTHLY FINANCE CHARGE = MONEY FACTOR x TOTAL FINANCED AMOUNT
= 0.001667 x $35700.00 = $59.51

Alternatively,

MONTHLY FINANCED AMOUNT = TOTAL FINANCED AMOUNT/200
= $35700.00/200 = $178.50

MONTHLY FINANCE CHARGE = MONTHLY FINANCED AMOUNT x APR/12
= $178.50 x 4.00/12 = $59.50

MONTHLY TAXABLE AMOUNT = MONTHLY DEPRECIATION FEE
+ MONTHLY FINANCE CHARGE)

MONTHLY SALES TAX = SALES TAX RATE x MONTHLY TAXABLE AMOUNT
= 0.07 x ($213.89 + $59.51) = $19.14

MONTHLY PAYMENT = MONTHLY DEPRECIATION FEE + MONTHLY FINANCE CHARGE + MONTHLY SALES TAX
= $213.89 + $59.51 + $19.14 = $292.54

TOTAL PAYMENTS = MONTHLY PAYMENT x TERM = $292.54 x 36 = $10531.44

TOTAL FINANCE CHARGE = MONTHLY FINANCE CHARGE x TERM
= $59.51 x 36 = $2142.36

TOTAL COST OF GAP INSURANCE = MONTHLY GAP INSURANCE COST x TERM
= $5.00 x 36= $180.00

EXCESS MILEAGE = (ACTUAL MILEAGE – MILEAGE LIMIT) x TERM/12
= (17000 – 15000) x 36/12 = 2000 x 3 = 6000 miles

EXCESS MILEAGE CHARGE = EXCESS MILEAGE RATE x EXCESS MILEA
= $0.15 x 6000 = $900.00

SITUATION 17 – OPTION L1 – CONTINUED

"You can blink now if you want to, Sweetie. How's that all look to you?"

After studying Dad's monitor for a few minutes, Nicole flips through her cheat sheet several times. Then she chimes in, "It's still not crystal clear to me, but I think I get the gist of it. The odd way they do the **TOTAL FINANCE CHARGE** still puzzles me. Given that, I followed the equations, numbers and calculations."

"That's good. It's why I put in the alternative calculation of the **MONTHLY FINANCE CHARGE**. It's also to check my answer.

"With the refresher stuff in hand, let's continue. Sam's **TOTAL FEES** include the following."

ACQUISITION FEE = $350.00
BANK FEE = $0.00
DEALER SERVICE FEE = $250.00
DISPOSITION FEE = $0.00
EARLY TERMINATION FEE = $0.00
TOTAL FEES = $600.00

SITUATION 17 – OPTION L1 – CONTINUED

"The seemingly endless fees are all there in plain sight, Dad. Just like you said, they do add up to a few bucks. And that's with most of them taken as $0.00."

"Yes, they do. If you aren't alert, the others can more than double the **TOTAL FEES**.

"Luckily, Sam returns the car in good condition without **EXCESS WEAR AND TEAR**.

"Considering all the costs we get the following."

TOTAL COST TO LEASE = CASH DOWN + TOTAL GAP INSURANCE
+ TOTAL PAYMENTS + TOTAL FEES
+ EXCESS MILEAGE COST CHARGE
+ EXCESS WEAR AND TEAR CHARGE
= $1600.00 + $180.00 + $10531.00 (rounded)
+ $600.00 + $900.00 + $0.00 = $13811.00

SITUATION 17 – OPTION L1 – CONTINUED

"Got that Ok, Sweetie?"

"Yes, I do Dad. I see it's a lot easier to calculate it than to describe it."

"That's great. Let's compare the **TOTAL COST TO LEASE** with the **TOTAL COST TO PURCHASE** in SITUATION 13

"Dad? There were a whole bunch of other **OPTIONS** in SITUATION 13. I hope you don't think I can remember all those results."

"Well, Smarter Pants, it would not surprise me if you did. For now, I'm only interested in **OPTION P1**."

"Ok, Dad. That softens the recall needed."

"Nicole, if you look back at SITUATION 13 - **OPTION P1**, you'll see that Sam's resulting **TOTAL COST TO PURCHASE** was $27500.00. How's that compare to the leasing alternative."

"I'm amazed! The **TOTAL COST TO LEASE** is only $13811.00. That's $13869.00 less than the **TOTAL COST TO PURCHASE**. That's a huge difference. Seriously, the **TOTAL COST TO PURCHASE** is about double the **TOTAL COST TO LEASE**. It seems his choice a no-brainer, Dad. It would be crazy for Sam not to lease the car."

"At face value, it's hard to argue with that observation, Peanut. However, taken alone, the preceding is a misleading comparison."

"Why's that?"

"At the end of the lease, Sam has only his **PRESENT CAR**. At the end of the purchase, Sam has his **PRESENT CAR** plus a **NEW CAR**. It's not a comparable result. What should we do to balance that out, Nicole?"

"I suppose we ought to look at what happens if Sam buys the leased car at the end of the **CAR LEASE**. Then we can compare the **TOTAL COST TO LEAST/PURCHASE** to the **TOTAL COST TO LEASE**?"

"That's interesting to know. But it's obvious the former will cost a lot more than the latter. Think a bit more. You almost have it, Smarty Pants. What's more important than the obvious?"

Pausing just a tad, Nicole observes, "You're right, that is obvious. It came to me as you spoke. We need to compare is **TOTAL COST TO LEASE/PURCHASE** to the **TOTAL COST TO PURCHASE**. That way we can see which of them is a more affordable path to owning a **NEW CAR**."

"Precisely! Let's do that.

"To compare correctly, assume that Sam purchases the leased car at the end of the lease for its **RESIDUAL VALUE**. Let's add in the resulting additional costs."

TOTAL COST TO LEASE = $13811.00
RESIDUAL VALUE = $14000.00
SALES TAX = 0.07 x $14000.00 = $980.00
PURCHASE OPTION FEE = $350.00
TOTAL COST TO LEASE/PURCHASE = $29141.00

SITUATION 17 – OPTION L1 – CONTINUED

"What do you see now, Peanut?"

"Hmm. Things really changed. The **TOTAL COST TO LEASE/PURCHASE** is higher than the **TOTAL COST TO PURCHASE** of $27500.00."

"Yes, it's actually $1641.00 higher. What do you deduce from that?"

"If I want to own a **NEW CAR**, then it makes more sense to buy it outright."

"Exactly! Of course it's a matter of the particular numbers we assumed. If we change some values it could go the other way. Commonly, I suspect that purchasing outright will be favorable over doing a lease/purchase. However, I have one more angle to look at."

"No surprise there, Dad. You always do. In fact, you always seem to think out everything."

"I suppose so. It's the only way I feel comfortable. Of course, if we are ball parking things, like we did back early in the game for your student loans, then I try to expedite by using approximate values and methods.

"Now, let's look at that 'one more angle'.

"An even fairer comparison is to assume that, in SITUATION 13 – **OPTION P1**, Sam finances his **CAR LOAN** for 36 months instead of 60 months. That would be consistent with the **TERM** of the **CAR LEASE**.

"In that case, for the **ANNUAL RATE OF INTEREST** of 4.00%, we get these results."

BASE LOAN MONTHLY PAYMENT = $28.64 + 0.50 x ($30.42 - $28.64) = $29.53

BASE LOAN CUMULATIVE INTEREST = $31.13 + 0.50 x ($95.19 - $31.13) = $63.16

From SITUATION 13 – OPTION P1: LOAN AMOUNT = 23422.00

SCALE FACTOR = 23.422

MONTHLY PAYMENT = 23.422 x $29.53 = $691.65

CUMULATIVE INTEREST = 23.422 x $63.16 = $1479.33

For the 36-month TERM:

TOTAL COST OF COST = 36 x $691.65 = $24899.00 (rounded)
= $1600.00 + $24899.00= $26499.00

SITUATION 17 – OPTION L1 – CONTINUED

"How's that result look, Sweetie?"

"I knew that question was coming, Dad. This time, I'm a step ahead. The **TOTAL COST TO PURCHASE** dropped from $27500.00 to $26499.00; by $1001.00. And the **TOTAL COST TO LEASE/PURCHASE** of $29141.00 is $2642.00 higher."

"Ok, Smarty Quick. Why does that happen?"

"I'm thinking the reduction in the **TOTAL COST TO PURCHASE** must be due to the lower **CUMULATIVE INTEREST** Sam pays for the shorter **TERM** of his car loan?"

"Terrific! I calculated it and the drop in **CUMULATIVE INTEREST** is indeed $1001.00. But there is a price to pay, too."

"What's that Dad?"

"Sam's **MONTHLY PAYMENT** increases from $431.67 to $691.65. To save the $1001.00 he would have to afford that amount. And if you look back, the **MONTHLY PAYMENT** for leasing is only $292.54. But that comes with the much higher **TOTAL COST TO LEASE/PURCHASE**. That's the subtle persuasion of ads for **CAR LEASES**.

"That '**low monthly payment of $292.54**' with the cost in the biggest, boldest print draws you in. They hope to have you lease the car than persuade you to purchase it once the lease ends. Further, the advertised amount might exclude the **SALES TAX** part of the **MONTHLY PAYMENT** for the lease. All the underlying costs must be fully calculated to have the full information. Then you can make a well informed choice. That's why I'm teaching you how to do it."

"As always, I really appreciate you spending time and energy on it, Dad. It has become a lot of fun to Skype with you. I learn so much faster than figuring things out entirely by myself; especially when it's the first time that I am venturing into new debt territory."

"I know you do and it makes me feel wonderful that you ask for some guidance before leaping into that new place. Let me close this example now.

"If Sam purchases the leased car, then it's likely he would finance all or part of the **RESIDUAL VALUE** plus **SALES TAX** cost of $14980.00. Without showing you the **AMORTIZATION SCHEDULE**, if he financed it for a 24-month **TERM** at the **ANNUAL RATE OF INTEREST** of 4.00%, then his **MONTHLY PAYMENT** = $650.51. He would incur **CUMULATIVE INTEREST** = $632.13. Adding that cost to it, the **TOTAL COST TO LEASE/PURCHASE** increases to $29773.13 over a 60-month period of time.

"For a 60-month **TERM** for the **CAR LOAN**, the **MONTHLY PAYMENT** drops to $275.88 but the **CUMULATIVE INTEREST** increases to $1527.77. That increases the **TOTAL COST TO LEASE/PURCHASE** to $30668.77."

"Dad, the **LEASE/PURCHASE** path is looking grimmer and grimmer. To me, all that does is delay owning the car and significantly increase the financial pain."

"Nicole, to make the comparison equal, for the **CAR LEASE** it was assumed that Sam pays all normal maintenance and repair costs. If he did not have to pay them then at face value, the **TOTAL COST TO LEASE/PURCHASE** would decrease by those costs. However, it's highly likely the dealership would either sell Sam a maintenance plan or raise the **SELLING PRICE** and/or **CASH DOWN** and **FEES** to offset incurring that cost."

"You never fail to carry things to the last detail. And I keep seeing more and more why I must do that myself. And I keep getting better at it. You're fantastic, Dad. Thank you."

"My pleasure! As always."

***Exercise 21:** Repeat SITUATION 17 – **OPTION L1** with the following changes. **CASH DOWN** = $0.00, **RESIDUAL VALUE** = $16000.00, **SALES TAX RATE** = 9.00%, **ANNUAL MILAGE LIMIT** =*

12000 miles, ***EXCESS MILEAGE RATE*** *= $0.10,* ***ANNUAL MILES USED*** *= 8000 miles,* ***GAP INSURANCE RATE*** *= $4.00,* ***MONEY FACTOR*** *= 0.003333 (****APR*** *= 8.00%),* ***ACQUISITION FEE*** *= $500.00, all other* ***FEES*** *= $0.00.*

Your partial results should be:

NET CAPITALIZED COST *= $23300,* ***MONTHLY FINANCED AMOUNT*** *= $196.50,* ***TOTAL PAYMENTS*** *= $13097.16,* ***TOTAL COST TO LEASE*** *= $13741.00,* ***TOTAL COST TO LEASE/PURCHASE*** *= $31181.00.*

"Nicole, as SITUATION 17 demonstrates, the complete calculations for **LEASE/PURCHASE** of a car are very lengthy and involved. Fortunately, I've extended the cheat sheet to include all these additional considerations. I'm E-mailing the additional steps to you right now. I included the numbers and results for SITUATION 17 – **OPTION L1**. Enjoy it!

"Thanks, Dad. As you went through the example, I was hoping you had one."

ASIDE: *The extended part of the cheat sheet is provided in* ***APPENDIX V****.*

"Sweetie, in our SITUATIONS, Sam leased the car outright. If Sam has a **PRESENT CAR** and either trades it in or sells it privately, it gets even more complicated. Last week, in SITUATION 13, we covered several **OPTIONS** involving those possibilities, when a **NEW CAR** is purchased. I want show you how to consider those other **OPTIONS** for a leased car.

"With so much done today, you need time for what I just covered settle in. In the meantime, you can review what we covered in SITUATION 13. You can look over the extended cheat sheet, too. It also applies to what we'll cover next time. Why don't we Skype again next Saturday?"

"That's would be great, Dad! Remember, I do have my very, very used **VW NEW BEETLE** to consider trading in or selling. My generation still calls them 'bugs'. Whatever they are called, I'll be armed and ready to go. Does 10:00 AM work for you?"

"That will be just fine, Sweetie. I'll see you then!"'

"Ok, I'll make the call and be ready to go."

LESSON 11 Car Leasing – What Am I to Do with My Present Car?

Nicole has spent the week busily reviewing SITUATION 13. Happy to have it, she has delved into Dad's expanded cheat sheet for **CAR LEASES**. She's anxious to learn about trading or selling her aged VW as part of leasing a **NEW CAR**. At 10:00 AM, promptly, she Skypes her Dad."

"Hi Dad! As promised, I'm ready to go. How about you?"

"I'm at the starting line, too. I can see the excitement in your face. I hope it lasts through this more involved topic."

"I'll try my best to keep smiling, Dad."

"In the SITUATION 17, Sam leases a car outright. He holds on to his **PRESENT CAR**. However, he could either trade it in or sell it and use the money to lower his **CAR LEASE** costs."

Net Capitalized Cost

"With a **PRESENT CAR** involved, this general equation is applicable."

NET CAPITALIZED COST = (SELLING PRICE + OPTIONS) – CASH REBATE
– CASH DOWN – CASH DOWN FROM
TRADE-IN (or SALE)

"As for purchasing a car, the last term applies for whichever one you do; **TRADE-IN** or **SALE**."

"I follow you on that, Dad. I do remember you mentioning that before."

"Exactly, Nicole. In the case of leasing you'll see the effects are similar. Let me continue.

Total Cost to Lease

"There's also a change to the **TOTAL COST TO LEASE**. Here's the modified equation."

TOTAL COST TO LEASE = CASH DOWN + TOTAL GAP INSURANCE
+ TOTAL PAYMENTS + TOTAL FEES
+ EXCESS MILEAGE CHARGE
+ EXCESS WEAR AND TEAR CHARGE
+ BOOK VALUE

"The term **BOOK VALUE** is what's new."

"Yes, I see that. You also added that when we talked about purchasing a **NEW CAR**. I reviewed it, but I was a bit fuzzy on exactly why you did."

"That's Ok, Sweetie. To recap it, if you have a **PRESENT CAR** and keep it, then you have retained it as a separate asset with some monetary value. For our purposes, that's the **BOOK VALUE**. If you either trade it in or sell it privately, then you have spent the entire value of the car. You no longer have the car, no matter what amount you trade it in or sell it for. You have used the entire asset, the entire **BOOK VALUE**. That's why I added the **BOOK VALUE** to the **TOTAL COST TO PURCHASE** The same effect occurs when you lease a **NEW CAR**. The **TOTAL COST TO LEASE** increases by the full **BOOK VALUE**."

.

"That's coming back to me, Dad."

"In SITUATION 13, we saw what happens for different trade-in or private sale **OPTIONS** relative to the **TOTAL COST TO PURCHASE** for purchasing a **NEW CAR**. Let's revisit those scenarios in the context of Sam leasing instead of purchasing. After each of them, I'll give you some homework exercises for later."

"It's Ok, Dad. I wouldn't expect less from you."

Trading in a Present Car

SITUATION 17 – OPTION L2

"Let's do the counterpart to SITUATION 13 – **OPTION P2**, in which Sam traded-in his **PRESENT CAR** for $4500.00; $2000.00 less than its full **BOOK VALUE**. That led to his highest **TOTAL COST TO PURCHASE**, $29024.00.

"For leasing, the first step is to calculate the **NET CAPITALIZED COST**. Which last term do we use in the equation, Nicole?"

"Since he traded in, we use the term **CASH DOWN FROM TRADE-IN**."

"That's right."

NET CAPITALIZED COST = (SELLING PRICE + OPTIONS) – CASH REBATE
– CASH DOWN – CASH DOWN FROM TRADE-IN
= \$24600.00 – \$1300.00 – \$1600.00 – \$4500.00
= \$17200.00

SITUATION 17 – OPTION L2 – CONTINUED

Except for the trade-in aspect of the **NET CAPITALIZED COST**, it's a repeat of the process we used in SITUATION 17 – **OPTION L1**."

NET VALUE = NET CAPITALIZED COST – RESIDUAL VALUE
= \$17200.00 – \$14000.00 = \$3200.00

MONTHLY DEPRECIATION FEE = NET VALUE/TERM = \$3200.00/36 = \$88.89
= \$17200.00 + \$14000.00 = \$31200.00

MONTHLY FINANCED AMOUNT = TOTAL FINANCED AMOUNT/200
= \$31200.00/200 = \$156.00

MONTHLY FINANCE CHARGE = MONEY FACTOR x TOTAL FINANCED AMOUNT
= \$31200.00 x 0.001667 = \$52.01

MONTHLY TAXABLE AMOUNT = MONTHLY DEPRECIATION FEE
+ MONTHLY FINANCE CHARGE
= \$88.89 + \$52.01 = \$140.90

MONTHLY SALES TAX = SALES TAX RATE/100 x FINANCE CHARGE
= 0.07 x \$140.91= \$9.86

MONTHLY PAYMENT = MONTHLY DEPRECIATION FEE + MONTHLY FINANCE CHARGE + MONTHLY SALES TAX
= \$88.89 + \$52.01 + \$9.86 = \$150.76
= \$150.76 x 36 = \$5427.36
= \$52.01 x 36 = \$1872.36

SITUATION 17 – OPTION L2 – CONTINUED

"Nicole, that's a lot all at once. Maybe it just whizzed by? Take a few moments to look at it closer and let me know if you are Ok with it."

After pausing to look it over, Nicole replies, "Yes, I'm Ok with it, Dad. I looked over each step carefully. I do see that everything following the calculation of the **NET CAPITALIZED COST** is the same sequence as before, but with different numbers and answers for each calculation."

"Good, Sweetie. Given those results, Sam would incur the following cost."

TOTAL COST TO LEASE = CASH DOWN + TOTAL GAP INSURANCE
+ TOTAL PAYMENTS + TOTAL FEES
+ EXCESS MILEAGE CHARGE
+ EXCESS WEAR AND TEAR CHARGE
+ BOOK VALUE

= \$1600.00 + \$180.00 + \$5427.00 (rounded) +\$600.00
+ \$900.00 + \$0.00 + \$6500.00
= \$15207.00

SITUATION 17– OPTION L2 – CONTINUED

"And what's different in that calculation, Sweetie?"

"That's where you added **BOOK VALUE** in at the end."

"And, what do you deduce from the result?"

"Again, I'm really amazed at the **TOTAL COST TO LEASE**. It's only \$15207.00, compared to purchasing the car for \$29024.00. That's \$13817.00 less. I know we need to properly compare apple with apples. And to do that the last step is to consider the cost of purchasing the leased car at the end of the lease."

"Exactly. Here it is."

TOTAL COST TO LEASE = \$15207.00
RESIDUAL VALUE = \$14000.00
SALES TAX = 0.07 x \$14000.00 = \$980.00
PURCHASE OPTION FEE = \$350.00
TOTAL COST TO LEASE/PURCHASE = \$30537.00

SITUATION 17 – OPTION L2 – CONTINUED

"Again, in SITUATION 13 – **OPTION P2**, Sam's resulting **TOTAL COST TO PURCHASE** was \$29024.00. How's this result compared to it, Nicole?"

"The **TOTAL COST TO LEASE/PURCHASE** is a higher amount. That tells me it's better to purchase the car instead of doing the **LEASE/PURCHASE**."

"That's right. It's $1513.00 higher. In other words, it costs $1513.00 less to purchase the car than to lease/purchase it.

"I also did a calculation for Sam financing his **CAR LOAN** for 36 months instead of 60 months. From SITUATION 13 – **OPTION P2**, the **LOAN AMOUNT** is $18922.00. Omitting the calculations, his **MONTHLY PAYMENT** = $558.17, **CUMULATIVE INTEREST** = $1185.11 and **TOTAL COST OF LOAN** = $20166.00 (rounded). Here's the effect on the overall cost."

TOTAL COST TO PURCHASE = CASH DOWN + BOOK VALUE
+ TOTAL COST OF LOAN
= $1600.00 + $6500.00 + $20166.00
= $28216.00

SITUATION 17 – OPTION L2 – CONTINUED

"How's that result affecting things, Sweetie?"

"The **TOTAL COST TO PURCHASE** is even more favorable, $28216.00 compared to $29024.00. Compared to the **TOTAL COST TO LEASE/PURCHASE** its $2321.00 less."

"And why does that happen?"

"As in **OPTION L1**, it's because less **CUMULATIVE INTEREST** was paid for the shorter loan **TERM**. However, his **MONTHLY PAYMENT** increases from $348.73 to $558.17."

"What happens if Sam decides to **LEASE/PURCHASE** and uses a **SUBSEQUENT CAR LOAN** to pay for it?"

"That's easy, Dad. The **CUMULATIVE INTEREST** paid on his **SUBSEQUENT CAR LOAN** will increase the **TOTAL COST TO LEASE/PURCHASE**."

"Perfect, Nicole. I see things are settling in for you."

***Exercise 22**: Repeat SITUATION 17 - **OPTION L2** using the following changes in values: **CASH DOWN** = $0.00, **RESIDUAL VALUE** = $16000.00, **SALES TAX RATE** = 9.00%, **ANNUAL MILAGE LIMIT** = 12000 miles, **EXCESS MILEAGE RATE** = $0.10, **ANNUAL MILES USED** = 8000 miles, **MONTHLY GAP INSURANCE COST** = $4.00, **MONEY FACTOR** = 0.003333 (**APR** = 8.00%), **ACQUISITION FEE** = $500.00, all other **FEES** = $0.00.*

Your partial results should be:

***NET VALUE** = $2800.00, **MONTHLY FINANCE CHARGE** = $115.99, **MONTHLY PAYMENT** = $144.00, **TOTAL COST TO LEASE/PURCHASE** = $32188.00.*

***Exercise 23**: To examine a very unfair circumstance, Repeat SITUATION 17- **OPTION L2** using the following changes in values: **CASH DOWN** = $0.00, **RESIDUAL VALUE** = 11000.00, **TRADE-IN** offered = $3000.00 (**VALUE** = $6500.00), **SALES TAX RATE** = 6.00%, **ANNUAL MILAGE LIMIT** = 9000 miles, **EXCESS MILEAGE RATE** = $0.18, **ANNUAL MILES USED** = 14000 miles, **MONTHLY GAP INSURANCE COST** = $6.00, **MONEY FACTOR** = 0.006667 (**APR** = 16.00%), **ACQUISITION FEE** = $400.00, **BANK FEE** = $250.00, **DEALER SERVICE FEE** = $500.00, **DISPOSITION FEE** = $200.00, **PURCHASE OPTION FEE** = $350.00. **EXCESS WEAR AND TEAR CHARGE** = $1100.00 (4 new tires), $600.00 (replace pinged window)*

***Your partial results should be**: **NET CAPITALIZED COST** =$20300.00, **MONTHLY PAYMENT** = $495.03, **TOTAL PAYMENTS** = $17821.08, **TOTAL COST TO LEASE** = $30287.00, **TOTAL COST TO LEASE/PURCHASE** = $42297.00.*

Selling a Present Car

"Nicole, we saw in purchasing a car that, if Sam traded in or sold his **PRESENT CAR** privately for full **BOOK VALUE**, then it became an advantage. Let's see what happens if he sells his **PRESENT CAR** and uses the money as **CASH DOWN FROM SALE** in leasing the car."

"Hmm, I remember that. You've got me really curious."

SITUATION 17 – OPTION L3

"In SITUATION 13 – **OPTION L3**, Sam sold his **PRESENT CAR** for its full **BOOK VALUE** of $6500.00. Using that as **CASH DOWN FROM SALE** led to a **TOTAL COST TO PURCHASE** of $26812.00.

"What changes in the leasing calculations, Sweetie?"

"I suppose we do similarly. We use the **CASH DOWN FROM SALE** term and the $6500.00 amount in calculating the **NET CAPITALIZED COST**. Then we repeat repeating the calculations you just showed me."

"That's right. Here are those numbers."

NET CAPITALIZED COST = (SELLING PRICE + OPTIONS) – CASH REBATE
– TRADE-IN – CASH DOWN
– CASH DOWN FROM SALE
= ($24600.00) - $1300.00 - $1600.00 - $6500.00
= $15200.00

NET CAPITALIZED COST = $15200.00

NET VALUE = NET CAPITALIZED COST – RESIDUAL VALUE
= $15200.00 – $14000.00 = $1200.00

MONTHLY DEPRECIATION FEE = NET VALUE/TERM = $1200.00/36 = $33.33
= $15200.00 + $14000.00 = $29200.00

MONTHLY FINANCE CHARGE = TOTAL FINANCED AMOUNT x MONEY FACTOR
= $29200.00 x 0.001667 = $48.68

MONTHLY TAXABLE AMOUNT = MONTHLY DEPRECIATION FEE
+ MONTHLY FINANCE CHARGE
= $33.33 + $48.68 = $82.01

MONTHLY SALES TAX = SALES TAX RATE/100 x MONTHLY TAXABLE AMOUNT
= 0.07 x $82.01 = $5.74

MONTHLY PAYMENT = MONTHLY DEPRECIATION FEE + MONTHLY
FINANCE CHARGE + MONTHLY SALES TAX
= $33.33 + $48.68 + $5.74 = $87.75

TOTAL PAYMENTS = TERM x MONTHLY PAYMENT = 36 x $87.75 = $3159.00

TOTAL FINANCE CHARGE = TERM x MONTHLY FINANCE CHARGE
= $48.68 x 36 = $1752.48

TOTAL COST TO LEASE = CASH DOWN + TOTAL GAP INSURANCE
+ TOTAL PAYMENTS + TOTAL FEES
+ EXCESS MILEAGE Charge
+ EXCESS WEAR AND TEAR CHARGE
+ BOOK VALUE
= $1600.00 + $180.00 + $3159.00 + $600.00 +900.00
+$0.00 + $6500.00
= $12939.00

TOTAL COST TO LEASE = $12939.00
RESIDUAL VALUE = $14000.00
SALES TAX = 0.07 x $14000.00 = $980.00
<u>PURCHASE OPTION FEE = $350.00</u>
TOTAL COST TO LEASE/PURCHASE = $28269.00

SITUATION 17 – OPTION L3 – CONTINUED

"Nicole, how does the **TOTAL COST TO LEASE/PURCHASE** compare to the **TOTAL COST TO PURCHASE** of $26812.00?"

"It's still greater, but by a smaller amount, $1457.00."

"That's right.

"Again the **TERM** for the **CAR LOAN** was 60 months. I redid calculation for Sam financing his **CAR LOAN** for 36 months for the **LOAN AMOUNT** = $16922.00. That's the amount in SITUATION 13 – **OPTION P3**.

"Without showing the calculations, his **MONTHLY PAYMENT** = $499.71, **CUMULATIVE INTEREST** = $1068.75 and **TOTAL COST OF LOAN** = $17990.00 (rounded). That changes the **TOTAL COST TO PURCHASE** to the following."

TOTAL COST TO PURCHASE = CASH DOWN + BOOK VALUE
+ TOTAL COST OF LOAN
= $1600.00 + $6500.00 + $17990.00
= $26090.00

SITUATION 17 – OPTION L3 – CONTINUED

"How's that result look, Sweetie?"

"The **TOTAL COST TO PURCHASE** of $26090.00 is even more favorable. Compared to $26812.00, it's $722.00 less."

"And why does that happen?"

"As in **OPTION L1**, it's because less **CUMULATIVE INTEREST** is paid for the shorter **TERM**. But his **MONTHLY PAYMENT** increases from $348.73 to $497.91."

"Perfect, Nicole.

"Now, comparing this **TOTAL COST TO LEASE/PURCHASE** result to the $30537.00 in **OPTION L2**, what do you see?"

"The $28269.00 for **OPTION L3** is a lot lower."

"Right, Nicole. It's $2268.00 lower. Can you surmise why it is?"

"I suppose it because he had $2000.00 more as **CASH DOWN FROM TRADE-IN**. The other $268.00 must be because of the lower **LOAN AMOUNT**."

"That's sort of right, Sweetie. For a **CAR LEASE** it's actually a lower **TOTAL AMOUNT**

FINANCED not a lower **LOAN AMOUNT**. And part of it is the reduced **SALES TAX**.

"Compare the **TOTAL PAYMENTS**. For **OPTION L2**, it's $5427.36. For **OPTION L3** it's $3159.00. That's a drop of $2268.00 rounded."

"Oops! You're right Dad. I did confuse the terminology, but I understand now."

Exercise 24: *Repeat SITUATION 17 -* ***OPTION L3*** *using the following changes in values:* ***CASH DOWN*** *= $0.00,* ***RESIDUAL VALUE*** *= $16000.00,* ***SALES TAX RATE*** *= 9.00%,* ***ANNUAL MILAGE LIMIT*** *= 12000 miles,* ***EXCESS MILEAGE RATE*** *= $0.10,* ***ANNUAL MILES USED*** *= 8000 miles,* ***MONTHLY GAP INSURANCE COST*** *= $4.00,* ***MONEY FACTOR*** *= 0.003333 (****APR*** *= 8.00%),* ***ACQUISITION FEE*** *= $500.00, all other* ***FEES*** *= $0.00.*

Your <u>partial</u> results should be:

NET VALUE *= $800.00,* ***MONTHLY FINANCE CHARGE*** *= $109.32,* ***MONTHLY PAYMENT*** *= $143.38,* ***TOTAL COST TO LEASE/PURCHASE*** *= $29746.00.*

"That's great, Nicole. Let's look at selling the **PRESENT CAR** for more than **BOOK VALUE**."

SITUATION 17 – OPTION L4

"In SITUATION 13 – **OPTION P4**, Sam sold his **PRESENT CAR** for $7500.00, $1000.00 more than **BOOK VALUE** and used that entire amount as **CASH DOWN FROM SALE**. The resulting **TOTAL COST TO PURCHASE** was $25706.00.

"Here's what happens if instead he leases the car and pays that amount as **CASH DOWN FROM SALE.**"

NET CAPITALIZED COST = (SELLING PRICE + OPTIONS) – CASH REBATE – CASH DOWN – CASH DOWN FROM SALE
= $24600.00 - $1300.00 - $0.00 – $1600.00 - $7500.00
= $14200.00

SITUATION 17 – OPTION L4 – CONTINUED

"What did I change here, Nicole?"

"I see the obvious. The **CASH DOWN FROM SALE** is $7500.00 instead of $6500.00. Is there anything I don't see?"

"Nope, that's all, Sweetie. Now what do we do?"

"The rest is the same routine for the calculations."

"Correct. Here are all of them."

NET VALUE = NET CAPITALIZED COST – RESIDUAL VALUE
= $14200.00 – $14000.00 = $200.00

MONTHLY DEPRECIATION FEE = NET VALUE/TERM = $200.00/36 = $5.56

TOTAL FINANCED AMOUNT = NET CAPITALIZED COST + RESIDUAL VALUE
= $14200.00 + $14000.00 = $28200.00

MONTHLY FINANCED AMOUNT = TOTAL FINANCED AMOUNT/200
= $28200.00/200 = $141.00

MONTHLY FINANCE CHARGE = TOTAL FINANCED AMOUNT x MONEY FACTOR
= $28200.00 x 0.001667 = $47.01

MONTHLY TAXABLE AMOUNT = MONTHLY DEPRECIATION FEE
+ MONTHLY FINANCE CHARGE
= $5.56 + $47.01 = $52.57

MONTHLY SALES TAX = SALES TAX RATE x MONTHLY TAXABLE AMOUNT
= 0.07 x $52.57 = $3.68

MONTHLY PAYMENT = MONTHLY DEPRECIATION FEE + MONTHLY
FINANCE CHARGE + MONTHLY SALES TAX
= $5.56 + $47.01 + $3.68 = $56.25

TOTAL PAYMENTS = TERM x MONTHLY PAYMENT
= 36 x $56.25 = $2025.00

TOTAL FINANCE CHARGE = MONTHLY FINANCE CHARGE x TERM
= $47.01 x 36 = $1692.36

TOTAL COST TO LEASE = CASH DOWN + TOTAL GAP INSURANCE
+ TOTAL PAYMENTS + TOTAL FEES
+ EXCESS MILEAGE CHARGE
+ EXCESS WEAR AND TEAR CHARGE
+ BOOK VALUE
= $1600.00 + $180.00 + $2025.00 + $600.00
+ $900.00 + $6500.00
= $11805.00

TOTAL COST TO LEASE = $11805.00
RESIDUAL VALUE = $14000.00
SALES TAX = 0.07 x $14000.00 = $980.00
PURCHASE OPTION FEE = $350.00
TOTAL COST TO LEASE/PURCHASE = $27135.00

SITUATION 17 – OPTION L4

"What's the bottom line outcome here, Sweetie?"

Being used to things whizzing by, Nicole is ready pretty quickly. "The **TOTAL COST TO LEASE/PURCHASE** of $27135.00 is higher than the **TOTAL COST TO PURCHASE** of $25706.00; by $1429.00.".

"Right. And if Sam finances his **CAR LOAN** for 36 months, the **TOTAL COST TO PURCHASE** is even lower. Without showing the details, here is the result."

TOTAL COST TO PURCHASE = CASH DOWN + TOTAL LOAN COST
+ BOOK VALUE
= $1600.00 + $16926.00 + $6500.00
= $25026.00

SITUATION 17 – OPTION L4 – CONTINUED

"How's that result look, Sweetie"

"The **TOTAL COST TO PURCHASE** dropped from $25706.00 to $25026.00, by $680.00. And now it's lower than the **TOTAL COST TO LEASE/PURCHASE** of $27135.00 by $2109.00."

"Exactly, it's a somewhat better result."

***Exercise 25**: Repeat SITUATION 17 - **OPTION L4** using the following changes in values: **CASH DOWN** = $0.00, **RESIDUAL VALUE** = $15000.00, **SALES TAX RATE** = 8.00%, **ANNUAL MILAGE LIMIT** = 9000 miles, **EXCESS MILEAGE RATE** = $0.10, **ANNUAL MILES USED** = 10000 miles, **MONTHLY GAP INSURANCE COST** = $7.00, **MONEY FACTOR** = 0.0025 (**APR** = 6.00%), **ACQUISITION FEE** = $600.00, **DEALER SERVICE FEE** = $200.00, all other **FEES** = $0.00.*

Your partial results should be:

***NET VALUE** = $800.00, **MONTHLY FINANCE CHARGE** = $77.00, **MONTHLY PAYMENT** =*

$107.16, ***TOTAL COST TO LEASE*** *= $1210.00,* ***TOTAL COST TO LEASE/PURCHASE*** *= $28410.00.*

"**OPTION L4** showed what happens if the **PRESENT CAR** sells for more than its **BOOK VALUE**. Now let's examine the calculations for a selling it for less than **BOOK VALUE**."

SITUATION 17 – OPTION L5

"In SITUATION 13 - **OPTION P5** Sam sold his car for $4500.00 and used that amount as **CASH DOWN FROM SALE.** That's $2000.00 less than the **BOOK VALUE** of $6500.00. His resulting **TOTAL COST TO PURCHASE** was $29204.00.

"For leasing, what changes at the outset, Nicole?"

"In calculating the **NET CAPITALIZED COST**, the **CASH DOWN FROM SALE** is $4500.00 instead of $7500.00. Then the calculations process is the same drill as before."

"Yes it is. And do we actually have to do them?"

Nicole knows the answer. Purposely, she pauses for a few minutes.

"Well? I'm waiting, Sweetie."

"I'm just teasing you, Dad. Everything is exactly the same as **OPTION L2**, except we use the term **CASH FROM SALE** instead of **CASH FROM TRADE-IN** for getting the **NET CAPITALIZED COST**."

"You caught me there. Here's the first step."

NET CAPITALIZED COST = (SELLING PRICE + OPTIONS) – CASH REBATE
– TRADE-IN – CASH DOWN
– CASH DOWN FROM SALE
= $24600.00 - $1300.00 - $0.00 – $1600.00 - $4500.00
= $17200.00

SITUATION 17 – OPTION L5 – CONTINUED

"And, as you surmised with a tease, all the subsequent calculations will produce the same numbers and results as we got in **OPTION L2**."

"Nicole, the **OPTIONS** we've looked at cover the typical monetary occurrences in leasing a car. There's no getting away from it involving more and more terminology and calculations as we went along. You've done great to follow it all and absorb it on the fly. Remember, I mentioned that the cheat sheet also applies to this topic."

"I did notice that as I studied and used it. It had some lines that were to be entered as 0 if no **PRESENT CAR** was involved. I suppose now those lines have to be filled in."

"I'm glad you noticed and you're correct. I'm going to send you it filled in for some of the **OPTIONS** we just covered. I certain you'll follow it easily.

"As follow-up for you, you can try using it for the others. I'm also suggesting you use it to give the exercises a try. They are a repeat of some aspects, but with some of the dollar amounts changed for the various lease conditions. I'll leave it up to you. If you try them and don't get my results or any part of them, just let me know. We can look into it together."

"Dad, as a teen, I battled a bit with you on doing your homework. I'm older now and this topic is very challenging. I may need to act on it soon for real. I'll give the exercises and try and let you know if I encounter difficulty."

"That's great, Nicole, we still have to look at one more possible monthly charge, **GAP INSURANCE**. We already discussed it in the context of car being purchased. If a leased car is either totaled or stolen, then the matter of paying off the **CAR LEASE** comes into play. **GAP INSURANCE** can also be obtained for a leased car. As you might imagine, that is a much more involved topic."

"Yikes! I can't even begin to imagine how complicated that must be."

"It does get a bit convoluted, Sweetie. Let's stop for today and cover that another time."

LESSON 12 Uh, Oh! I Totaled My Leased Car

"Good morning, Peanut! Are you ready to discuss how **GAP INSURANCE** applies to a leased car?"

"Hello, Dad. I think I am. I can't even imagine the horror of totaling a leased car and facing the consequences. I've reviewed what you covered before about **GAP INSURANCE** for a **CAR LOAN**. At least I'm pretty clear on that part. It was always worrisome to deal with the insurance aspects of a rental car. The rental agent always asked if I wanted to add some sort of damage insurance. I could either accept to or waive it. Is that done for a leased car?"

"The rental car insurance you alluded to is the **COLLISION DAMAGE INSURANCE** offered to you. Typically, your **STANDARD CAR INSURANCE** policy with your own insurance agency will cover it. A lot of credit cards provide it, if you use their card to pay the rental costs. Either way, you can choose to decline that option by initialing a **COLLISION DAMAGE WAIVER**."

"Yeah, Dad, that's exactly what I've encountered with rental cars. I just followed my company policy on it."

"For a leased car, it is your responsibility to provide **STANDARD CAR INSURANCE** for it. You should have arranged that insurance before you drive the leased car off the lot.

"For a **CAR LEASE** they almost certainly will require that you have **C&CD INSURANCE**, especially if it is a **NEW CAR**. For your own protection, you should also consider including each of the other optional coverages.

"Typically, the **C&CD INSURANCE** coverage amounts required by the leasing party will significantly exceed those required by the state laws. They are likely to exceed the even higher amounts a person might normally carry. On the other hand, some leases might indicate base amounts that are less than required by the state laws. You'd have to be alert to it and purchase the necessary amounts."

"Ok, that's logical and I'll be careful about it."

"That's good. Let's get into the details of the **GAP INSURANCE**."

Buying Out of a Car Lease

"If a leased car is either totaled or stolen, you still will owe the dealership the remaining costs of the **CAR LEASE**."

"That feels like an awful thing to face, Dad. My legs are even starting to wobble. How are the remaining costs determined?"

"Typically, a so-called **BUYOUT AMOUNT** is calculated by the dealership."

"How does the leasing dealership determine it?"

- Determining the Buyout Amount -

"Basically, you have to compensate the dealership for the remaining value of the leased car. The **BUYOUT AMOUNT** includes the remaining **MONTHLY PAYMENTS**, the **RESIDUAL VALUE** and some other lesser costs. Some questions arise about these other things.

"One question is whether the dealership will treat the circumstance as you having done a **LEASE/PURCHASE** or not. If they do, then they would have to add the **SALES TAX** onto the **RESIDUAL VALUE**.

"Another question is whether the dealership will add in the **PURCHASE OPTION FEE** and/or the **EARLY TERMINATION FEE**. The latter one can be a substantial fee. If they do charge those, then will your **STANDARD CAR INSURANCE** cover them?

"The answers should be clearly discussed with the dealership and your insurance agent. Then, you need to negotiate **CAR LEASE** language about them that is consistent with your insurance coverage. If you overlook these matters and your leased car is either totaled or stolen, then you can have a big surprise."

"I can't imagine facing those things, too. I'm glad you mentioned them, and I'll be alert to them."

"For our need now, I'll assume that the **BUYOUT AMOUNT** includes the remaining **MONTHLY PAYMENTS**, the **RESIDUAL VALUE** and **SALES TAX** on it, and the **PURCHASE OPTION FEE**. Including the **EARLY TERMINATION FEE** for a totaled or stolen car seems unfair. I'll exclude it as having been negotiated out of the **CAR LEASE**

"Here are the equations we we'll use."

REMAINING MONTHLY PAYMENTS = MONTHLY PAYMENT x REMAINING MONTHS

BUYOUT AMOUNT = REMAINING MONTHLY PAYMENTS + RESIDUAL VALUE + SALES TAX + PURCHASE OPTION FEE

"They make sense to me, Dad."

"There are two other considerations. **EXCESS MILEAGE** may have occurred. A precise, picky dealership could get the mileage reading at the time of the loss and charge for any **EXCESS MILES**. I doubt they would do that. We'll exclude it. The **EXCESS WEAR AND TEAR** is not a factor. The car is gone and **C or CD INSURANCE** is in play. There is no way to assess it anyway."

"As always, Dad, you think of everything. I would be pretty upset if they attempted either of those charges."

"I would be, too. Let's look at a numerical example of calculating the **BUYOUT AMOUNT**."

- **Example**

SITUATION 18

"One year into his **CAR LEASE**, Sam of SITUATION 17 – **OPTION L1** is involved in accident. The leased car is totaled. His **CD INSURANCE** is in play.

"From before, for his **CAR LEASE**, the **NET CAPITALIZED COST** = \$21700.00, the **MONTHLY PAYMENT** = \$292.54, the **RESIDUAL VALUE** = \$14000.00 with a **SALES TAX** = \$980.00, and the **PURCHASE OPTION FEE** = \$350.00.

"Assume the **MONTHLY PAYMENTS** are made at the end of each month into the lease. Sam has twenty-four months of **REMAINING MONTHLY PAYMENTS**. Here's the calculation of the **BUYOUT AMOUNT**."

REMAINING MONTHLY PAYMENTS = MONTHLY PAYMENT x REMAINING MONTHS
= \$292.54 x 24 = \$7021.00 (rounded)

BUYOUT AMOUNT = REMAINING MONTHLY PAYMENTS + RESIDUAL VALUE
+ SALES TAX + PURCHASE OPTION FEE
= \$7021.00 + \$14000.00 + \$980.00 + \$350.00 = \$22351.00

"Gosh, Dad, that's a huge amount of money."

"Yes it is. But his **CD INSURANCE** will cover most of it. Let's look at that process."

Exercise 26: *For SITUATION 18, calculate the* ***BUYOUT AMOUNT*** *if the car is totaled two years into the* ***CAR LEASE****.*

Your result should be: BUYOUT AMOUNT *= \$18440.00.*

Insurance Claim Process

- C or CD Insurance -

"Nicole, when a leased car is damaged by your fault, but is not totaled, **CD INSURANCE** will apply and an insurance claim can be made. The **CD PAYOUT** will cover the **REPAIR COST** minus the **CD DEDUCTIBLE** on the policy. The **CD DEDUCTIBLE** becomes an out of pocket expense to the lessee. Depending on the type and extent of the damage, the damage event may or may not have to be reported to the lessor.

"If a leased car is either stolen or totaled, then the lessor is owed the **BUYOUT AMOUNT**. The **C or CD INSURANCE** claim can be made for that amount. For ease of terminology, I'll assume it was totaled and use the **CD INSURANCE** setting in everything I describe. For events involving the **C INSURANCE**, everything is the same except for the use of **C INSURANCE** and the associated **C** terminology.

"Just as for your own car, the **CD PAYOUT** will provide coverage up to the **DEPRECIATED VALUE** of the leased car minus the **CD DEDUCTIBLE.**"

CD PAYOUT = DEPRECIATED VALUE – CD DEDUCTIBLE

"After that, **GAP INSURANCE** might come into play."

"When does that happen, Dad?"

- Gap Insurance -

"Once the **CD PAYOUT** occurs, if any remaining portion of the **BUYOUT AMOUNT** remains, it must be paid by the lessee. He or she can use **GAP INSURANCE** to cover that cost.

"Essentially, the **GAP INSURANCE** process for a **CAR LEASE** is the same as for a **CAR LOAN**. Instead of serving to pay off the **OUTSTANDING BALANCE** of a **CAR LOAN**, it serves to pay off the **BUYOUT AMOUNT** of a **CAR LEASE**. The equations used are the same. We just replace the **OUTSTANDING BALANCE** term with **BUYOUT AMOUNT**."

GAP AMOUNT = BUYOUT AMOUNT – DEPRECIATED VALUE

CD PAYOUT = DEPRECIATED VALE – CD DEDUCTIBLE

AMOUNT STILL OWED = BUYOUT AMOUNT – CD PAYOUT

"Instead of a **NEW OUTSTANDING BALANCE**, there is a **REMAINING BUYOUT AMOUNT**."

REMAINING BUYOUT AMOUNT = AMOUNT STILL OWED – GAP PAYOUT

"If the **GAP INSURANCE** covers the **CD DEDUCTIBLE**, then

GAP PAYOUT = AMOUNT STILL OWED

"The **REMAINING BUYOUT AMOUNT** will be $0.00. Otherwise,

GAP PAYOUT = AMOUNT STILL OWED – CD DEDUCTIBLE

REMAINING BUYOUT AMOUNT = CD DEDUCTIBLE

"For any event for which the **C INSURANCE** comes into play, the **C DEDUCTIBLE** applies in place of the **CD DEDUCTIBLE**."

"Sweetie, do you see the similarity to **GAP INSURANCE** for a **CAR LOAN**?"

"Yeah, I do. Everything seems straight-forward. Your general explanation is not causing my legs to wobble."

"Well, I'm really happy about that."

"Let's look at a numerical example. I'll use three-quarters of the **% CUMULATIVE DEPRECIATION** of the Nissan 370z example of Lesson 8."

- **Example**

<u>**SITUATION 19**</u>

"Sam, of SITUATION 18, purchases a **GAP INSURANCE** policy from his insurance company for an **ANNUAL GAP INSURANCE RATE** of \$60.00. That's a **MONTHLY GAP INSURANCE RATE** of \$5.00. It is paid at the end of each month of the **CAR LEASE**. Sam's **GAP INSURANCE** <u>does not include</u> repayment of the **CD DEDUCTIBLE**.

"One year into the **CAR LEASE** the car is totaled. Sam has paid **TOTAL MONTHLY PAYMENTS** = \$292.54 x 12= \$3510.00 (rounded) on his **CAR LEASE**. The car had depreciated by 0.75 x 19.00% = 14.00% (rounded) to a **DEPRECIATED VALUE** of \$21156.00.

"Sam's **CD DEDUCTIBLE** is \$1000.00. The **CD PAYOUT** = \$21156.00 – \$1000.00 = \$20156.00.

"The **BUYOUT AMOUNT** is \$22351.00, which includes the cost of purchasing the leased car, which no longer exists. The **BUYOUT AMOUNT** exceeds the **DEPRECIATED VALUE** by a **GAP AMOUNT** = \$22351.00 – \$21156.00 = \$1195.00.

"A **GAP INSURANCE** claim can be, and is, made."

AMOUNT STILL OWED = BUYOUT AMOUNT – CD PAYOUT
= \$22351.00 – \$21156.00 = \$2195.00

GAP PAYOUT = AMOUNT STILL OWED – CD DEDUCTIBLE
= \$2195.00 – \$1000.00 = \$1195.00

REMAINING BUYOUT = AMOUNT STILL OWED – GAP PAYOUT
= $2195.00 - $1195.00 = $1000.00

SITUATION 19 - CONTINUED

"Combining the **CD PAYOUT** and **GAP PAYOUT**, the dealership was paid $21156.00 + $1195.00 = $21351.00. The dealership also was paid the **CASH DOWN** = $1600.00 and the **TOTAL MONTHLY PAYMENTS** = $3510.00. Sam pays them $22351.00 – $21351.00 = $1000.00, the amount of the **CD DEDUCTIBLE**. Collectively, the dealership was paid $27461.00 for a car originally worth $26400.00.

"Sam also paid one year of **GAP INSURANCE** ($5.00 x12 = $60.00). His **TOTAL SPENT** = $1000.00 + $1600.00 + $3510.00 + $60.00 = $6170.00.

"**GAP INSURANCE** saved Sam $1256.00 – $60.00 = $1196.00. If his **GAP INSURANCE** policy paid the **CD DEDUCTIBLE**, then his **TOTAL SPENT** would drop to $5170.00.

"Sam also has paid twelve months of his **STANDARD CAR INSURANCE POLICY**. Assuming the same car, the amount would be the same whether he leased or purchased it."

"Do you understand all of that, Nicole?"

"Generally, I followed it. It's just like we did before for **CAR LOANS**. I'd have to take time to check the calculated values. You only stated the amount of the **BUYOUT AMOUNT.** Where did that value come from?"

"The given information is the same as in SITUATION 18. Those calculations and the resulting **BUYOUT AMOUNT** carry over to SITUATION 19."

"I didn't notice that, but get it now."

- ### Effect of Time into the TERM

"In SITUATION 19, Sam benefited from having **GAP INSURANCE**. Let's look at what happens later in the **TERM** of the **CAR LEASE**. I extended the time into the **CAR LEASE** to 1.5 years and used 0.75 x **% CUMULATIVE DEPRECIATION** of the Nissan example. By interpolation, it's 0.75 x 25.00% = 19.00% (rounded). Here's a look at the outcome."

SITUATION 19A

"Sam's car is totaled 1.5 years into the lease. He has paid **TOTAL MONTHLY PAYMENTS** = $292.54 x 18 = $5265.00 (rounded). Skipping the calculations, the **BUYOUT AMOUNT** is $20596.00.

"The car has depreciated 19.00% to a **DEPRECIATED VALUE** of $19926.00. The **CD PAYOUT** = $19926.00 - $1000.00 = $18926.00.

"The **GAP AMOUNT** = **BUYOUT AMOUNT** – **DEPRECIATED VALUE** = $20596.00 – $19926.00 = $670.00.

"A **GAP INSURANCE** claim is made."

AMOUNT STILL OWED = BUYOUT AMOUNT – CD PAYOUT
= $20596.00 – $18926.00 = $1670.00

GAP PAYOUT = AMOUNT STILL OWED – CD DEDUCTIBLE
= $1670.00 – $1000.00 = $670.00

REMAINING BUYOUT AMOUNT = AMOUNT STILL OWED – GAP PAYOUT
= $1670.00 – $667.00 = $1000.00

SITUATION 19A - CONTINUED

"Combining the **CD PAYOUT** and **GAP PAYOUT**, the dealership was paid $18926.00 + $670.00 = $19596.00. The dealership also was paid the **CASH DOWN** = $1600.00 and the **TOTAL MONTHLY PAYMENTS** = $5265.00. Sam pays them $1000.00, the amount of the **CD DEDUCTIBLE**. Collectively, the dealership was paid $27461.00.

"Sam also paid eighteen months of **GAP INSURANCE** ($5.00 x 18 = $90.00). His **TOTAL SPENT** = $1000.00 + $1600.00 + $5265.00 + $90.00 = $7955.00.

"**GAP INSURANCE** saved Sam $670.00 – $90.00 = $580.00. If his **GAP INSURANCE** policy paid the **CD DEDUCTIBLE**, then his **TOTAL SPENT** would drop to $6955.00.

"Sam also has paid twelve months of his **STANDARD CAR INSURANCE POLICY**."

"What stands out for you, Nicole?"

"Seeing the calculations, it is a lot clearer to me how **GAP INSURANCE** works. At 1.5 years, Sam had less benefit from it, $580.00 compared to $1195.00. I see that Sam's **TOTAL SPENT** is $7955.00, compared to $6170.00 after one year. That's obvious, as he is further into the **CAR LEASE** period."

"Your spot on, Sweetie."

"Notice that the collective amount the dealership was paid did not change. It's $27461.00."

"I did catch that, but I don't know why?"

"It's because the **TOTAL COST OF THE LEASE** is a set amount. It's not affected by how far it is into the lease. The same **TOTAL COST OF THE LEASE** has to be paid. It's just paid by a different sequence in each case.

"At one year, the **CASH DOWN** + **CD PAYOUT** + **GAP PAYOUT** + **TOTAL MONTHLY PAYMENTS** =$1600.00 + $21351.00 + $3510.00 = $26461.00. Atop that, Sam paid the **CD DEDUCTIBLE** = $1000.00. **TOTAL COST OF THE LEASE** = $26461.00 + $1000.00 = $27461.00.

"At 1.5 years, **GAP INSURANCE**. The **CASH DOWN** + **CD PAYOUT** + **TOTAL MONTHLY PAYMENTS** = $1600.00 + $19596.00 + $5265.00 = $26461.00. Atop that, Sam paid the **CD DEDUCTIBLE** = $1000.00. **TOTAL COST OF THE LEASE** = $26461.00 + $1000.00 = $27461.00

"Does that make sense, Peanut?"

"Now that you explained it, it does. It would have taken me a while to figure it out on my own. Maybe I would have."

"I have no doubt you would have, Sweetie."

Exercise 27: *Sam's car is stolen 1.25 years (fifteen months) into the lease. The car has depreciated 16.50% to a* ***DEPRECIATED VALUE*** *of $20541.00. He also has paid 1.25 years of* ***GAP INSURANCE*** *at cost of $75.00. The* ***BUYOUT AMOUNT*** *on his* ***CAR LEASE*** *is $21473.00. Calculate his out of pocket expenses a) without reimbursement of his* ***C DEDUCTIBLE****, b) with reimbursement of his* ***C DEDUCTIBLE****.*

Your results should be*: a) $7063.00, b) $6063.00*

▪ Effect of Higher % Cumulative Depreciation

"Now, let's take a look at what happens for SITUATION 19A, if we use the higher **% CUMULATIVE DEPRECIATION** of the Nissan example, 25.00%."

SITUATION 19B

"Sam's car is totaled 1.5 years into the lease. As before, he has paid **TOTAL MONTHLY PAYMENTS** = $5265.00 (rounded) and the **BUYOUT AMOUNT** is $20596.00.

"The car has depreciated 25.00% to a **DEPRECIATED VALUE** of $18450.00. The **CD PAYOUT** = $18450.00 - $1000.00 = $17450.00. Because the **BUYOUT AMOUNT** exceeds the **DEPRECIATED VALUE** by a **GAP AMOUNT** = $20596.00 - $17450.00 = $2146.00, a **GAP INSURANCE** claim can be made."

AMOUNT STILL OWED = BUYOUT AMOUNT – CD PAYOUT
= $20596.00 – $17450.00 = $3146.00

GAP PAYOUT = AMOUNT STILL OWED – CD DEDUCTIBLE
= $3146.00 - $1000.00 = $2146.00

REMAINING BUYOUT AMOUNT = AMOUNT STILL OWED – GAP PAYOUT
= $3146.00 - $2146.00 = $1000.00

SITUATION 19B - CONTINUED

"The **GAP INSURANCE** saved Sam $2146.00 - $120.00 = $1926.00.

"Sam owes $1000.00. Sam also has paid the **CASH DOWN** ($1600), **TOTAL MONTHLY PAYMENTS** ($5265), and 1.5 years of **GAP INSURANCE** ($90). That's a **TOTAL SPENT** of $7955.00.

"The dealership was paid $17450.00 + $2146.00.0 = $19596.00 from the insurance payouts. Collectively, the dealership was paid **CASH DOWN** + **CD PAYOUT** + **GAP PAYOUT** + **TOTAL MONTHLY PAYMENTS** + **CD DEDUCTIBLE** = $27461.00."

"Nicole, despite the difference in **% CUMULATIVE DEPRECIATION**, the dealership was still paid $27461.00. Why do you suppose that happened?"

After a short, but deep moment of thought, Nicole sheepishly replies, "I suppose it's because the difference in **% CUMULATIVE DEPRECIATION** does not change the **TOTAL COST OF THE LEASE**?"

Grinning, Dad reacts, "That's it. I had no doubt you would figure it out. And, it didn't take a while, Smarty Pants."

"Nicole, notice that Sam's **TOTAL SPENT** is the same amount as for the lower **% CUMULATIVE DEPRECIATION**. Why do you suppose it would be?"

"You've got me thinking about it, Dad."

After a few moments pausing, Nicole adds, "I see it now. The actual **% CUMULATIVE DEPRECIATION** did not affect any of his costs. Regardless of what the **% CUMULATIVE DEPRECIATION** is, Sam pays the same amounts for **CASH DOWN**, **TOTAL MONTHLY PAYMENTS**, **TOTAL MONTHLY PAYMENTS, CD DEDUCTIBLE** and 1.5 years of **GAP INSURANCE** ($90)."

"Perfect, again."

- **When CD Payout Exceeds Buyout Amount**

"Sweetie, I played around with the numbers a bit, and found an interesting circumstance. Let's extend the time into the **CAR LEASE** to 2.5 years and used 0.75 times **% CUMULATIVE DEPRECIATION** of the Nissan example. By interpolation, it's 27.00% (rounded). Here's a look at the outcome."

SITUATION 19C

"Sam's car is totaled 2.5 years into the lease. He has paid **TOTAL MONTHLY PAYMENTS** = $292.54 x 30 = $8776.00 (rounded). Skipping the calculations, the **BUYOUT AMOUNT** is $17085.00.

"Assume the car has depreciated 27.00% to a **DEPRECIATED VALUE** of $17958.00. The **CD PAYOUT** = $17958.00 – $1000.00 = $16958.00.

"The **GAP AMOUNT** = **BUYOUT AMOUNT** – **DEPRECIATED VALUE** = $17085.00 – $17958.00 = -$873.00. In other words, the **DEPRECIATED VALUE** exceeds the **BUYOUT AMOUNT** by $873.00. Because there is no **GAP AMOUNT**, a **GAP INSURANCE** claim cannot be made. In effect, Sam did not need **GAP INSURANCE** and could have saved the $150.00 cost, if he did not buy it."

AMOUNT STILL OWED = BUYOUT AMOUNT – CD PAYOUT
= $17098.00 – $16958.00 = $127.00

GAP PAYOUT = $0.00

REMAINING BUYOUT AMOUNT = AMOUNT STILL OWED – GAP PAYOUT
= $127.00 - $0.00 = $127.00

SITUATION 19C - CONTINUED

"The dealership is paid the **CD PAYOUT** of $16958.00. Sam pays the $127.00. Collectively, the dealership was paid $27461.00. As expected that amount did not change."

"Sam also paid the **CASH DOWN** ($1600), **TOTAL MONTHLY PAYMENTS** ($8776), and 2.5 years of **GAP INSURANCE** ($150). Those plus the $127.00 is a **TOTAL SPENT** of $10653.00."

"Sweetie, how do these **GAP INSURANCE** results compare to 1 year and 2 years?"

"If I recall right, for those years, Sam benefited because the **GAP INSURANCE** came into play. He had less benefit at 1.5 years. At 2.5 years, the **GAP INSURANCE** did not apply. He has a no benefit. It illustrates your point that, the longer is the time period into the lease, the less the **GAP INSURANCE** is needed."

"That's right. Sometime between 1.5 years and 2.5 years, if his car has not been totaled or stolen, then he should cancel the **GAP INSURANCE**. Playing around, I found that he should do that at 2 years. In this case, because he only spent $120.00 on the **GAP INSURANCE**, its cost is not a big factor.

"There's a subtle point to mention. Even though there wasn't a **GAP AMOUNT**, Sam still owed the dealership $127.00 of the **BUYOUT AMOUNT**. That's due to the **DEDUCTIBLE** on his **CD INSURANCE**. Had there been no **CD DEDUCTIB**LE, then the **CD PAYOUT** would have been $17958.00, $873.00 more than the **BUYOUT AMOUNT** of $17085.00. Sam would owe nothing. Instead, the **CD DEDUCTIBLE** reduced the $873.00 by $1000.00, leaving $127.00 still owed.

"How's all that sound, Peanut?"

Scratching her head Nicole replies, "Actually, I got a bit lost in your explanation. I trust you on it and know it's worth figuring out why you mentioned it. I'll keep thinking on it later and maybe it will sink in."

"That's why I said it was subtle, really subtle. I know it will sink in later and you'll have an Aha moment. Here's another way to see it.

"Had the **BUYOUT AMOUNT** been $873.00 higher, $17958.00, this would be the result."

AMOUNT STILL OWED = BUYOUT AMOUNT – CD PAYOUT
= $17958.00 – $16958.00 = $1000.00

GAP PAYOUT = AMOUNT STILL OWED – CD DEDUCTIBLE
= $1000.00 - $1000.00 = $0.00

REMAINING BUYOUT AMOUNT = AMOUNT STILL OWED – GAP PAYOUT
= $1000.00 - $0.00 = $1000.00

"Sam would owe the entire **CD DEDUCTIBLE**."

"Gee, Dad. I see the $1000.00 staring me in the face. It should mean something. I'll add it to my thinking cap."

"Ok, give it time, and your light bulb will go on."

"I can hardly wait for that to happen, Dad."

Exercise 27A: *Sam's car is stolen two years into the lease. The car has depreciated 23.00% to a **DEPRECIATED VALUE** of $18942.00. The **BUYOUT AMOUNT** on his **CAR LEASE** is $18840.00. Calculate his out of pocket expenses a) without reimbursement of his **C DEDUCTIBLE**, b) with reimbursement of his **C DEDUCTIBLE**.*

Your results should be: *a) $9639.00, b) $8639.00 Note: **CDPAYOUT** = $17942.00 and **GAP PAYOUT** = $0.00.*

"Nicole, I redid SITUATION 19C with one change. The accident occurs just before the **CAR LEASE** ends. Here's what I got."

SITUATION 19D

"Sam's car is totaled 35 months (2.917 years) into the lease. He has paid **TOTAL MONTHLY PAYMENTS** = $292.54 x 35 = $10239.00 (rounded). The car has depreciated 31.00% to a **DEPRECIATED VALUE** of $16974.00. Skipping the calculations, the **BUYOUT AMOUNT** is $15623.00.

"The **GAP AMOUNT** = $15623 - $16974.00 = -$1351.00. In other words, the **DEPRECIATED VALUE** exceeds the **BUYOUT AMOUNT**. There is no **GAP AMOUNT** and **GAP INSURANC**E does not apply. If he did not buy the car, Sam could have saved $175.00.

"Sam's **CD INSURANCE** has a **CD PAYOUT** = $16974.00 - $1000.00 = $15974.00. That amount is greater than the **BUYOUT AMOUNT**. Because of that, the **CD PAYOUT** is reduced to $15623.00, which is paid to the dealership. The **AMOUNT STILL OWED** is $0.00.

"Nicole, are you with me and do you follow the logic of the results?"

"I follow your calculations all right, Dad. It's just different numbers that result. I still have to let the logic sink in, though.

"I do notice one difference. It puzzles that in SITUATION 19C there was no **GAP AMOUNT** and the **CD PAYOUT** was not reduced. And Sam owes nothing. What's going on here?"

"You're catching a subtlety. There is no inconsistency. In SITUATION 19C, the **CD PAYOUT** was less than the **BUYOUT AMOUNT**. As a result the **CD PAYOUT** was not reduced. And Sam had to pay the remainder of the **BUYOUT AMOUNT**. The does not happen here. The reduced **CD PAYOUT** was large enough to pay the entire **BUYOUT AMOUNT** Sam owes them $0.00.

"Sam paid for the **CASH DOWN** ($1600), **TOTAL MONTHLY PAYMENTS** ($10239), and the **GAP INSURANCE** ($175). His **TOTAL COST** is $12014.00. His **CD DEDUCTIBLE** did not come into play."

"I follow that now, Dad. I also see that Sam made more **MONTHLY PAYMENTS** and his **TOTAL**

COST increased. That's because he is further into the **CAR LEASE**,"

"Righto, Sweetie! Nice observation!

"The main point is that, even with the **CD DEDUCTIBLE** excluded, the **CD PAYOUT** alone was sufficient to pay the **BUYOUT AMOUNT**. Unlike before, he does not owe the dealership any part of the $1000.00. In SITUATION 19C, he had to pay $127.00."

Exercise 28: *Sam's car is stolen 34 months into the* ***CAR LEASE****. The car has depreciated 30.00%. The* ***BUYOUT AMOUNT*** *on his* ***CAR LEASE*** *is $15915.00. Calculate his out of pocket expenses.*

Your result should be: *$11716.00*

- Total Cost of Gap Insurance over Time –

"Sweetie, we've covered a lot. To see it in summary, I tabulated the primary results for Sam's SITUATION.

"I also calculated and included them for zero months and for two years. I've also assumed the **CD PAYOUT** pays the full **GAP AMOUNT** even if the **CD PAYOUT** is greater than the **BUY OUT AMOUNT**. Some private insurers would actually do that.

"With the results, we can see the trends over time in the **DEPRECIATED VALUE, BUY OUT AMOUNT, GAP AMOUNT, CD PAYOUT, GAP PAYOUT**, what **SAM OWES**, and the **TOTAL SPENT**."

INITIAL VALUE	24600	24600	24600	24600	24600	24600
YEARS	0.000	1.000	1.500	2.000	2.500	2.917
% CUMULATIVE DEPRECIATION = 0.75 x % CUMULATIVE DEPRECIATION of NISSAN EXAMPLE (ROUNDED)	7.00	14.00	19.00	23.00	27.00	31.00
DEPRECIATED VALUE (REALISTIC)	22878	21095	19926	18942	17866	16974
BUYOUT AMOUNT	25861	22351	20596	18840	17085	15623
GAP AMOUNT	2983	1195	670	-102	-873	-1351
CD PAYOUT	21878	20156	18926	17942	16958	15974
GAP PAYOUT	2983	1195	670	0	0	0
TOTAL INSURANCE PAYOUT	24861	21351	19596	17881	16958	15974
BUYOUT AMOUNT – TOTAL INSURANCE PAYOUT	1000	1000	1000	898	127	-315

SAM OWES	**1000**	**1000**	**1000**	**898**	**127**	**0**
TOTAL SPENT	**2600**	**6170**	**7955**	**9639**	**10653**	**12014**

"It helps to see it all at once, Dad. Without your examples, I probably would be very confused by what Sam owes when the **BUYOUT AMOUNT** becomes negative. I'm pretty sure I see the entire picture, now."

"That's great. Let's take a closer look at what is going on. Recall the equation for the **GAP AMOUNT**."

GAP AMOUNT = BUY OUT AMOUNT – DEPRECIATED VALUE

"As time moves along, the **DEPRECIATED VALUE** gets lower and lower. So does the **BUY OUT AMOUNT** of the lease. The difference in the two amounts is the **GAP AMOUNT**. And our table shows the **GAP AMOUNT** is decreasing. Eventually it goes negative. At that point the value of buying **GAP INSURANCE** ends.

"Anyway, it tells us that as time moves along, the **CAR LEASE** is being paid off faster than the car is depreciating in value. In math terms, the **BUYOUT AMOUNT** in the equation is getting smaller and smaller. The **DEPRECIATED VALUE** is also getting smaller and smaller, but more slowly. That's why the **GAP AMOUNT** eventually became negative."

"The math logic about the equation spins my head a bit. But, I get the general point."

"That's fine, Peanut. It's just me thinking out loud. I also did a table for the higher **% CUMULATIVE DEPRECIATIONS** of the Nissan example."

INITIAL VALUE	**24600**	**24600**	**24600**	**24600**	**24600**	**24600**
YEARS	**0.00**	**1.000**	**1.500**	**2.000**	**2.500**	**2.917**
% CUMULATIVE DEPRECIATION (NISSAN EXAMPLE)	**9.00**	**19.00**	**25.00**	**31.00**	**36.00**	**41.00**
DEPRECIATED VALUE (NISSAN EXAMPLE)	**22386**	**19926**	**18450**	**16974**	**15744**	**14514**
BUYOUT	**25861**	**22351**	**20596**	**18840**	**17085**	**15623**
GAP AMOUNT	**3182**	**2425**	**2146**	**1866**	**1341**	**1109**
CD PAYOUT	**21386**	**18926**	**17450**	**15974**	**14744**	**13514**
GAP PAYOUT	**3182**	**2425**	**2146**	**1866**	**1341**	**1109**
TOTAL INSURANCE PAYOUT	**24861**	**21351**	**19596**	**17840**	**16085**	**14623**
BUYOUT AMOUNT – TOTAL INSURANCE PAYOUT	**-1000**	**-1000**	**-1000**	**-1000**	**-1000**	**-1000**

SAM OWES	**1000**	**1000**	**1000**	**1000**	**1000**	**1000**
TOTAL SPENT	**2600**	**6170**	**7956**	**9741**	**11526**	**13014**

"Sweetie, the pattern of a declining **GAP AMOUNT** is evident, too. However, notice the **GAP AMOUNTS** are higher than before and the value never goes negative. That's the effect of the higher **% CUMULATIVE DEPRECIATION**."

"Yes, I see that Dad. And the **GAP INSURANCE** has more pay off than in the first table."

"That's right. And in all cases, Sam's **GAP INSURANCE** is in play. He always ends up paying the **CD DEDUCTIBLE**.

"Do you notice anything striking about the **TOTAL AMOUNT SPENT**? Take a look at both results."

Pausing a bit, Nicole then points out, "Yeah, Dad. Some of them have identical amounts in both tables. Others do not. That's puzzling me. You showed me before that even though the **% CUMULATIVE DEPRECIATION** was changed, Sam's **TOTAL SPENT** was the same. Why are some of them different here?"

"Well, Sweetie, when did that happen?"

"Gosh, I see it happens for those cases when the **GAP AMOUNT** was negative in the first table. I don't see why?"

"Well, let's look at it for 2 years into the **CAR LEASE**. The difference between the first table entries and second table entries is $9639 - $9741 = -$102. For 2.5 years, it's $10653 - $11526 = -$871. Where did you see those numbers?"

"Hmm, they're the **GAP AMOUNTS** in table 1? But, I still don't get it?"

"Sweetie, let me help. In the first table, the **CD PAYOUT** overpaid the **BUYOUT AMOUNT** by $102 and $871, respectively. In the second table, that did not happen. Had it, the **TOTAL SPENT** amounts would be the same. Because it didn't happen, Sam had to pay that much more himself.

"I realize that taxes your brain a bit, at least it did mine. Nonetheless, do you generally follow my explanation?"

"Actually, it makes sense, Dad. It's only because you explained it."

"Nicole, let's look at 2.917 years. The difference is $12014 - $13014 = -$1000. I won't tax your brain on it. In this case, for the first table, the **CD PAYOUT** was $1351.00. It was enough to cover the $1000.00 **CD DEDUCTIBLE** that Sam would have owed the dealership. The dealership got an extra $351.00. In the second table, that did not happen and Sam paid $1000.00 more. The dealership did not get an extra $351, either!"

"I've got to let the settle in a bit, Dad."

"I'm sure it will, Sweetie.

"I want to reiterate the main overall point about **GAP INSURANCE**. The **GAP AMOUNT** is highest at the outset and then declines. Since the **GAP INSURANCE** pays for it, it's most beneficial the sooner the car is either stolen or totaled. I don't mean to say it's a good thing to happen at all. Because, then you don't have a car and have to start all over. The point is that **GAP INSURANCE** has the most effect early in the game. After a while it is not needed at all."

"I can see that clearly now, Dad."

Cost of Gap Insurance

"Nicole, some leases will automatically include the **GAP INSURANCE** and its cost. If not then the dealership might try to sell **GAP INSURANCE** to you. It will be at much higher cost than using your own insurance company. A **TOTAL COST OF GAP ISURANCE** of $450.00 to $675.00 for a 3-year lease would not be unusual.

"Some dealerships might try to collect the entire **GAP INSURANCE** up front. Don't do that. Pay it monthly. Later in the **TERM** you will not need it and can cancel it. If you have paid it up front then the dealership may not refund any of it.

"Some dealerships might include or offer a so-called **GAP WAIVER**, which means they waive (forgive) the **GAP AMOUNT**. There is added lease cost for that. Likely, it's a little higher than their usual cost of **GAP INSURANCE**. It's negotiable.

"One advantage of purchasing **GAP INSURANCE** from a private insurance company is it can be bought at any time, not necessarily at the outset of the lease. You can take your chances for a while and purchase it after some of the depreciation occurs. But, the longer you wait, the less you need it. It is better to buy it right away. That's because you can also cancel it any time. Once the **GAP AMOUNT** reaches $0.00, you can and should cancel it. You have to keep a financial eye on the changing amounts of the **BUYOUT AMOUNT** and **DEPRECIATED VALUE** of the car as you move further in time into the **TERM**."

"That makes total sense, Dad. It's kind of like watching those repayment brackets when I had to be careful not to just spill into a higher one by borrowing one dollar too much."

"Good point and recall, Sweetie!"

- Cost versus Benefit -

"Now let's answer the basic question. Should you purchase **GAP INSURANCE** for a **CAR LEASE**?"

"Yeah, that's the whole point. What would you do, Dad?"

"There you go, putting pressure on me again. That's Ok. It's a matter of cost versus benefit over time. I did a table to show that."

YEARS INTO THE CAR LEASE	0.000	1	1.500	2	2.5	2.917
COST-PRIVATE GAP INSURANCE	5	60	90	120	150	175
COST-DEALERSHIP GAP INSURANCE	15	180	270	360	450	525
GAP PAYOUT (REALISTIC)	2983	1195	670	0	0	0
GAP PAYOUT (NISSAN EXAMPLE)	3182	2425	2146	1866	1341	1109

"I got some of the values from our prior SITUATIONS. I calculated the others. You know the drill."

"Wow, Dad. 'Know the drill'? You surprised me with that phrase."

"I'm not that old. Even my generation uses it."

"For various **YEARS INTO THE CAR LEASE**, I listed the **COST-PRIVATE GAP INSURANCE** and the **COST-DEALERSHIP GAP INSURANCE**. I assumed it is paid monthly, starting the month before the **CAR LEASE** begins. I made the dealership cost three times as much."

"Consider the **COST-PRIVATE GAP INSURANCE** amounts compared to the **GAP PAYOUT (REALISTIC)**. At 0 years you've paid $5.00 for $2983.00 of benefit. At 1.5 years you've paid $90.00 for $670.00 of benefit. After that, you've gotten no benefit. At worst, you've spent $175.00 for no benefit. What's that tell you?"

"Well, Dad. It's sort of a no-brainer. I would buy the **GAP INSURANCE**. And, if I can drop it after 1.5 years or so, then I would."

"I would, too.

"Look at the **GAP PAYOUT (NISSAN EXAMPLE)**. You get a benefit all the way through. At 0 years, it's $3182.00 for a cost of $15.00 At 2.917 years (35 months) it's $1109.00 for a cost of $175.00. That's really good. The underlying **% CUMULATIVE DEPRECIATION** values might be unrealistic. However, if they happen, then you are protected."

"I suppose so, especially since I would pay for it gradually and not all at once. And once I don't need it, I can cancel it."

"Good point, Sweetie. What about the **COST-DEALERSHIP GAP INSURANCE**?"

"Well, it just means I pay three times as much for the same benefits

"For the **GAP PAYOUT (REALISTIC)**, at 1.5 years, I've paid $270.00 for a $670.00 benefit. At 2 years, I've paid $360.00 for no benefit. Maybe, I just skip the **GAP INSURANCE**. If the dealership wanted to collect the entire $525.00 cost up front, I'd definitely pass on it.

"For the **GAP PAYOUT (NISSAN EXAMPLE)**, at 0 years, I've paid $15.00 for a $3182.00 benefit. At 2.917 years, I've paid $525.00 for an $1109.00 benefit. Even if the dealership collected it up front, it seems to pay off well. I'm inclined to buy it, even if I couldn't drop it. Because those **% CUMULATIVE DEPRECIATION** values are so iffy, I would have to think about it real hard."

"That's terrific, Sweetie. I agree with everything you said."

"There's another dilemma you need to know regarding the **CASH DOWN** aspect of **CAR LEASES**. Let's take break and I'll work up some numbers to look at. I should be ready in a couple hours or so."

"That'll be fine Dad. I'll see you later."

"Nicole, similar to when you purchase a car, you can put **CASH DOWN** when you lease a car. Commonly, the dealership will require a specific amount, perhaps several thousands of dollars. Optionally, you can put **EXTRA CASH DOWN** atop that. There are pros and cons to doing that."

Extra Cash Down

"Assume you lease a car with no **PRESENT CAR** involved. If you put **EXTRA CASH DOWN**, then this equation applies."

NET CAPITALIZED COST = (SELLING PRICE + OPTIONS) – CASH REBATE – CASH DOWN – EXTRA CASH DOWN

"A positive is that, if you put **EXTRA CASH DOWN**, then the **NET CAPITALIZED COST** for the **CAR LEASE** will be reduced. Consequently, the **MONTHLY PAYMENT** will be lowered. That's a choice you can make."

Overage Amount

"There is a rub to paying a lot of up-front money, though. And, it's a big rub."

"You've got me wondering on this one, Dad."

"The rub arises if your leased car is either totaled or stolen. At the time that happens, if you've put **EXTRA CASH DOWN**, then it will be reflected in the remaining cost of the **CAR LEASE**. The higher is the **EXTRA CASH DOWN**, the lower is the remaining cost of the lease."

"Hmm, Dad. That seems like a good thing to me. Wouldn't that mean I could buy less **GAP INSURANCE**?"

"Actually, you couldn't. Likely the insurer won't know about your **EXTRA CASH DOWN** and wouldn't care anyway. Recall, the insurer bases the insurance cost on the projected **DEPRECIATED VALUE** of the specific leased car. They don't care who paid what, their only concern is what they would pay out if the car is either totaled or stolen. There is no effect on what they charge you for the **GAP INSURANCE**. And the cost is minor, anyway."

"Then, what's the problem?"

"Peanut, I've never faced the circumstance of a totaled or stolen leased car myself. From what I've read at different websites, here's what I found.

"Assume the leased car is totaled. There's an issue as to who receives the **CD PAYOUT** money. On the one hand, the lessee purchased the insurance. As the insured party it would seem the lessee should receive the money. However, the dealership owns the car and holds the **TITLE**. On that basis, the **CD PAYOUT** should go to the dealership. If that happens, then the lessee can lose money."

"How so, Dad?"

"Let's look back at SITUATION 19C. Sam's **CD INSURANCE** could have had a **CD PAYOUT** of $17958.00. Because the **BUYOUT AMOUNT** of $17085.00 was less than that amount, the **CD PAYOUT** was reduced to $17085.00. It was paid to the dealership. That's fine.

"However, some private insurers would payout the entire **CD PAYOUT** of $19958.00. If that's the case, then the risk in putting **EXTRA CASH DOWN** comes into play. It's important to know why and how."

"I'm all ears now, Dad. Whenever you say something is important it always is very important."

"Ok, Nicole. Let me take advantage of that to cover a tricky point.

"Again, by paying **EXTRA CASH DOWN**, the lessee reduces the remaining cost of the **CAR LEASE**, the **BUYOUT AMOUNT**. The higher is the **EXTRA CASH DOWN** the lower is the **BUYOUT AMOUNT**.

"The **CD PAYOUT** is a fixed amount based on the **DEPRECIATED VALUE** of the car. The higher is the **EXTRA CASH DOWN**, then the higher is the amount by which the **CD PAYOUT** exceeds the **BUYOUT AMOUNT**. If the dealership receives the **CD PAYOUT**, then the dealership can pocket the **OVERAGE AMOUNT**. That **OVERAGE AMOUNT** includes some or all of your **EXTRA CASH DOWN**.

"The insurance company may or may not pass the **CD PAYOUT** through the lessee. Even though you paid the insurance company, technically it goes to the holder of the car's **TITLE**, the dealership. Unless they either do pay it to the lessee or the dealership reimburses the **OVERAGE AMOUNT**, the lessee loses the money. In my view, the dealership should only get the **BUYOUT AMOUNT**, no more. Any **OVERAGE AMOUNT** should belong to the lessor."

"I get the general point, Dad. That would sure steam me up. How much money is involved?"

"A high **EXTRA CASH DOWN** puts you at significant risk early in the **TERM** of the **CAR LEASE**. If the leased car is totaled or stolen very early in the **TERM**, then it will be very costly. It takes an example to see how it plays out. I was about to do that. Here goes."

- Example (with Extra Cash Down) –

SITUATION 19E

"Assume Sam of SITUATION 19C puts **EXTRA CASH DOWN** of $5000.00. Without the details here are the main results."

NET CAPITALIZED COST = (SELLING PRICE + OPTIONS) – CASH REBATE – CASH DOWN – EXTRA CASH DOWN CASH
= $24600.00 – $1300.00 – $1600.00 – $5000.00
= $16700.00

MONTHLY PAYMENT = $135.01

SITUATION 19E – CONTINUED

"Sam totals his leased car immediately after driving it off the lot. For consistency, let's say the car has depreciated 0.75 x 9.00% = 7.00% (rounded) to a **DEPRECIATED VALUE** of $22878.00. Sam has paid no **MONTHLY PAYMENTS.** Here's what happens monetarily."

REMAINING MONTHLY PAYMENTS = MONTHLY PAYMENT x REMAINING MONTHS
= $135.01 x 36 = $4860.00 (rounded)

BUYOUT AMOUNT = REMAINING MONTHLY PAYMENTS + RESIDUAL VALUE + SALES TAX + PURCHASE OPTION FEE
= $4860.00 + $14000.00 + $980.00 + $350.00 = $20190.00

AMOUNT STILL OWED = BUYOUT AMOUNT – CD PAYOUT
= $20190.00 - $21878.00 = -$1688.00

GAP AMOUNT = BUYOUT AMOUNT - DEPRECIATED VALUE
= $20190.00 - $22878.00 = -$2688.00

SITUATION 19E – CONTINUED

"The **DEPRECIATED VALUE** exceeds the **BUYOUT AMOUNT**, resulting in a negative **GAP AMOUNT**. In other words, **GAP INSURANCE** does not apply. Assume the entire **CD PAYOUT** = $22878.00 - $1000.00 = $21878.00 and is paid to the dealership. The **AMOUNT STILL OWED** is -$1688.00. The negative result means they received an **OVERAGE AMOUNT**= $21878.00 - $20190.00 = $1688.00.

"The dealership also was paid the **CASH DOWN** = $1600.00 and **EXTRA CASH DOWN** = $5000.00. Collectively, the dealership was paid $28478.00 for a car worth $26400.00.That's $2140.00 extra profit made in an instant.

"Even though the **CD PAYOUT** reflected his **CD DEDUCTIBLE** of $1000.00, Sam owes nothing to the dealership. He paid his **CASH DOWN** ($1600.00), **EXTRA CASH DOWN** ($5000.00), **TOTAL MONTHLY PAYMENTS** ($0.00), and **GAP INSURANCE** ($0.00). His **TOTAL SPENT** = $6600.00. He has spent a lot of money for nothing! And, he has no car and must begin again.

"The **GAP INSURANCE** did not come into play, it was not needed. Sam could have saved $5.00. But that is a tiny, tiny solace."

"What do you take from that outcome, Nicole?"

Feeling almost speechless, Nicole expresses, "That's incredible, in a huge negative way. It kind of makes me not want to lease a car."

"Indeed it is astonishing. Despite the low risk of a totaled or stolen car, it is a big worry. If either the **CAR LEASE** specified it, or it was graciously returned, getting the $2140.00 back from the dealership would make Sam's **TOTAL SPENT** = $4460.00. But he still gets nothing for it!"

Exercise 29: *Repeat SITUATION 19E, except there is no* ***CASH REBATE****. The resulting* ***MONTHLY PAYMENT*** *= $175.96.*

Your <u>partial</u> result should be: GAP AMOUNT *= –$1275.00 (rounded). Sam's* ***TOTAL SPENT*** *= $6600.00.*

"But getting back to our assumptions, Nicole, what was the major monetary factor involved? And what does that lead us to do?"

"Of course, I forgot about main aspect of the example. He paid the **EXTRA CASH DOWN** of $5000.00. It turned to be foolish to do so. I suppose we should look at what happens if he does not do that?"

"Exactly, Smarty Pants. Let's take a look it."

- Example (without Extra Cash Down) -

<u>SITUATION 19F</u>

"Assume Sam only pays the required **CASH DOWN** of $1600.00. He experiences the immediate crash and totaled car. As before, the **CD PAYOUT** = $21878.00. From SITUATION 19, the **NET CAPITALIZED COST** = $21700.00 and his **MONTHLY PAYMENT** = $292.54. Here are the changes in outcome."

TOTAL MONTHLY PAYMENTS = 0 x $292.54 = $0.00

REMAINING MONTHLY PAYMENTS = MONTHLY PAYMENT x REMAINING MONTHS
= \$292.54 x 36 = \$10531.00 (rounded)

BUYOUT AMOUNT = REMAINING MONTHLY PAYMENTS + RESIDUAL VALUE
+ SALES TAX + PURCHASE OPTION FEE
= \$10531.00 + \$14000.00 + \$980.00 + \$350.00 = \$25861.00

AMOUNT STILL OWED = BUYOUT AMOUNT – CD PAYOUT
= \$25861.00 - \$21878.00= \$3983.00

GAP AMOUNT = BUYOUT AMOUNT - DEPRECIATED VALUE

= \$25861.00 – \$22878.00 = \$2983.00

<u>SITUATION 19F – CONTINUED</u>

"In this case **GAP INSURANCE** comes into play. The **GAP PAYOUT** = **AMOUNT STILL OWED** – **CD DEDUCTIBLE** = \$3983.00 - \$1000.00 = \$2983.00, and is payed to the dealership. There is no **OVERAGE AMOUNT**."

"Let's add things up.

"The dealership was paid \$21878.00 + \$2983.00 = \$24861.00 from the insurance payouts. Sam pays them \$25861.00 - \$24861.00 = \$1000.00, the amount of the **CD DEDUCTIBLE**. The dealership also was paid the **CASH DOWN** = \$1600.00. Collectively, the dealership was paid \$27461.00. Sam's **TOTAL SPENT** = \$2600.00. If the **CD DEDUCTIBLE** is covered, then the dealership gets that \$1000.00 directly from the insurer. Sam's **TOTAL SPENT** becomes \$1600.00."

"Sweetie, let's compare the results to when Sam paid **EXTRA CASH DOWN** of \$5000.00.

"In that case, the dealership was paid \$28478.00. Here, they were paid \$27461.00, \$1079.00 less for the \$26400.00 car.

"And, previously, Sam had a **TOTAL SPENT** of \$6600.00. How's that compare?"

"Hmm, now it's \$4000.00 less. That's whole lot better, but he still has no car and must start over."

"Indeed he does. On the positive side, technically, he has the \$4000.00 to use."

"Yeah, I guess that's right."

With a quizzical look, Nicole asks, "Dad, I'm thinking about the \$4000.00. If Sam put down \$5000.00 less, why isn't the **TOTAL SPENT** less by \$5000.00?"

"Super question!

"If you look back at it, in SITUATION 19E, Sam did not have to pay the **CD DEDUCTIBLE** of $1000.00. Here, he does. That's why; relative to that example, the reduction in **TOTAL COST** is only $4000.00."

"Ok, I see it now."

"This logic applies to the normal required **CASH DOWN** as well. Sam would do even better if he did not have to put down the $1600.00 either?"

"Yeah, I guess that's right, too. Don't tell me you checked that out? It wouldn't surprise me."

"Indeed, I did. But you get the picture and the calculation process, Smarty Pants. I won't go through it again. If you run the numbers, then you'll find out that the dealership was paid a total of $27676.00, exactly the **BUYOUT AMOUNT**. And, Sam has a **TOTAL SPENT** = $1000.00, which is the **CD DEDUCTIBLE**. It's $6600.00 – $1000.00 = $5600.00 less than when he paid the **EXTRA CASH DOWN** of $5000.00. He has that much more to use toward getting another car, whether leased or purchased."

Exercise 30: *Confirm Dad's results for Sam putting **TOTAL CASH DOWN** = $0.00. The resulting **MONTHLY PAYMENT** = $342.95.*

***Your result should be: GAP AMOUNT** = $4798.00(rounded). Sam's **TOTAL SPENT** = $1000.00.*

"I really get the point now, Dad. Paying no **CASH DOWN** and no **EXTRA CASH DOWN** limits my immediate risk to just having to pay my **CD DEDUCTIBLE** and the single **MONTHLY PAYMENT**. What are the chances the dealership would accept no **CASH DOWN**?"

"You can try to negotiate that to a lower amount, maybe not $0.00. Still, negotiating it out with the dealership might not be easy. They run their numbers, too. Even so, I would try."

Effect of Time into TERM

"Dad, your SITUATIONS 19E and 19F assumed the car was totaled immediately. What happens to the **OVERAGE AMOUNT** if the car is totaled further into the **CAR LEASE**?"

"It's sort of like **GAP INSURANCE**. The longer you get into the lease, the less is the risk involved in putting **EXTRA CASH DOWN**. That's because ultimately the **CAR LEASE** ends. You have simply sped up the payment of the full terms. Once it ends, there is no risk.

"I've looked into the monetary aspects of having the car totaled further into the **TERM** of the **CAR LEASE**. I used the realistic **% CUMULATIVE DEPRECIATION** values of the Nissan example. Here are the main results for Sam paying <u>no</u> **TOTAL CASH DOWN**."

MONTHS INTO CAR LEASE	TOTAL CASH DOWN	BUY OUT AMT.	DEPRECIATED VALUE	GAP AMT.	CD PAYOUT	OVERAGE AMT.	TOTAL SPENT
0	0	27676	22878	4798	21878	-	1000
12	0	23561	21156	2405	20156	-	5175
24	0	19445	18942	503	17942	-	9351
36	0	15330	16974	-1644	15974	644	13526

"The **MONTHS INTO THE LEASE** mean the accident occurred just after that number of months. For example, the second line means it happened momentarily into the **MONTH 13**.

"Do the trends in the various columns make sense to you?"

After a pause, with hand on cheek, Nicole says, "I guess the obvious things are the **BUYOUT AMOUNT** and **DEPRECIATED VALUE** each get lower and lower. That's because Sam makes more and more **MONTHLY PAYMENTS** and the car is getting older. Of course, as time moves along, the **TOTAL SPENT** by Sam increases, too."

"What about the **GAP AMOUNT**?"

Thinking longer, Nicole then replies, "Well, thinking back, you pointed out the **BUYOUT AMOUNT** drops faster than the **DEPRECIATED VALUE**. That means the **GAP AMOUNT** would get smaller and smaller. And that's what is happening."

"Right. What about the negative value, the -$1644?"

"I think that means the **CD PAYOUT** was larger than the **BUYOUT AMOUNT**. The dealership ended up getting that additional money. You called it an **OVERAGE AMOUNT**."

"Exactly! As you see, I listed that **OVERAGE AMOUNT**. It's $644.00.

"Dad, why isn't it $1644.00.?"

"It's because the **CD PAYOUT** is the **DEPRECIATED VALUE – CD DEDUCTIBLE** = $15974.00. The **OVERAGE AMOUNT= CD PAYOUT – BUYOUT AMOUNT** = $15974.00 - $15330.00 = $644.00.

"Oh, yeah. I overlooked that, Dad."

"Let's look at what happens when Sam pays **TOTAL CASH DOWN** of $6600.00."

MONTHS INTO CAR LEASE	TOTAL CASH DOWN	BUY OUT AMT.	DEPRECIATED VALUE	GAP AMT.	CD PAYOUT	OVERAGE AMT.	TOTAL SPENT
0	6600	20190	22878	-2688	21878	1688	6600
12	6600	18570	21156	-2586	20156	1586	8280
24	6600	16950	18942	-1992	17942	992	9960
36	6600	15330	16974	-1644	15974	644	11640

"For the **BUYOUT AMOUNT**, **DEPRECIATED VALUE** and **TOTAL SPENT**, the trends are the same. What do you notice about the **GAP AMOUNT** trend?"

After smiling, Nicole exclaims, "All of them are negative. I guess there is no **GAP AMOUNT**. The **CD PAYOUT** covered the entire **BUYOUT AMOUNT** and resulted in an **OVERAGE AMOUNT**. I see those amounts listed."

"And what happens over time?"

"The dealership is getting less and less **OVERAGE AMOUNT**."

"Precisely! What about the **OVERAGE AMOUNT** of $644.00 for Month 36? It's the same as before."

"Oh, I see that. Well, we already saw the reason why a higher **% CUMULATIVE DEPRECIATION** does not affect the outcome at the end of the **TERM**. I guess it's the same reason for the **TOTAL CASH DOWN**."

"Super!"

"That's all great. Let's compare the **TOTAL SPENT**. Here the two results side by side."

MONTHS INTO CAR LEASE	TOTAL CASH DOWN	TOTAL SPENT	TOTAL CASH DOWN	TOTAL SPENT	DIFFERENCE IN TOTAL SPENT
0	6600	6600	0	1000	5600
12	6600	8280	0	5523	2757
24	6600	9960	0	9699	-39
36	6600	11640	0	13526	-1886

"Expectedly, the **TOTAL SPENT** gets larger and larger in both cases. I listed the difference in the two amounts. What's interesting about those values, Sweetie?"

"Well, the difference is getting smaller and smaller. Then it goes negative."

"What's the smaller and smaller tell us?"

"Well, I guess it means that the longer the time is before the accident, the closer are the **TOTAL SPENT** amounts for the two cases."

"Yes, and what does that suggest about paying **CASH DOWN**?"

Hand on forehead and after a long pause, "Hmm, Dad, I guess it means the longer is the time to the accident, the less is the risk of losing the **CASH DOWN**. That's because the difference in the **TOTAL SPENT** is becoming less and less."

"Great, my budding genius! That's it exactly. In fact, that last value of -$1886.00 means that in the end you are actually $1886.00 better off, if you did have **CASH DOWN** of $6600.00.

"What's interesting is that, in the early months, more is spent by putting **TOTAL CASH DOWN** of $6600.00. At some point before Month 24, that reverses. The negative entries for **DIFFERENCE IN TOTAL SPENT** indicate that.

"I have another question for you, Sweetie. Why is the final **TOTAL SPENT** larger for no **CASH DOWN**?"

After thinking hard on it, "You've got me there, Dad. I have no clue."

"The difference is due to paying more interest. Oops, I mean finance charge, in leasing lingo. In this case, it's $1886.00 more. That happens because when you don't pay any **CASH DOWN** the **NET CAPITALIZED AMOUNT** is larger than if you do. You end up paying a higher **MONTHLY FINANCE CHARGE**, and thus **TOTAL FINANCE CHARGE**.

"Now that you say all that, it's kind of obvious. Maybe I'm a mid-size genius."

"I won't dispute you on that, Sweetie."

"Dad, I need to ask again. What would you do regarding **CASH DOWN** and **EXTRA CASH DOWN**?"

"It boils down to this. If I want to risk not having a car totaled or stolen car at all, then I'd put **TOTAL CASH DOWN** of $6600.00. If I don't put anything down, then at the end it only costs me $1886.00 more. Even though the chances of either happening is very small, especially for happening the instant you drive of the lot, why use up $6600.00 up front to save $1886.00 over three years of time?

"I'd pay for the inexpensive **GAP INSURANCE**. I would ask that the required **CASH DOWN** of $1600.00 be rolled into the **MONTHLY PAYMENTS** and keep the $5000.00 safely in my bank account. It will earn a little interest over three years, and then I could use it to either lease another car or purchase one.

"Of course, I likely would not buy the leased car at the end of the **CAR LEASE**. I clearly showed that was a very costly step. As the end of the **CAR LEASE** approaches I would check the current **BOOK**

VALUE compared to the **RESIDUAL VALUE**. If I felt I could sell it to my advantage, then I might purchase it and resell it."

"Thank you, Dad. I tend to agree with that path. That's if I were to consider leasing a car at all."

"Nicole, the **TOTAL SPENT** amounts are based on the dealership keeping the **OVERAGE AMOUNT**. If Sam got that refunded, the amounts would be a lot lower by the **OVERAGE AMOUNT**. Taking those into account I got these results."

MONTHS INTO CAR LEASE	TOTAL CASH DOWN	OVERAGE AMT.	TOTAL SPENT - OVERAGE AMT.	TOTAL CASH DOWN	OVERGAGE AMT.	TOTAL SPENT - OVERAGE AMT.	DIFFERENCE IN (TOTAL SPENT - OVERAGE AMT.)
0	6600	1750	4850	0	-	1000*	3850
12	6600	1525	6755	0	-	5175*	1580
24	6600	931	9029	0	-	9351*	-322
36	6600	521	11119	0	521	13005	-1886

*** For these entries, there was no OVERAGE AMOUNT.**

"Other than lower values, there's nothing new about the trends. However, the **DIFFERENCE IN (TOTAL SPENT – OVERAGE AMOUNT)** value of -1886.00 for MONTH 36 is the same as before. For MONTH 36, the same **OVERAGE AMOUNT** was subtracted from each of the **TOTAL SPENT** amounts. That was not the case for the other three **MONTHS**.

"I get it, Dad. That's interesting."

"Your earlier question about the possibility of the dealership negotiating the normal **CASH DOWN** prompts me to another point. When we began our discussion of **CAR LEASES**, I gave an example ad prompt: 2017 Dodge Dart, SXT MSRP $21140, Stock #3260, $149/mo. 3-yr lease, $2229 down, accompanying photo. The dealership has configured the overall terms of the anticipated **CAR LEASE** to reflect getting that **CASH DOWN** of $2229.00. If you negotiate it out, they probably will offset the effect."

"What do you mean by 'offset the effect'?"

"By getting up-front **CASH DOWN**, the dealership has it available to either use or to earn bank interest. If you tried to remove it, then they likely would adjust aspects like fees and the **RESIDUAL VALUE**, to offset the effect of not having that money. You would end up with an increased **MONTHLY PAYMENT**. That $2229.00 is not at risk money. One way or another you are going to pay it. It's any **EXTRA CASH DOWN** you elect to add to the required up-front **CASH DOWN** that is at risk. Does that make sense, Nicole?"

"I can see that point, Dad. And I guess I should avoid paying any **EXTRA CASH DOWN**?"

"Not necessarily, Sweetie. If I could, and wanted to, pay **EXTRA CASH DOWN**, I would negotiate for the dealership to roll it into the **CAR LEASE** by spreading it out over the **TERM**. They can do that simply by adding 1/36 of the **EXTRA CASH DOWN** to each **MONTHLY PAYMENT**. In other words, instead of paying an up-front **EXTRA CASH DOWN**, I would add that **MONTHLY EXTRA CASH DOWN** to the normal **MONTHLY PAYMENT**. That has two benefits."

"Hmm, that's got me curious. What are they?"

"The extra payment is similar to accelerating repayment of a loan to pay it off sooner. For a **CAR LEASE** it does that as well. You will pay off the **CAR LEASE** before the end of its **TERM**. More importantly, the **MONTHLY EXTRA CASH DOWN** flows into the entire **CAR LEASE**. It sets the pattern of the **BUYOUT AMOUNT** being less than if there was no **CASH DOWN**. It gradually decreases the **BUYOUT AMOUNT** in play to be steadily lower than usual each month. The effect is to make the risk consistent with the passing of time."

Wincing her eyes, Nicole asks, "Why's that so, Dad?"

"If the leased car is totaled or stolen early in the **TERM**, you have paid very few **MONTHLY CASH DOWN** amounts. As time passes, you pay more and more. The current **BUYOUT AMOUNT** is decreasing simultaneously and faster than otherwise. The later the car is totaled or stolen, the greater the reduction in the amount you owe on the **CAR LEASE** is, compared to no **MONTHLY EXTRA CASH DOWN**."

"Couldn't I do that with the required up-front **CASH DOWN**, too?"

"You could try to roll that into the **MONTHLY PAYMENTS**, too. Again, the dealership likely would make adjustments to the other terms to compensate. At the end, you would pay about the same **TOTAL COST**.

"Of course, there is another step one can take with **EXTRA CASH DOWN** funds. The money could just be set aside in a bank account. Then 1/36 of the money could be withdrawn monthly and applied toward reducing the ongoing out of pocket normal **MONTHLY PAYMENTS**. It has no consequence to the **TOTAL COST** of the **CAR LEASE**."

Loose Ends

"Nicole, there a few loose ends to mention.

"For a leased car, an alert is needed regarding the purchasing **DEALERSHIP GAP INSURANCE.** "The dealership might also imply, or directly say, you must buy its **DEALERSHIP GAP INSURANCE**. It might be illegal for them to do so. For example, I found that the state of New York prohibits any person, firm, association or corporation from acting as an insurance agent or insurance broker in New York without an appropriate license. You do not have to accept their offer and can walk away from the deal if you choose to do so."

"Until you said the last part, my nervous legs started to wobble."

ASIDE: *http://www.dfs.ny.gov/insurance/ogco2008/rg080320.htm is the source of the statement regarding the state of New York. Quoting that source, "Only a licensed insurance agent or broker may offer gap insurance on behalf of an insurer, because Insurance Law § 2102(a)(1) prohibits any person, firm, association or corporation from acting as an insurance agent or insurance broker in New York without an appropriate license." If the **CAR LEASE** indicates the dealership **GAP INSURANCE** is offered through a licensed insurance agency, then it is likely legal.*

"You also have to be aware that, for a totaled or stolen car, the lessor will expect you to keep making payments until your insurance claims are settled and paid to them. That's no surprise and they should refund them to you once that happens. Be sure the **CAR LEASE** indicates they will do so.

"Another loose end is the possibility is your leased car is totaled due to the fault of another driver. If that happens, then that driver's insurance company will become responsible to paying claims to your lessor. That driver's **CD INSURANCE** will come into play. It can get pretty involved and time consuming for all of that to play out. If that driver does not have the coverage, then your standard policy's **UNINSURED MOTORIST COVERAGE** will take care of that possibility.

"Let me add something making a large **DOWN PAYMENT** on a purchased car. It's similar to putting **CASH DOWN** on **CAR LEASE**. Until the **CAR LOAN** is paid off, the lender holds the **TITLE** and owns the car. If you total the car or it's stolen, then you have exactly the same risk of having paid a large **DOWN PAYMENT.** You'll still be still left with loan payments. The **CD PAYOUT** could favor the lender with an **OVERAGE AMOUNT.**

"But a bank is more likely to transfer those funds to you. Indeed, they might be required to do so by law. That's because at the moment when the loan is paid off with the insurance funds, the car is yours and you should get the **OVERAGE AMOUNT**. In fact, the insurer might make the **CD PAYOUT** directly to you and then you pay off the loan. More likely the insurer interacts with both you and the lender to work things out. Or, they simply make the **CD PAYOUT** equal to the **OUTSTANDING BALANCE**. If so, then no **OVERAGE AMOUNT** arises.

"Ok, that's logical and I'll be careful about it."

Playing the Odds

"Of course, the counter point is that if the car is neither totaled nor stolen, then the **CAR LEASE** runs its full **TERM**. In that highly likely case, it's good to put as much **CASH DOWN** and **EXTRA CASH DOWN** as possible. There is a tug between the two extremes. You have to play with the numbers to determine a **CASH DOWN** that fits your comfort zone. That's why I showed you how do that.

"It's sort of like betting on a horse race. The favorite could win in a safe ride, or place second, or show for third. It's also possible the favorite could stumble out of the gate and get hurt and not finish at all. If any of the former happens, then you'd be glad you made a large bet. If the latter happens, you be glad you made a small bet, or didn't bet at all."

"That makes sense, Dad."

"The analogy is that, if you never have the car totaled or stolen, then you wouldn't need **GAP INSURANCE**. Of course, you cannot know that in advance. Maybe you chance it, maybe you don't. What are the odds of either one happening?"

"I don't have any idea, Dad."

"I researched it. According to the National Insurance Crime Bureau statistics I found at www.nicb.org/newsroom/news-releases/historical-look-at-vehicle-theft-in-the-u-s the percentage of registered cars stolen is very low. In 2102 it was only 0.285%.

"The only statistics I could find on totaled cars were about percentages of insurance accident claims that resulted in the car being totaled. I didn't find anything about the actual numbers of accident claims, themselves. Perhaps, for competitive reasons, that's confidential information.

"I can only venture a guess. There are several hundred fatalities nationally each July 4 holiday. The number of accidents on that day is surely a lot higher. Maybe it's a few thousand. That's the worst accident day of the year. I'd bet there are lot less totaled cars annually than stolen cars. I have walked the Earth for 70+ years. I don't know of anyone besides myself that ever had a car totaled by an insurance company. Based on wrecks seen along the highway others might deduce the opposite. Without data one really cannot know.

"In any case, if you want to take your chances and not get **GAP INSURANCE** the odds that you won't need it are very high. For the low cost, However, I would still buy it whatever the odds are.'

"Ok, Sweetie. We covered a lot of territory about purchasing a car compared to leasing one. I'd like you to speed review everything for the general gist of it. Let's break for a bit and then take a look at all of it in summary. I have some tables to pull up and discuss."

"That sounds good, Dad. Let's break for a couple hours. That'll give me time to skim through everything. It takes me back to my college days when I used to do that just before an exam."

LESSON 14 Now what? Purchase? Lease? Lease/Purchase?

Nicole has quickly looked over everything her Dad covered on **CAR LOANS** and **CAR LEASES**. With that done their Skype chat restarts.

Grinning, Dad greets Nicole, "Hi Sweetie, long time, no see!"

Smilingly, "Ha! Ha! I still recognize you, Dad."

"And I think I know you, too. Let's start by summarizing the things we covered about the costs of **CAR LOANS** and **CAR LEASES**. Then as sort of a review quiz, as we move along, I'll ask you some things."

"Ok, I'll try my best to pass."

"In SITUATION 13 of Lesson 7, we examined various **OPTIONS** to purchase a **NEW CAR** using a **CAR LOAN**. The loan costs were calculated for a **TERM** of 60 months. That reflected the reality that the high cost of **NEW CAR** leads to many buyers taking out a **CAR LOAN** for as long as possible.

"Then, the corresponding results for a **TERM** of 36 months were calculated. The main trade-off is the lower **MONTHLY PAYMENT** and higher **CUMULATIVE INTEREST** of the 60-month **TERM** compared to the 36-month **TERM**.

"This table compares the two outcomes."

TOTAL COST OF LOAN: EFFECT OF LOAN TERM

OPTION	*ACTION	CASH DOWN T or S	LOAN AMT	LOAN TERM = 60			LOAN TERM = 36		
				MP	CI	TOTAL COST OF LOAN	MP	CI	TOTAL COST OF LOAN
1	P	0	23422	431.67	2478.52	25900	691.65	1479.33	24899
2	T or S	4500	18922	348.73	2002.33	20924	558.17	1185.11	20116
3	Tor S	6500	16922	311.87	1790.69	18712	499.71	1068.75	17990
4	T or S	7500	15922	293.44	1684.87	17606	470.18	1005.63	16926

*P = PURCHASE OUTRIGHT T = TRADE IN PRESENT CAR S =SELL PRESENT CAR PRIVAYELY

"We covered a lot, Dad. It's helpful to see all the numbers in one place."

"Yes we did. What do you see regarding the **CASH DOWN**?

Peering at the table for a few moments, Nicole replies, "I see that, whether the **PRESENT CAR** is traded in or sold privately, the higher is the amount of **CASH DOWN**, the lower is the **TOTAL COST OF LOAN**. But, that's obvious."

"You're correct. We examined the corresponding costs of doing a **CAR LEASE** and then purchasing it via a **LEASE/PURCHASE**. This table lists that comparison for each of the **LOAN TERMS** used."

TOTAL COST: TO PURCHASE vs.TO LEASE vs. TO LEASE/PURCHASE

			LOAN TERM = 60		LOAN TERM = 36		LOAN TERM =36	
OPTION	ACTION	CASH DOWN T or S	TOTAL COST OF CAR LOAN	TOTAL COST TO PURCHASE	TOTAL COST OF CAR LOAN	TOTAL COST TO PURCHASE	TOTAL COST TO LEASE	TOTAL COST TO LEASE/ PURCHASE
1	P	0	25900	27500	24899	26499	13811	29141
2	T or S	4500	20924	29024	20116	28216	15207	30537
3	T or S	6500	18712	26812	17990	26090	12939	28269
4	T or S	7500	17606	25706	16926	25026	11805	27135

"Nicole, what's it show about the total costs?"

"The **TOTAL COST TO LEASE** is always dramatically lower than the **TOTAL COST TO PURCHASE**. The negative is that, at the end of the lease, the leased car is returned. If, instead, the leased car is purchased outright at the end of the lease, then the **TOTAL COST TO LEASE/PURCHASE** is always greater than the **TOTAL COST TO PURCHASE**. Again, it's obvious. At the time you covered it, it really surprised me."

"Sweetie, the **TOTAL COST TO LEASE/PURCHASE** assumes you have the cash to pay the **RESIDUAL VALUE**. Many buyers would likely finance that subsequent purchase with a **SUBSEQUENT CAR LOAN**. The **CUMULATIVE INTEREST** paid would be an added cost. We calculated that effect before.

"Since a 3-year (36-month) **TERM** was used for the **CAR LEASE**, the **TERM** of the **SUBSEQUENT CAR LOAN** was taken as 2 years (24 months). That made the combined duration 5 years (60 months), which enabled a comparison with an outright purchase (no lease) for a **CAR LOAN** with a 5-year **TERM** (**OPTION 1** in the preceding table)."

"I remember you doing that and seeing it increased the **TOTAL COST TO LEASE/PURCHASE** by a small amount."

"That's right, Nicole. However, conceivably, the **SUBSEQUENT CAR LOAN** could be taken out with a 5-year **TERM**, making the total time for the **LEASE/ PURCHASE** 8 years (96 months). While likely an impractical and more expensive choice, the choice does exist.

"I did a table listing the costs of the **SUBSEQUENT CAR LOAN** for each of the two **SUBSEQUENT CAR LOAN TERMS**. They're based on a **SUBSEQUENT CAR LOAN AMOUNT** equal to the projected **RESIDUAL VALUE** agreed to in the **CAR LEASE**.

"The resulting **CUMULATIVE INTEREST** was added to the prior **TOTAL COST TO LEASE/ PURCHASE** (preceding table), to get the extended **TOTAL COST TO LEASE/ PURCHASE** reflecting the **SUBSEQUENT CAR LOAN.**"

TOTAL COST OF LEASE PURCHASE: EFFECT OF SUBEQUENT LOAN TERM

OPT.	ACTION	CASH DOWN FROM T or S	SUBEQUENT CAR LOAN TERM = 24				SUBEQUENT CAR LOAN TERM = 60			
			MP	CI	*TOTAL COST OF SUBS. CAR LOAN	TOTAL COST TO LEASE/ PURCHASE	MP	CI	*TOTAL COST OF SUBS. CAR LOAN	TOTAL COST TO LEASE/ PURCHASE
1	P	0	651	632	15612	29773	276	1528	16553	30669
2	T or S	4500	651	632	15612	31169	276	1528	16553	32065
3	T or S	6500	651	632	15612	28901	276	1528	16553	29797
4	T or S	7500	651	632	15612	27767	276	1528	16523	28623

*SUBSEQUENT CAR LOAN AMOUNT = RESIDUAL VALUE ** MP, CI VALUES ARE ROUNDED TO FIT COLUMN WIDTH

"What changes in the results, Sweetie?"

"I see that for a **SUBSEQUENT CAR LOAN TERM** of 24 months, only $632.00 is added to the **TOTAL COST TO LEASE/ PURCHASE.** For a **SUBSEQUENT CAR LOAN TERM** of 60 months, it increases to $1528.00 being added to the **TOTAL COST TO LEASE/ PURCHASE.**"

"That's right. It's a modest amount, but an extra cost. How can you lower it?"

"One way would be by paying a **DOWN PAYMENT** to lower that **SUBSEQUENT LOAN AMOUNT**. You could also accelerate its repayment by making larger **MONTHLY PAYMENTS.**"

"Correct again!

"You might wonder about the assumption that the **SUBSEQUENT LOAN AMOUNT** is equal to the **RESIDUAL VALUE.** After all, the **RESIDUAL VALUE** is negotiated at the outset of the **CAR LEASE.** It is an estimate of the **DEPRECIATED VALUE** the car will have at the end of the lease. At that time, the leased car is worth its actual **DEPRECIATED VALUE.** The common measure of that is its **BOOK VALUE.**"

Looking quizzical, Nicole chimes in, "Yeah, I never would have thought about it. It would be incredible coincidence if the **BOOK VALUE** equals the **RESIDUAL VALUE.**"

"Yes, Nicole. Almost invariably, they will be different. The result would be either a gain or a loss in paper value for the individual (in this case, Sam). Regardless, the lessor would be paid the agreed to **RESIDUAL VALUE.** To do so, I've assumed he or she borrows the needed money.

"A caution is in play. The **BOOK VALUE** of the leased car could be less than the **RESIDUAL VALUE.** Likely, only the lesser **SUBSEQUENT LOAN AMOUNT** would be approved. Out of pocket money would be needed to pay the shortage to the lessor."

"That's interesting to know. It makes sense."

"Dad, it seems to me that, if you like to frequently change to a different **NEW CAR**, a sequence of **CAR LEASES** does that. And a **CAR LEASE** has a much lower **MONTHLY PAYMENT** for its **TERM** than a **CAR LOAN**. And it cost less than purchasing the car outright."

"I tend to agree with you, Sweetie.

"There are some negatives to car leasing. What are they?"

After pausing to ponder it, Nicole gives a flurry of negatives.

"For one thing, you have a required **CASH DOWN**, and need up-front money for it. It can be a lot of money.

"You also may need to purchase more standard car insurance than for a purchased car.

"Then there's that **GAP INSURANCE**. Unless you have it, a stolen or totaled leased car leads to huge headaches, added costs and no car to drive anymore. Even with **GAP INSURANCE**, it is a difficult thing to deal with.

"Another concern is that leasing might or might not cover the costs of maintenance and usual repairs during its **TERM.**

"Oh, unless you strictly control mileage and avoid overuse, the charges for **EXCESS MILEAGE** and **EXCESS WEAR AND TEAR** may be huge surprises in costs.

"You also have to steadfastly resist all the extra front end and back end **FEES**. You might or might not succeed.

"And, after 3 years you've spent a lot of money and don't own a car."

"Wow! Sweetie, you certainly absorbed all the bad stuff. What do you think about purchasing the car for its **RESIDUAL VALUE** at the end of the **CAR LEASE**?"

"Dad, one thing rang out loud and clear. For purchasing the leased car, the **TOTAL COST TO LEASE/PURCHASE** is significantly higher than the **TOTAL COST TO PURCHASE.** I suppose it's possible the **RESIDUAL VALUE** is lower than the **BOOK VALUE** at the time**.** Like you said, I could purchase and resell it. I doubt even that would motivate me to do a **LEASE/PURCHASE**.

"Another thing is that when you do a **LEASE/PURCHASE** the **MANUFACTURER'S WARRANTY** has run out. You could face subsequent repairs for a car. Unless you purchase an **EXTENDED WARRANTY**, you pay for them yourself. As time goes on, they can become more frequent and more expensive costs.

"Yikes! I've brought back all those worries that made my knees wobbly."

"Sweetie, hearing your litany made mine wobbly, too. The good thing is that, clearly you are fully armed with awareness now.

"I've shared everything I can think of about purchasing or leasing a **NEW CAR**. When the time comes for you to purchase a **NEW CAR**, there are lots of decisions to make. Whichever you do, you have to decide either to trade-in, privately sell or keep your VW.

"Can you afford the high costs of **NEW CARS** these days? And depreciation will hit in a big way. Maybe a **USED CAR**, and its separate concerns, become reality.

"If affording the **MONTHLY PAYMENT** on a purchased car is an issue, then you will have to get a long-term **CAR LOAN.** In that case, leasing a car may be more beneficial if you don't need the car for more than a few years. It is surely has much lower ongoing and total costs.

"At the end of the **CAR LEASE,** you will be left with a dilemma. Clearly, you should walk away and not purchase the leased car. If you walk away, then you begin again deciding whether to lease again or purchase another car. If you want to purchase another one, then you have nothing to sell or trade-in."

"If you need a car for the foreseeable future, and will be using it for more than 15000 miles a year, perhaps you should think about buying a car outright. You won't have that long list of negative worries that make your knees wobble. You won't be watching mileage like a miser. You won't be feeling you threw money away with nothing to show for it at the end.

"Those are the larger things that come to mind. You will have a lot to think about, but I'm very confident in you. My Smartest Pants daughter will do it carefully and make the Smartest Decisions by herself."

"Dad, I can't possibly say thank you enough for preparing me to take on those decisions. When we began, I was just sitting in the dugout and hoping to play. Now I'm ready to take the field, step up to the plate, and swat one toward the fence. I'll do my best to make the ball go over it."

"I'm sure you will, Sweetie. I'm very sure you will!"

Epilogue

—By Nicole Ehrlich

It is a Saturday afternoon and Nicole is visiting her parents for a long weekend. Dad knows she is coming and is waiting on the front porch, reading the paper. Nicole has told him that she has a big surprise for him, so he's doubly excited to see her.

Dad hears a sound and looks up from his paper to see Nicole pulling into the driveway behind the wheel of a new car, a huge grin on her face. She hops out of the car, almost trembling with excitement.

"Hi Dad!" she smiles guiltily as she comes up to hug her Dad."

"Hi Peanut! I see you more than just 'thought' about which path you were going to take for getting a car," Dad chuckles in disbelief.

Nodding happily Nicole replies, "After working through all those examples, I had a fairly good idea of what path I would to take. I just wanted to research it a little more on my own before I told you. But once I was approved for a loan from my bank and went to the dealership, it all happened so fast—my friends were definitely right about that! I'll tell you all about it after I see mom and we catch up."

After Nicole, Dad, and Mom have lunch and catch up, they go to Dad's office. Nicole jumps into Dad's big chair with a smile on her face.

"I'm going to be the teacher today," she announces, "It's time for you to sharpen your pencils Dad!"

Chuckling, Dad complies and sits in the smaller chair next to her. "Alright, show me what you got."

"Alright. After we went through all the car leasing stuff I decided that wasn't for me. Even though it seemed like a deal to pay half of the car price, I didn't want to be left with nothing at the end of three years except $10000+ less. If I bought the car, I would be able to sell it down the road for some money, even if it was significantly less than what I paid for it new."

"That makes sense Sweetie. Personally, I would have been deterred by the uncertainty of insuring a leased car. **GAP INSURANCE** can give you some protection, but I would still be worried about totaling the car or having it stolen early on in the lease."

"I agree Dad. That was another reason I was uncomfortable with it.

"It wasn't the only deciding factor for choosing a **NEW CAR** though. I also thought about the warranty you talked about. The **USED CARS** made me worry that something might go wrong with them sooner rather than later. I've had friends buy **USED CARS** only to find that the car was a 'lemon' and they had to sink thousands of dollars into it to keep it running. That was not a position I wanted to be put in. If I got a **NEW CAR** I knew it would be reliable and I wouldn't have to worry about that."

"I've seen several people get 'lemons' for cars as well. They generally end up having to sell them or salvage what they can to get another car, so another good decision Peanut!"

"Thanks Dad! Next on my wish list was gas mileage. It's a big deal to me since I have to commute into the city 5 days a week for work. Stopping by the gas station every week to fill up my car because it only gets 20 miles a gallon hasn't been fun. I've seen so many **NEW CARS** that advertise getting 30+ mpg in the city and sometimes around 40 mpg on the highway! That sounded like a dream. I added this as the last item on my wish list.

"This brings me to one big concern I had in buying a **NEW CAR**—losing thousands of dollars when I drove it off the lot. Even though I saw buying as a better choice than leasing, I wanted to reduce the impact of this potential loss as much as possible. I remembered you mentioned that some cars depreciate faster than others. I wanted to find a car that would depreciate the slowest. My hope was, down the road, I would be able to sell it if I wanted to upgrade.

"I used these as my starting point to find what car would fit my needs best. After hours of research, I zeroed in on an electric car. It seemed to fit my life perfectly! With it, I never would have to go to the gas station again."

"Sounds like you had a lot figured out before we were done with our lessons!" Dad laughed.

"You explained things well enough as we went along, I knew what I could and couldn't discount as right for me. It wasn't too hard after that."

"Well, I'm happy to have such a good student!"

"And I such a good teacher," Nicole smiled. "Anyway, before I went too much into deciding what car I wanted, I knew I needed to sell my **VW NEW BEETLE**. Selling it first would give me a better idea of what I could afford. Trading it in didn't seem like the best choice for the money. For this reason, I put an add up on Craigslist, marketing it a bit high so people could negotiate down to a price I was comfortable with. I also thought this would allow the buyer to feel like they were getting a good deal.

"This part happened pretty fast! I got several calls the first few days and ended up selling it for $3750, which was about the Kelly Blue Book value. And don't worry, I was safe and met the people during the day time in well populated areas!"

"I'm glad to hear that Peanut."

“Now that I had my car sold, I ended up renting one for $200 a week, which I realized wasn’t cheap, but I wanted to go about the process in a way I felt comfortable.”

“I agree. Though that seems like a lot of money, as long as you didn’t keep it up for too long it isn’t too much.”

“Thanks Dad.

“At that point I started to look more into electric cars. I found that a lot of them seem to lose value quickly, which almost made me backtrack and start again. It was then that I found the Tesla cars. They have been holding their value better than any other electric cars on the market.

“I first found the Model S and Model X, which were way out of my price range. Then, however, I found the Model 3. It’s MSRP was $35000 going in, which was at the cap of what I was willing to pay. Since the car seemed to fit my needs so well, however, I decided to see if I could make it happen.

“From there I went to my bank to see what kind of loan I could obtain. My banker made it fairly easy, and I found that I qualified for a $30,000 loan at 3.2% interest for 48 months. At first, I was a little bummed that it wasn’t the full $35000 of the suggested retail of the car, but then I remembered you talking about cash rebates when buying a new car. I figured a $5000 rebate was reasonable. I also had the money from the sale of my VW BEETLE to apply to it, as well as $4250 I had saved up for the down payment. I knew that wouldn’t cover the entire price of car, plus the tax, plus all the registration fees. Thus this was yet another reason I wanted to negotiate with the dealer. If I couldn’t negotiate the price down at least a few thousand dollars, then I wouldn’t be able to get my new dream car!”

Aside: The Model 3 has not yet come out, but production starts in mid-2017. The expected incentives for this car are $7500. Since this is not set in stone, 2/3 was taken for this value.

“The negotiation is key, and difficult for many, but with those kinds of encouragements I bet you did well Sweetie!”

“Well, I tried! Before I went to the dealership I was fairly nervous about the negotiation. I wasn’t sure what to expect and I didn’t want to come out of the process feeling like I hadn’t made the best deal just because I wasn’t assertive enough. This lead me to read a few psychology articles on how to deal with car salesmen, which were extremely helpful. I then walked bravely into the dealership, feeling more confident that I could make a deal I’d be happy with.”

“It sounds like you may have been reaching a bit to get this dream car, but I’m happy with the precautions you took!” Dad said.

Nicole smiled and breathed a sigh of relief. “When I sat down with the closer, he certainly tried to have me order all the bells and whistles for the car. I couldn’t add too much on because I knew

I couldn't afford it. Ultimately, I added $1200 of options that I really wanted.

"I then found out I was right about the $5000 cash rebate I could apply to the price of the car. They tried pretty hard to get me to finance with them. At first I wasn't wild about the idea, but then decided to use it as a negotiation tactic. They offered me a loan for 4.0% **ANNUAL INTEREST** with a 48-month term and taking $2000 off the car if I did the financing through them. The **ANNUAL INTEREST** seemed quite a bit higher than the bank, but I didn't have a good feel for how it would ultimately affect the price of the car. It was then they left me in an office alone to think over what course of action I wanted to take.

"I pulled out my phone and a copy of the **CAR-BASE LOAN TABLE** I brought with me, then did the calculation on how much it would cost to turn down their offer and finance with the bank."

Pulling out a thumb drive, Nicole navigates through Dad's computer to pull up her prepared spreadsheets."

SITUATION N1

"The **SELLING PRICE** of the car is $35000, at a 7.5% tax, $1200 of options are added, $4250 **CASH DOWN**, and $3750 **CASH DOWN FROM SALE**. The **TERM** of the loan is 48 months and the terms indicated 3.2% **ANNUAL INTEREST**."

SALES TAX = $35000 x 7.5/100 = $2625

LOAN AMOUNT = $35000 + $1200 + $2625 - $5000 - $4250 - $3750 = $25825

SCALING FACTOR = 25.825

SITUATION N1 – CONTINUED

"Now I will interpolate since my **ANNUAL RATE OF INTEREST** isn't one of the given values. I need to look at the **CAR-BASE LOAN TABLE** values for 2.00% and 6.00%. Then 3.2% is 1.2/4 = 3/10 between those. Here are my calculations."

MONTHLY PAYMENT AT 2.00% = 25.825 x $21.70 = $560.40

CUMULATIVE INTEREST AT 2.00% = 25.825 x $41.37 = $1068.38

MONTHLY PAYMENT AT 6.00% = 25.825 x $23.49 = $606.63

CUMULATIVE INTERESTAT 6.00% = 25.825 x $127.28 = $3287.01

SITUATION N1 – CONTINUED

"Now I need to interpolate for 3.2%. My calculations are as follows."

MONTHLY PAYMENT = $560.40 + 3/10 ($606.63 - $560.40) = $574.27

CUMULATIVE INTEREST = $1068.38 + 3/10 ($3287.01 - $1068.38) = $1733.97

TOTAL LOAN COST = $25825 + $1733.97 = $27558.97

"How am I doing so far Dad?"

"Very well Sweetie! Please, keep going!"

"Okay, then I did the calculation for how much it would cost me to accept the higher **ANNUAL RATE OF INTEREST**, but also get $2000 off the total price of the car."

SITUATION N2

The **SELLING PRICE** of the car is $33000, at a 7.5% tax, $1200 of options are added, $4250 **CASH DOWN**, and $3750 **CASH DOWN FROM SALE**. The term of the loan is 48 months.

SALES TAX = $33000 x 7.5/100 = $2475

LOAN AMOUNT = $33000 + $1200 + $2475 - $5000 - $4250 - $3750 = $23675

SCALING FACTOR = 23.675

SITUATION N2 – CONTINUED

"Again I have to interpolate looking at the **CAR BASE LOAN TABLE** values for 2.00% and 6.00%. Then 3.5% is 1.5/4 = 3/8 between those. First are my calculations for 2.00%."

MONTHLY PAYMENT AT 2.00% = 23.675 x $21.70 = $513.75

CUMULATIVE INTEREST AT 2.00% = 23.675 x $41.37 = $979.43

MONTHLY PAYMENT AT 6.00% = 23.675 x $23.49 = $556.13

CUMULATIVE INTEREST AT 6.00% = 23.675 x $127.28 = $3013.35

SITUATION N2 - CONTINUED

"Finally, I can interpolate for 3.50%."

MONTHLY PAYMENT AT 3.50% = $513.75 + 3/8 ($556.13 - $513.75) = $529.64

CUMULATIVE INTEREST AT 3.50% = $979.43 + 3/8 ($3013.35- $979.43) = $1742.15

TOTAL LOAN COST = $23675 + $1742.15 = $25417.15

"What did you observe from the alternative Sweetie?"

"I found that accepting their offer would save me $27558.97 - $25417.15 = $2141.82. I saw that I would be paying $1742.15 - $1733.97 = $8.18 more in **CUMULATIVE INTEREST**. I was also paying $2625 - $2475 = $150 less in sales tax. The difference was surprisingly insignificant to me! Therefore, I deemed the deal a fair one, and one I would be proud of."

"Why do you think the **CUMULATIVE INTEREST** was so close in these two cases Peanut?"

"This actually made me pause when I was in the dealership. It seemed so odd that an **ANNUAL RATE OF INTEREST** increase of 0.8% could lead to such a small difference. Then I realized I was paying the higher interest on a smaller amount of money. That's why in the end it came out to be about the same thing."

"Very good Smarty Pants! Please continue on with your tale."

"Once the closer came back in, I happily accepted their financing offer with the dealership to finance the car. From there, it was signing a bunch of papers and then them handing me the key!"

"It was very smart of you to think about using their financing as a tool for negotiation. I hadn't ever thought about doing that! I may have to try that with the next car I buy."

"Are you saying I outsmarted you, Dad?" Nicole asked with a grin.

“In a way, I suppose so Sweetie. More so, however, I would say you bested the dealership by being so well prepared.

“I do have to admit that I haven’t thought too much about electric cars and may have to look into one for my next car. Right now the leap scares me a bit. Perhaps I will have to do more research and figure everything out I can about them.”

Nicole smiled, “I guess I’ll just have to keep trying to outsmart you. I’m glad I got you thinking about electric cars! They’re an excellent choice.

“Also, I would like to thank you for everything you have taught me thus far. You made the scary, complex process much simpler than most people experience. If I was worried about all the numbers going over my head, I think I would have gotten flustered and not been able to make a decision I was proud of. Thank you Dad.”

“I’m happy to hear you say that. Thank you for being open to my guidance and jumping in with both feet. It’s fulfilling for me to see you becoming more and more financially responsible as an adult.”

“It feels good to not be so scared of debt anymore. You know, I used to think of it as one of the four letter words you never let me say as a kid. You’ve made me comfortable enough with it I realize it isn’t always a bad thing. As long as I know how to deal with it and keep paying off my loans, I will be fine in the long run!”

“I’m sure that you will be.”

“I suppose I won’t need any more lessons for a while, but in good time I may be back with questions about buying a condo or house when I can financially afford it. Do you think you can help me with that too?”

With a smile on his face Dad nods, “Whenever that day comes, just send your dear old Dad an SOS.

Evening Gazette

Got a new car on your mind? Buying a new car - Part 1 of a two-part series

FICTIONAL NICOLE

FICTIONAL NICOLE@EVENINGAZETTE.COM

Your aged, non-vintage VW bug is nearing the sputtering stage. Its odometer is showing a scary number. The only car you've ever had is headed for extinction. You've got a NEW CAR on your mind. Dad bought the bug. It's your turn, now. You're entering the first-time buyer world. There's a bunch to handle and think about Help! Here's some guidance.

Ghost of Car Buying Past: Traditionally, you searched tons of newspaper car ads. On Sundays, you walked the lots to check out cars. Honed in on one, you needed to visit the dealership and encounter a car salesperson for the first time. You were nervous and feeling anxiety. You had heard it's pretty intimidating. And that a sale can happen quickly and without fully understanding everything that transpired.

A cheery salesperson greeting comes, "Can I help you? What kind of car are you looking for?" Succumbing, you gave base details. The car selling process had begun. Getting an honest and fair deal can be a heavy duty mental endeavor. That's why a lot of people loath having to buy a car.

Skipping the woes, and worries we all have in navigating through that process; you've settled on a car you want. Skipping further along, the day to buy arrived. The salesperson has achieved his or her task - motivating you to buy a car. Having mostly floundered through MANUFACTURER'S SUGGESTED RETAIL PRICE, BASE PRICE, FACTORY INVOICE PRICE, ASKING PRICE, CASH REBATES etc., you needed to arrive at a PURCHASE PRICE you're willing and able to pay.

You were asked how much CASH DOWN you will be paying. I hope you had a solid figure or narrow range determined. If you are trading in your VW bug, a trade-in value was offered. You needed to be wary of a low-ball offer. Hopefully, you researched actual value and negotiated a fair amount of CASH DOWN FROM TRADE-IN. Subtracting those payments yielded the LOAN AMOUNT you needed.

Entered the "finance person" whose task was to get you do any needed financing via a loan from the dealership. Hopefully, you had already arranged a pre-approved LOAN AMOUNT from your bank or credit union and could compare. Maybe the dealership offered similar or better

Past that hurdle, entered the "closer" who tried to sell add-ons; (service and maintenance plan? extended warranty?) and settle any negotiation issues.

The outcome was a SELLING PRICE plus OPTIONS. The SALES TAX monster added to that cost. That all done, you signed the PURCHASE AGREEMENT. Likely it left you feeling a bit unsettled and captured? Did you get the best deal possible?

Ghost of Car Buying Present:

Fortunately, times have changed. The physical leg work and mental worries of car buying have almost become extinct. That dinosaur age has succumbed to the digital-electronic age. There are lots of resources your Dad didn't have when he bought your bug. When he was the first time buyer himself, he probably had none of them. Nowadays you can even buy a car and never step on to a car lot.

Print ads are augmented by digitally formatted ads on the dealership website, photographs included. For many, 3-D virtual imagery allows you remotely walk around the car. Using online tools at *www.kbb.com*, the website of Kelley Blue Book, you can estimate the range of market value for a NEW CAR or a USED CAR.

Websites of the National Auto Dealers Association (www.nada.com) and Edmunds, Inc. (www.edmunds.com) are popular, too. Both enable you to find dealerships in your locale offering the make, model and year of cars you specify. Edmunds offers you a quote to purchase it, via them, on-line. Of course, at either, you can assess the trade-in value of your VW.

CARFAX, Inc. markets CARFAX VEHICLE HISTORY REPORTS via www.carfax.co. A CARFAX report provides the damage and repair and servicing history of specific cars.

Planning to go to a dealership? auto.howstuffworks.com/buying selling/car-buying.htm and www. Car buying tips.com help you with understanding the nitty gritty of the buying process. The latter helps you with the nervous, scary aspects of going through it and to avoid pitfalls.

Looking to avoid all the work? You can by having a CAR BROKER to do everything for you, on your behalf. Similar to a real estate broker being paid a fee to help you buy a home and do all the legal paper work, a CAR BROKER finds cars meeting your specifications. He or she brings them to you to look at and test drive. To buy one, you do all the negotiating and sales transactions through the CAR BROKER. You buy the car at his or her location. You never have to step foot on a car lot.

How's that for progress? I bet you can't wait to tell your Dad. Maybe you'll outsmart him. I keep trying to outsmart mine on a financial matter. So far I haven't been able to do that, Maybe one of us will get it done, sooner rather than later. If you do outsmart yours, then please let me in on your secret.

Evening Gazette

Got a new car on your mind? Leasing a new car - Part 2 of a two-part series

FICTIONAL NICOLE

FICTIONAL.NICOLE@EVENINGAZETTE.COM

Judging from the car ads in the Evening Gazette, leasing dominates them. If you've never looked into it, here's what it's all about.

Unlike daily or weekly car rentals, the time period for leasing a car is three years. That coincides with the period of the manufacturer's warranty. Although you don't borrow money, it is a loan. You are borrowing a car and will be financing through a CAR LEASE. By signing one, you incur the indicated MONTHLY PAYMENT and some fees. Sounds simple. It isn't.

Leasing is very involved. For newbies,www.edmunds.com/car-leasing/10-steps-to-leasing-a-new-car. html summarizes the steps. Sub-links like "pros and cons of leasing" give detailed content. www.carbuying tips .com/lease2.html covers "ins-and outs" of getting a fair outcome. Its "Auto Lease Glossary" defines terminology, with alerts about "Don't..." and "Never..." Let's take on terminology. Take a deep breath.

During the TERM of the CAR LEASE, you pay a MONTHLY DEPRECIATION FEE. It's for the decreasing market value. It's based on the CAPITALIZED COST = SELLING PRICE + OPTIONS value of the car. You might get a CASH REBATE, put CASH DOWN and CASH DOWN FROM TRADE-IN. Subtracting those gives the NET CAPITALIZED COST.

RESIDUAL VALUE is the market value at the end of the TERM. Subtracting it from the NET CAPITALIZED COST gives the NET VALUE. That's what you borrow and pay back over time. Divide it by 36 to get the MONTHLY DEPRECIATION FEE. For NET CAPITALIZED COST of $30000 and RESIDUAL VALUE of $20000, the MONTHLY DEPRECIATION FEE = $10000/36 = $277.78.

The lessor charges a MONTHLY FINANCE CHARGE and it's done in an odd way. The TOTAL FINANCED AMOUNT is the sum of the NET CAPITALIZED COST and the RESIDUAL VALUE of the car. In our case, TOTAL FINANCED AMOUNT = $50000.00. The TOTAL FINANCED AMOUNT is divided by 200 to get the MONTHLY FINANCED AMOUNT CHARGE = $50000.00/200 = $250.00. Then you multiply by the MONTHLY RATE OF INTEREST, which is ANNUAL RATE OF INTEREST/12. For an ANNUAL RATE OF INTEREST of 3.00%, MONTHLY FINANCE CHARGE = $250.00 x (3/12) = $62.50. The TOTAL FINANCE CHARGE = $62.50 x 36 months = $2250.00

Confusingly, in the CAR LEASE it is done differently. A MONEY FACTOR is used. The MONEY FACTOR is the ANNUAL RATE OF INTEREST divided by 2400. Multiplying it times the TOTAL FINANCED AMOUNT gives the MONTHLY FINANCE CHARGE. MONEY FACTOR = 3.00/2400 = 0.00125 and MONTHLY FINANCE CHARGE = 0.00125 x $50000.00 = $62.50. If the 200 and 2400 mystify you, you're not alone.

Unsurprisingly, a MONTHLY SALES TAX is charged on the MONTHLY TAXABLE AMOUNT = MONTHLY DEPRECIATION FEE + MONTHLY FINANCE CHARGE. For a SALES TAX RATE of 6.00%, the MONTHLY SALES TAX = (6.00/100) x ($277.78 + $62.50) = $20.42.TOTAL SALES TAX = MONTHLY SALES TAX x 36 months = $735.12. Beware, in some states, the CASH REBATE is taxed. Some states tax the entire CAPITALIZED COST. All CASH DOWN is ignored.

Combining the three monthly amounts gives the MONTHLY PAYMENT of $360.70. The TOTAL PAYMENTS = $360.70 x 36 months = $12985.20.

Over the lease TERM, there will be some NORMAL WEAR AND TEAR.
An example is worn carpeting. For all EXCESS WEAR AND TEAR you'll pay an EXCESS WEAR AND TEAR CHARGE. An example is a broken CD player. Get written criteria for both.

The manufacturer's warranty will cover the major unexpected repairs. If the car incurs any damage, then you must make, and pay, for repairs needed. If caused in an accident, then the STANDARD CAR INSURANCE, which you must buy, covers them. At the end of the CAR LEASE, you will be charged for any existing RESIDUAL DAMAGE. That's anything that did not exist when you leased the car. Resist any an up-front SECURITY DEPOSIT for possible EXCESS WEAR AND TEAR and/or RESIDUAL DAMAGE.

Your lease should specify who is responsible for usual maintenance costs and how frequently. If they try to sell you a maintenance service plan, be wary about possible inflated prices. You cannot drive endless miles. CAR LEASES include a MILEAGE LIMIT. Typically, it's 10,000 to 15,000 miles per year. For EXCESS MILEAGE you incur an EXCESS MILEAGE CHARGE. Commonly, the EXCESS MILAGE RATE is about $0.10 to $0.20 per excess mile. If the MILEAGE LIMIT is 10000 miles and at the end of the CAR LEASE, it has been driven 35000 miles, then the EXCESS MILEAGE is 5000 miles. For an EXCESS MILEAGE RATE of $0.15 per mile, the EXCESS MILEAGE CHARGE = $0.15 x 5000 = $750.00.

Watch out for fees. An ACQUISITION FEE might be charged for processing. You might encounter a BANK FEE and a DEALER SERVICE FEE. A DISPOSITION FEE might be charged at the end for preparing it for resale. If you want or have to terminate a lease early, an EARLY TERMINATION FEE might be charged. Some fees are minor, some are steep. Some are negotiable. Give it a try.

Oh, how did I find out all this stuff? Dad, thank you for teaching me all of it. When I began dreaming of a NEW CAR, I sought and got your great advice, as always. ! Now that I've learned how to do it, I'm about to get a new car myself, on my own. I might even outsmart you, finally.

ACKNOWLEDGEMENTS

The cornerstone for my book series is my immediate family. All of its content reflects attentively addressing common place financial matters experienced during my long-time marriage to my loving and caring wife, Irene, and our raising my wonderful daughter, Jody Zorn. Through those years, and still, I have been and am deeply committed to maintaining our familial financial well-being. Evolving greater and greater understanding of everyday debt situations and properly handling them is quintessential to our monetary security. Having them in my life led to my wanting to write about the techniques and insights I evolved over the years in order to accomplish that.

Being, in large part, pragmatic and mathematical, I have always seen proper handling of debt needs as a requiring understanding how the numerical aspects are calculated, ability to check or do them myself, and skilled application of that knowledge. While not a passion for them, Irene and Jody lived with and accepted this mathematical-oriented husband and Dad. I cannot help analyzing anything and everything involving numbers. In this case, the numbers were valuable dollars and cents. It is an understatement to say they had to "bear with me" for all those years. Indeed they did, sometimes with quizzical looks or frowns. But, they did. And I am deeply thankful for their understanding and patience with me. They endured spreadsheet after spreadsheet after spreadsheet and tedious explanations that came with almost every financial planning decision of importance. Each was done with my love and wish for wise decisions on their behalves. In writing my book series, I sought to share that wish with each of my readers.

In volume one, **THE COLLEGE EXPERIENCE**, I conveyed my appreciation to many individuals encountered along the path of writing it, who contributed directly and indirectly to its content, clarity, realism and my will and spirit to complete it. It was expressed in an extended way and, hopefully, you have seen and read it. If not, then I invite you to read it on my author website (www.debtisafourletterword.net). Some of them, and others, contributed similar spark, attentiveness, and help with content to volume two.

As related to this volume two, **THE CAR FINANCING EXPERIENCE**:

As a high school student, Timea ("Timi") Balogh was a reviewer for the first volume. Her math acumen served me well. Via her reads, I was better able to present numerical material effectively for the 16 to 18-year old readers. Equally important, as an avid, voracious reader, Timi let me know whenever my wording was off target for young people like her. Post publication, and now in college, she helped in other ways. She shared the table at my first formal book signing at the Loveland Library and handled the Square device more adeptly than I could. She also partnered as the fictional daughter, Nicole, with me (as the fictional Dad) in a reading of an excerpt from the book for attenders. Nearly bowing out at the 11th hour, she overlooked/overcame fever etc. to enable the show to go on. It was an impressive commitment and made for a wonderful experience. Thank you!,Timi.

I gave my fictional Nicole her name on behalf of the very real and indispensable Nicole Erhlich. Now a college graduate, during her prior studies she was my other young person reviewer, and a tad older than Timi. She's been my dedicated sidekick through both volumes.

From my post http://www.writingbugncw.com/2017/04/from-professor-to-publisher.html#links, "As juxtaposition, I hired a trusted college student to proofread and advise me. I gave her my red pen. She uses it well. The result: She helped make it fit the intended young reader, her generation." From my post http://www.writingbugncw.com/2017/04/from-professor-to-publisher.html#links." My skilled college kid sidekick, Nicole, helps reconcile my past with my present. A part of that younger me has returned. Nicole reads drafts, edits like a caring critic, and provides lost pieces. Need a synonym? She provides a link to contemporary on-line tools. Erred in punctuation? When did they drop they double-space after a period? Nicole knows."

Nicole and I joust on wording. Nicole would never say auto. To her it's a car. My initial use of "auto" changed to "car". My fictional daughter becomes more current and realistic. My fictional Dad communicates with her more effectively. They have fun. I enjoyed and treasured Nicole's backstopping my entire volumes 1 and 2. Lesson, hire a college kid at affordable cost to help get the manuscript ready for professional copy editing etc. For me it's easy, I hired and worked with many of them in my academic career. I loved giving them a wee bit of financial aid.

Oh, Nicole is brainy and technical. Numbers and prudence in monetary matters are her things, too. She majored in mathematics and minored in physics. As a result, math errors usually caught her attention and corrections were made. And she fully understood "acceleration". Joining her and her family at her college Commencement was a very special day in my life. Congratulations again, Nicole.

ASIDE: Methinks (knows) Nicole is a fine writer herself and I hope she tweaks some published works into her very full and intensive life. It's why I invited her to write the Epilogue to volume two. I am grateful she accepted. She wrote a superb one. It made me smile a lot. Now my readers also know she is a fine writer.

Graciously, Chelsea Creekmore (financial service consultant at Public Service Credit Union) read an early draft of this volume. Conversations with her updated me on the relationship between FICO SCORES, AGE OF VEHICLE, and TERM of car loans in setting loan interest rates at her institution. She handles many of my own loans and periodic chats added to that and details about loans in general. I also learned that PSCU offers GAP INSURANCE, as likely do other banking institutions. She also pointed me in the direction of Jay Nelson.

It's fair to say most people, including myself, experience hesitancy when it comes to stopping in at a used car dealership. Negative anecdotes abound and if feels like "hit or miss" when chancing to do so. For volume 2, I actually interviewed one, sort of. Jay Nelson, operator of Northern Auto Brokers in Fort Collins, Colorado primarily brokers car. He also has some used car stock on site for sale. Amidst ongoing customer traffic, he generously and graciously gave me about 2 hours of his time in conversation. He corroborated much of my understanding of car brokering and car leasing. Atop that he added new information which improved my content. I am indebted and grateful to him for much of what I wrote regarding car brokering. He's the reason I wrote, "Look for signs of a good person and displays of family photos etc. Get a good inner feeling and sense of peace of mind." He exemplified that and the several photos of his family and children said a lot. His sleepy dog at my foot added to my positive impression.

In a recent hailstorm, Irene's aging car (2003 Toyota Highlander, 200,000+ miles) was heavily damaged. That led to it being "totaled" by her insurance carrier. While not "totaled", my daughter and son-in-law's (Jody and Zach Zorn) two cars were damaged, too. Consequently, I got first-hand experience in car insurance coming into play for those circumstances. Negotiating all the involved steps was helpful to improving book content on the subject of car leasing.

Conversations with my State Farm insurance agent, Gary Cramer, provided detailed insight into handling a claim resulting in a totaled car and the implications of its salvage value. His advice on forfeiting vs. keeping the totaled car and the implications of each were invaluable. I worked some of it into the coverage of the insurance consequences of a totaled car.

Our insurer offered a $7136.00 insurance payout and they take the car vs. $4357.00 ($2779.00 salvage subtracted) and we keep the car. The best salvage value we could find ourselves was $2000.00. We took the $7136.00. Related to that, Jody and Zach's 2014 Honda Pilot had two months remaining on a car lease. Irene and I purchased that car, as they chose to lease a new one. They listened to my advice, given in Lesson 11, about not purchasing it themselves at the end of the car lease. Jody and Zach, I thank you for making the deal and working through this. As they say, it's a Win-Win!

As in volume 1, there are no formal referenced publications behind this book series. I simply wrote my story as the reflection of my personal experiences and growth in managing my personal debt for my family, and viewpoints, approaches and techniques I evolved over time. Perusing the web was involved. Of course, in doing searches, uncountable items come up as related to any topic being searched. They varied from useful to somewhat pertinent to odd and way off target. Mostly, the pertinent ones were overlapping and/or somewhat repetitive. Those which gave me added insight and information or were used directly are cited in the body.

As I wrote this book, I continued my regimen (essentially every other Thursday) of writing stints in the lounge at a local Marriott hotel. It has stretched to three or four years. Cleaning people shoving me out of my home base necessitated that regimen. Numerous Marriott staff people have grown accustomed to my laptop and I hanging around. I was never asked to leave. To the contrary, it seemed I was very welcomed to be there. They got to know this fellow and any absences were surely noticed. When I was there, writing was smooth and easy.

Barista Diane Curry still brought me my usual "diet Pepsi and martini glass of salty snacks" and served my occasional lunch orders - always with a smile and well wishing. She got occasional sneak-peeks or readings of some passages and reacted. Her smiles or laughs at intended humorous ones told me to keep them as is. I'm very thankful for her putting up with my omnipresence and having let me take up the same old seat almost every time.

I am immensely indebted to and appreciative of Kerrie Flanagan; my consultant, writing coach and editor for this book series. She founded Northern Colorado Writers, a group that supports and encourages writers of all levels and genres, and was its Director for eight years. Kerrie is also the publisher of Hot Chocolate Press. She's an author and freelance writer and a very busy person. You'd never know it from her calm, patient, welcoming personality and manner. When meeting with her, her at-large world seemed invisible and my little writing task was her caring focus. I am indebted for her contribution to the launch of this book and preparation for its marketing and promotion.

Following a busy family and business relocation from Denver to the suburbs (with my grand-baby and grand-toddler in tow to adjust and resettle), Jody and Zach of Zorn Photography did the photo shoot for the front and back cover photos. Previously, they did my author's photo. Jody also formatted the written matter for the cover, spine and back of the book. It was deeply special to have them team with me and dedicate their great talents to those key pieces of the book. Jody also set up my initial webs and Kerrie Flanagan updated it for the release of this volume.

High school student Sophia Alcott (daughter of my CrossFit pal, Katherine) posed as the fictional daughter, again. It was a fun session and I am deeply grateful to her and her parents' willingness and her courage to participate that way and her sister Amanda for cheering her on.

Most importantly I close just as I did in volume 1. Writing a book is an intensive, time consuming process. Writing a book is also a mix of inspiration, labor of good will, determination, persistence, and seemingly endless revisions and refinements. The goal is to "get it right" for the readership. Writing a book of this type also flows through frequent frustrations and setbacks. There are lots of repeated minutiae tasks: rechecking all data and math, correcting discovered mistakes, checking consistency of formats, renumbering Situations and Exercises, etc. Then interest rates and other parameters change periodically. One redoes a lot of numbers and exhaustive tables. Seemingly, when the book is just about completed, new information happens to arise and requires last minute additions. No author survives the gauntlet without periodic visible and auditory expression of desire to figuratively heave things. I was no exception. Above all appreciations, I love my wife for her patience, understanding and ability to block out temperamental moments and frustrated phases when they came along and her caring to tell me to carry on.

APPENDIX I – ALTERNATE SOLUTION TO SITUATION 12 - LESSON 6

STEP 1:

From the **CAR-BASE LOAN TABLE**, for an **ANNUAL RATE OF INTEREST** = 2.00% and a **TERM** of 36 months:

BASE LOAN MONTHLY PAYMENT = $28.64

BASE LOAN CUMULATIVE INTEREST = $31.13

For a **TERM** of 48 months:

BASE LOAN MONTHLY PAYMENT = $21.70

BASE LOAN CUMULATIVE INTEREST = $41.37

For a **TERM** of 42 months:

BASE LOAN MONTHLY PAYMENT = $28.64 + 1/2(21.70 – $28.64) = $25.17

BASE LOAN CUMULATIVE INTEREST = $31.13 + 1/2 ($41.37 – $31.13) = $36.25

STEP 2:

From the **CAR-BASE LOAN TABLE**, for an **ANNUAL RATE OF INTEREST** = 6.00% and a **TERM** of 36 months:

BASE LOAN MONTHLY PAYMENT = $30.42

BASE LOAN CUMULATIVE INTEREST = $95.19

For a **TERM** of 48 months:

BASE LOAN MONTHLY PAYMENT = $23.49

BASE LOAN CUMULATIVE INTEREST = $127.28

For a **TERM** of 42 months:

MONTHLY PAYMENT = $30.42+ 1/2(23.49 – $30.42) = $26.96

BASE LOAN CUMULATIVE INTEREST = $95.19 + 1/2 ($127.28 - $95.19) = $111.24

SUMMARIZING:

For 2.00% and 42 months,

BASE LOAN MONTHLY PAYMENT = $25.17

BASE LOAN CUMULATIVE INTEREST = $36.25

For 6.00% and 42 months,

BASE LOAN MONTHLY PAYMENT = $26.96

BASE LOAN CUMULATIVE INTEREST = $111.24

STEP 3: The approximate results for 3.00% are 1/4 of the way between those two results.

BASE LOAN MONTHLY PAYMENT = $25.17 + 1/4(26.96 – $25.17) = $25.62

BASE LOAN CUMULATIVE INTEREST = $36.25 + 1/4(111.24 – $36.25) = $55.00

STEP 4: Scaling the results.

MONTHLY PAYMENT = 7.50 x $25.62 = $192.15

CUMULATIVE INTEREST = 7.50 x $55.00 = $412.50

APPENDIX II - CHEAT SHEET FOR CAR LOAN COSTS AND SELECTED EXERCISES

NOTE: Heavy BOLD block applies to LESSON 6. For Lesson 5, enter zeros.

GIVEN INFORMATION	CALCULATED RESULTS

GIVEN INFORMATION		CALCULATED RESULTS	
SELLING PRICE			
OPTIONS			
		SELLING PRICE + OPTIONS	
CASH REBATE			
CASH DOWN			
*BOOK VALUE OF PRESENT CAR			
*CASH DOWN FROM TRADE-IN			
or *CASH DOWN FROM SALE			
** IF NO PRESENT CAR INVOLVED: ENTER 0*			
		LOAN AMOUNT = SELLING PRICE + OPTIONS - CASH REBATE - CASH DOWN - CASH DOWN FROM TRADE-IN - CASH DOWN FROM SALE	
APR(%)			
TERM (MONTHS)			
BASE MONTHLY PAYMENT			
*CAR BASE-LOAN TABLE: CUMULATIVE INTEREST			
* VALUE TAKEN FROM TABLE and, if necessary, by also using INTERPOLATION		SCALING FACTOR = LOAN AMOUNT/1000	
		MONTHLY PAYMENT = SCALING FACTOR x BASE MONTHLY PAYMENT	
		PRECISE AMORTIZED VALUE	
		CUMULATIVE INTEREST = SCALING FACTOR x BASE CUMULATIVE INTEREST	
		PERCENT CUMULATIVE INTEREST = (CUMULATIVE INTEREST /LOAN AMOUNT) x 100	
		TOTAL LOAN COST = LOAN AMOUNT + CUMULATIVE INTEREST	
ALTERNATE CALCULATION (DONE AS A CHECK) (ROUNDED-OFF, MIGHT DIFFER SLIGHTLY)		TOTAL LOAN COST = MONTHLY PAYMENT x TERM	
		TOTAL COST TO PURCHASE = CASH DOWN +TOTAL LOAN COST + BOOK VALUE	

SOLUTION TO: LESSON 5 - SITUATION 6

GIVEN INFORMATION

*SELLING PRICE	7500
*OPTIONS	0
SALES TAX RATE	0

* INCLUDES SALES TAX

CASH REBATE	0
CASH DOWN	0
*BOOK VALUE OF PRESENT CAR	0
*CASH DOWN FROM TRADE-IN	0
or *CASH DOWN FROM SALE	0

** IF NO PRESENT CAR INVOLVED: ENTER 0*

APR(%)	6
TERM (MONTHS)	48
BASE MONTHLY PAYMENT	23.49
*CAR BASE-LOAN TABLE: CUMULATIVE INTEREST	127.28

* VALUE TAKEN FROM TABLE and, if necessary, by also using INTERPOLATION

CALCULATED RESULTS

*SELLING PRICE + *OPTIONS	7500
SALES TAX	0

LOAN AMOUNT = SELLING PRICE + OPTIONS + SALES TAX - CASH REBATE - CASH DOWN - CASH DOWN FROM TRADE-IN- CASH DOWN FROM SALE	7500

SCALING FACTOR = LOAN AMOUNT/1000	7.5
MONTHLY PAYMENT = SCALING FACTOR x BASE MONTHLY PAYMENT	176.18
PRECISE AMORTIZED VALUE	*176.14*
CUMULATIVE INTEREST = SCALING FACTOR x BASE CUMULATIVE INTEREST	954.6
PERCENT CUMULATIVE INTEREST = (CUMULATIVE INTEREST /LOAN AMOUNT) x 100	12.73
TOTAL LOAN COST = LOAN AMOUNT + CUMULATIVE INTEREST	8454.6

ALTERNATE CALCULATION (DONE AS A CHECK) (ROUNDED-OFF, MIGHT DIFFER SLIGHTLY)	TOTAL LOAN COST = MONTHLY PAYMENT x TERM	8456.64

TOTAL COST TO PURCHASE = CASH DOWN +TOTAL LOAN COST + BOOK VALUE	8454.60

SOLUTION TO: LESSON 5 - SITUATION 7

GIVEN INFORMATION

*SELLING PRICE	7500
*OPTIONS	0
SALES TAX RATE	0

* INCLUDES SALES TAX

CASH REBATE	0
CASH DOWN	0
*BOOK VALUE OF PRESENT CAR	0
*CASH DOWN FROM TRADE-IN	0
or *CASH DOWN FROM SALE	0

** IF NO PRESENT CAR INVOLVED: ENTER 0*

APR(%)	4
TERM (MONTHS)	48
*CAR BASE LOAN TABLE: MONTHLY PAYMENT	22.6
*CAR BASE-LOAN TABLE: CUMULATIVE INTEREST	84.33

* VALUE TAKEN FROM TABLE and, if necessary, by also using INTERPOLATION

CALCULATED RESULTS

SELLING PRICE + OPTIONS	7500
SALES TAX	0

LOAN AMOUNT = SELLING PRICE + OPTIONS + SALES TAX - CASH REBATE - CASH DOWN - CASH DOWN FROM TRADE-IN- CASH DOWN FROM SALE	7500

SCALING FACTOR = LOAN AMOUNT/1000	7.5
MONTHLY PAYMENT = SCALING FACTOR x BASE MONTHLY PAYMENT	169.5
PRECISE AMORTIZED VALUE	*169.34*
CUMULATIVE INTEREST = SCALING FACTOR x BASE CUMULATIVE INTEREST	632.48
PERCENT CUMULATIVE INTEREST = (CUMULATIVE INTEREST /LOAN AMOUNT) x 100	8.43
TOTAL LOAN COST = LOAN AMOUNT + CUMULATIVE INTEREST	8132.48

ALTERNATE CALCULATION (DONE AS A CHECK) (ROUNDED-OFF, MIGHT DIFFER SLIGHTLY)	TOTAL LOAN COST = MONTHLY PAYMENT x TERM	8136.00

TOTAL COST TO PURCHASE = CASH DOWN +TOTAL LOAN COST + BOOK VALUE	8132.48

SOLUTION TO: LESSON 5 - SITUATION 11

GIVEN INFORMATION

*SELLING PRICE	10000
*OPTIONS	0
SALES TAX RATE	0
* INCLUDES SALES TAX	

CASH REBATE	0
CASH DOWN	0
*BOOK VALUE OF PRESENT CAR	0
*CASH DOWN FROM TRADE-IN	0
or *CASH DOWN FROM SALE	0
IF NO PRESENT CAR INVOLVED: ENTER 0	

APR(%)	12
TERM (MONTHS)	54
*CAR BASE LOAN TABLE: MONTHLY PAYMENT	24.33
*CAR BASE-LOAN TABLE: CUMULATIVE INTEREST	300
* VALUE TAKEN FROM TABLE and, if necessary, by also using INTERPOLATION	

ALTERNATE CALCULATION (DONE AS A CHECK) (ROUNDED-OFF, MIGHT DIFFER SLIGHTLY)	

CALCULATED RESULTS

SELLING PRICE + OPTIONS	10000
SALES TAX	0

LOAN AMOUNT= SELLING PRICE + OPTIONS + SALES TAX - CASH REBATE - CASH DOWN - CASH DOWN FROM TRADE-IN- CASH DOWN FROM SALE	10000

SCALING FACTOR = LOAN AMOUNT/1000	10
MONTHLY PAYMENT = SCALING FACTOR x BASE MONTHLY PAYMENT	243.3
PRECISE AMORTIZED VALUE	*240.57*
CUMULATIVE INTEREST = SCALING FACTOR x BASE CUMULATIVE INTEREST	3000
PERCENT CUMULATIVE INTEREST = (CUMULATIVE INTEREST /LOAN AMOUNT) x 100	30
TOTAL LOAN COST = LOAN AMOUNT + CUMULATIVE INTEREST	13000
TOTAL LOAN COST = MONTHLY PAYMENT x TERM	13138.20
TOTAL COST TO PURCHASE = CASH DOWN + TOTAL LOAN COST + BOOK VALUE	13000.00

SOLUTION TO: LESSON 6 - SITUATION 13 - OPTION 1

GIVEN INFORMATION

*SELLING PRICE	23200
*OPTIONS	1400
SALES TAX RATE	7

* INCLUDES SALES TAX

CASH REBATE	1300
CASH DOWN	1600
*BOOK VALUE OF PRESENT CAR	0
*CASH DOWN FROM TRADE-IN	0
or *CASH DOWN FROM SALE	0

** IF NO PRESENT CAR INVOLVED: ENTER 0*

APR(%)	4
TERM (MONTHS)	60
*CAR BASE LOAN TABLE: MONTHLY PAYMENT	18.43
*CAR BASE-LOAN TABLE: CUMULATIVE INTEREST	105.82

* VALUE TAKEN FROM TABLE and, if necessary, by also using INTERPOLATION

ALTERNATE CALCULATION (DONE AS A CHECK) (ROUNDED-OFF, MIGHT DIFFER SLIGHTLY)

CALCULATED RESULTS

SELLING PRICE + OPTIONS	24600
SALES TAX	1722

LOAN AMOUNT = SELLING PRICE + OPTIONS + SALES TAX - CASH REBATE - CASH DOWN - CASH DOWN FROM TRADE-IN- CASH DOWN FROM SALE	23422

SCALING FACTOR = LOAN AMOUNT/1000	23.422
MONTHLY PAYMENT = SCALING FACTOR x BASE MONTHLY PAYMENT	431.67
PRECISE AMORTIZED VALUE	*431.35*
CUMULATIVE INTEREST = SCALING FACTOR x BASE CUMULATIVE INTEREST	2478.52
PERCENT CUMULATIVE INTEREST = (CUMULATIVE INTEREST /LOAN AMOUNT) x 100	10.58
TOTAL LOAN COST = LOAN AMOUNT + CUMULATIVE INTEREST	25900.52
TOTAL LOAN COST = MONTHLY PAYMENT x TERM	25900.20
TOTAL COST TO PURCHASE = CASH DOWN + TOTAL LOAN COST + BOOK VALUE	27500.52

SOLUTION TO: LESSON 6 - SITUATION 13 - OPTION 2

GIVEN INFORMATION

*SELLING PRICE	23200
*OPTIONS	1400
SALES TAX RATE	7

* INCLUDES SALES TAX

CASH REBATE	1300
CASH DOWN	1600
*BOOK VALUE OF PRESENT CAR	6500
*CASH DOWN FROM TRADE-IN	4500
or *CASH DOWN FROM SALE	0

** IF NO PRESENT CAR INVOLVED: ENTER 0*

APR(%)	4
TERM (MONTHS)	60
*CAR BASE LOAN TABLE: MONTHLY PAYMENT	18.43
*CAR BASE-LOAN TABLE: CUMULATIVE INTEREST	105.82

* VALUE TAKEN FROM TABLE and, if necessary, by also using INTERPOLATION

CALCULATED RESULTS

SELLING PRICE + OPTIONS	24600
SALES TAX	1722

LOAN AMOUNT = SELLING PRICE + OPTIONS + SALES TAX - CASH REBATE - CASH DOWN - CASH DOWN FROM TRADE-IN- CASH DOWN FROM SALE	18922

SCALING FACTOR = LOAN AMOUNT/1000	18.922
MONTHLY PAYMENT = SCALING FACTOR x BASE MONTHLY PAYMENT	348.73
PRECISE AMORTIZED VALUE	348.48
CUMULATIVE INTEREST = SCALING FACTOR x BASE CUMULATIVE INTEREST	2002.33
PERCENT CUMULATIVE INTEREST = (CUMULATIVE INTEREST /LOAN AMOUNT) x 100	10.58
TOTAL LOAN COST = LOAN AMOUNT + CUMULATIVE INTEREST	20924.33

ALTERNATE CALCULATION (DONE AS A CHECK) (ROUNDED-OFF, MIGHT DIFFER SLIGHTLY)	TOTAL LOAN COST = MONTHLY PAYMENT x TERM	20923.80

TOTAL COST TO PURCHASE = CASH DOWN + TOTAL LOAN COST + BOOK VALUE	29024.33

SOLUTION TO: LESSON 6 - SITUATION 13 - OPTION 3

GIVEN INFORMATION

*SELLING PRICE	23200
*OPTIONS	1400
SALES TAX RATE	7
* INCLUDES SALES TAX	
CASH REBATE	1300
CASH DOWN	1600
*BOOK VALUE OF PRESENT CAR	6500
*CASH DOWN FROM TRADE-IN	0
or *CASH DOWN FROM SALE	6500
IF NO PRESENT CAR INVOLVED: ENTER 0	
APR(%)	4
TERM (MONTHS)	60
*CAR BASE LOAN TABLE: MONTHLY PAYMENT	18.43
*CAR BASE-LOAN TABLE: CUMULATIVE INTEREST	105.82
* VALUE TAKEN FROM TABLE and, if necessary, by also using INTERPOLATION	
ALTERNATE CALCULATION (DONE AS A CHECK) (ROUNDED-OFF, MIGHT DIFFER SLIGHTLY)	

CALCULATED RESULTS

SELLING PRICE + OPTIONS	24600
SALES TAX	1722
LOAN AMOUNT = SELLING PRICE + OPTIONS + SALES TAX - CASH REBATE - CASH DOWN - CASH DOWN FROM TRADE-IN- CASH DOWN FROM SALE	16922
SCALING FACTOR= LOAN AMOUNT/1000	16.922
MONTHLY PAYMENT = SCALING FACTOR x BASE MONTHLY PAYMENT	311.87
PRECISE AMORTIZED VALUE	311.64
CUMULATIVE INTEREST = SCALING FACTOR x BASE CUMULATIVE INTEREST	1790.69
PERCENT CUMULATIVE INTEREST = (CUMULATIVE INTEREST /LOAN AMOUNT) x 100	10.58
TOTAL LOAN COST = LOAN AMOUNT + CUMULATIVE INTEREST	18712.69
TOTAL LOAN COST = MONTHLY PAYMENT x TERM	18712.20
TOTAL COST TO PURCHASE = CASH DOWN + TOTAL LOAN COST + BOOK VALUE	26812.69

APPENDIX III – SOLUTIONS TO EXERCISES 17A AND 17B

Solution to Exercise 17A:

DEPRECIATED VALUE = (1 - 0.3500) x $29873.00 = $19417.00

GAP AMOUNT = BUYOUT AMOUNT - DEPRECIATED VALUE

= $24647.00 - $19417.00 = $5230.00

CD PAYOUT = DEPRECIATED VALUE – ~~CD DEDUCTIBLE~~

= $19417.00 - $0.00 = $19417.00

AMOUNT STILL OWED = OUTSTANDING PRINCIPAL – CD PAYOUT

= $24647.00 - $19417.00 = $5230.00

GAP INSURANCE: GAP PAYOUT = $5230.00

LOAN/LEASE INSURANCE: L/L CAP = 0.25 x $19417.00 = $4854.00.00 < GAP AMOUNT

L/L PAYOUT = $4854.00

GAP INSURANCE provides more coverage than LOAN/LEASE INSURANCE!

Solution to Exercise 17B:

DEPRECIATED VALUE = (1- 0.3300) x $29873= $20015.00

GAP AMOUNT = OUTSTANDING PRINCIPAL - DEPRECIATED VALUE

= $24847.00 - $20015.00 = $4632.00

CD PAYOUT = DEPRECIATED VALUE – ~~CD DEDUCTIBLE~~

= $20015.00 - $0.00 = $20015.00

AMOUNT STILL OWED = OUTSTANDING PRINCIPAL – CD PAYOUT

= $24647.00 - $20015.00 = $4632.00

GAP INSURANCE: GAP PAYOUT = GAP AMOUNT = $4632.00

LOAN/LEASE INSURANCE: L/L CAP = 0.25 x $20015.00 = $5004.00.00 > GAP AMOUNT

L/L PAYOUT = GAP AMOUNT = $4632.00

GAP INSURANCE provides more coverage than LOAN/LEASE INSURANCE!

APPENDIX IV – SOURCE OF MONEY FACTOR EQUATIONS

"Dad, I follow the number in your calculations all right, but the terminology and equations have to sink in. And I still have to trust you on the use of a **MONEY FACTOR**."

"Don't worry on the terminology and equations. Over time it will all sink in. As to that **MONEY FACTOR**, here's what I found out about it.

"We know the following is how it is used."

MONTHLY FINANCE <u>CHARGE</u> = TOTAL FINANCED AMOUNT x MONEY FACTOR

"In some websites it was mentioned that the **MONEY FACTOR** is obtained from this equation.

MONEY FACTOR = APR/2400

"That indicates the magnitude of the **MONEY FACTOR** reflects the **APR** you are being charged in the lease. As I understand from various websites it's not clear where this relationship comes from. But here is my try at it."

"First I made the following modification."

MONEY FACTOR = APR/2400 = APR/(12 x 200) = (APR/12)/200

"Then I made the following series of math modifications to the form of the equation for the **MONTHLY FINANCE <u>CHARGE</u>**."

MONTHLY FINANCE CHARGE = TOTAL FINANCED AMOUNT x MONEY FACTOR

= TOTAL FINANCED AMOUNT x (APR/12)/200

= TOTAL FINANCED AMOUNT x (APR/12)/(100 x2)

= (TOTAL FINANCED AMOUNT/2) x (APR/12)/100

"With that last form I observed that the **TOTAL FINANCED AMOUNT/2** is the **AVERAGE FINANCED AMOUNT** over the **TERM** of the lease. I say that because the intent is to pay the initial **TOTAL FINANCED AMOUNT** down to 0 at the end of the lease. In math steps it means the following."

AVERAGE FINANCED AMOUNT = (TOTAL FINANCED AMOUNT + 0)/2

= TOTAL FINANCED AMOUNT/2

"Then I observed that **(APR/12)/100** is essentially the **MONTHLY RATE OF INTEREST** expressed as a **FRACTION**. That indicates that the **MONTHLY FINANCE CHARGE** is obtained by multiplying **AVERAGE FINANCED AMOUNT** by the **MONTHLY RATE OF INTEREST**. That explains where the relationship **MONEY FACTOR = APR/2400** comes from."

"Whoa! Dad I kind of follow your modifications and your explanation. But why did you figure out all of it?"

"Commonly, in a **LEASE AGREEMENT** they simply state a numerical value for the **MONEY FACTOR**. Usually, when a person reads that the **MONEY FACTOR** = 0.00250 or whatever he or she scratches their head. That's what happened to me when I first read about it. There's no mention of an **APR** value at all and certainly not that **MONEY FACTOR** = **APR/2400**. My sense is the lessor tries to hide a high **APR** value.

"It's hard for me to use anything I don't understand. At first it stumped your dear old Dad. But my curiosity and persistence won out. I kept trying until if figured it out what I just showed you. Maybe you have that trait as well."

"I don't have your math wizardry, Dad. But I have the same determination when it comes to my journalism tasks. I guess I got it from watching you."

"Maybe so, Peanut. It's more important that you have it than where it might have come from.

"On several websites I also saw mention of the following equation without any explanation of its source."

MONTHLY FINANCED AMOUNT = TOTAL FINANCED AMOUNT/200

"I got curious and figured out where that came from too."

"Dad, before you show that what's meant by the **MONTHLY FINANCED <u>AMOUNT</u>?** How is it different from the **MONTHLY FINANCE <u>CHARGE</u>**?

"Super question! In fact, answering it leads into my explanation.

"The **MONTHLY FINANCE <u>CHARGE</u>** is the interest paid each month. The **MONTHLY FINANCED <u>AMOUNT</u>** is the amount of money the **MONTHLY RATE OF INTEREST** is applied to in order determine it. This is it in equation form."

MONTHLY FINANCE <u>CHARGE</u> = MONTHLY RATE OF INTEREST
x MONTHLY FINANCED <u>AMOUNT</u>

"And the **MONTHLY RATE OF INTEREST = APR/12**. That means the following."

MONTHLY FINANCE CHARGE = (APR/12) x MONTHLY FINANCED AMOUNT

"In the last equation, the **APR/12** is in %. There is no division by 100 to get a **RATIO**. Odd as it is, that's correct. I put the equation in italics, so I can refer to it later.

"Now, I just showed the source of the equation **MONTHLY FINANCED AMOUNT = TOTAL FINANCED AMOUNT/2400**. In doing that I did the following."

MONTHLY FINANCE CHARGE = TOTAL FINANCED AMOUNT x MONEY FACTOR

= TOTAL FINANCED AMOUNT x (APR/12)/200

"That last equation can be rewritten as follows."

MONTHLY FINANCE CHARGE = (APR/12) x (TOTAL FINANCED AMOUNT/200)

MONTHLY FINANCE CHARGE/(APR/12) = TOTAL FINANCED AMOUNT/200

"Remember that,

MONTHLY FINANCE CHARGE = (APR/12) x MONTHLY FINANCED AMOUNT

"Revising it gives,

MONTHLY FINANCE CHARGE/(APR/12) = MONTHLY FINANCED AMOUNT

"That means that the equation,"

MONTHLY FINANCE CHARGE/(APR/12) = (TOTAL FINANCED AMOUNT/200

converts to,

MONTHLY FINANCED AMOUNT = TOTAL FINANCED AMOUNT/200

"That's show how they got the equation."

"Whoa! Whoa! Dad, my head is twisting and turning like a tornado again. I'm having a really hard time following the twists and turns in your math steps. Together with a sea of terminology it's boggling my mind."

"It did that to me too even as I wrote it. I figured out all of this background to demonstrate to myself where the equation came from. Math types would love it. All that matters now is you take my word that the equation is valid and not a hocus-pocus magical trick."

"I have to admit your math is like a magician taking a bunny out of top hat. I don't know how he or she did it, but I know it was done somehow and I only saw the bunny."

"Ok, very good Nicole. Again, in time I'm sure the terminology will eventually sink in for you. That probably will happen when you actually go about considering leasing a car."

"Earlier, I italicized this equation."

MONTHLY FINANCE CHARGE = (APR/12) x MONTHLY FINANCED AMOUNT

"I pointed out that the **APR/12** was in % and did not have to be divided by 100. Here's how. I divided it by 100 and did the same math. At the end I got,

MONTHLY FINANCED <u>AMOUNT</u>/100 = TOTAL FINANCED <u>AMOUNT</u>/200

MONTHLY FINANCED <u>AMOUNT</u> = TOTAL FINANCED <u>AMOUNT</u>/2

"The second equation indicates **MONTHLY FINANCED <u>AMOUNT</u>** is half the **TOTAL FINANCED <u>AMOUNT</u>.** That's nonsense. I dug deeper.

"Earlier we had this equation."

MONTHLY FINANCE CHARGE = (APR/12) x (TOTAL FINANCED <u>AMOUNT</u>/200)

Which means,

MONTHLY FINANCE <u>CHARGE</u> = (APR/12)/100 x (TOTAL FINANCED <u>AMOUNT</u>/2)

"The **(APR/12)/100** is the **MONTHLY FINANCE RATE**. But in the prior form the **'/100'** is embedded in the **'/200'**. It's also embedded in the **'/200'** in the following equation."

MONTHLY FINANCED AMOUNT = TOTAL FINANCED AMOUNT/200

"Well, Dad. Wasn't there a famous magician named, 'Houdini'? Are you, him?"

"Fortunately, I'm not. You wouldn't want me to make you disappear, would you?"

"Right now, with all this math you showed, I wish you could."

"Fair enough! There's actually a simpler way to show it."

"The **MONEY FACTOR** is sort of a gimmick used to calculate the **MONTHLY FINANCE CHARGE**. In my day, we called that sort of thing 'a fudge factor'. It meant that it seemed like the real thing was covered up by a simpler thing that nobody understood. Let's look at a more understandable way of calculating it.

"Hidden in the **MONEY FACTOR** 'fudging' is an actual **ANNUAL RATE OF INTEREST** in play in **CAR LEASE** financing. Knowing that, we could get the corresponding **MONTHLY RATE OF INTEREST** by dividing it by 12. Then, if we knew the **MONTHLY FINANCED AMOUNT** we could do the following calculation."

MONTHLY RATE OF INTEREST = APR/12

MONTHLY FINANCE CHARGE = (MONTHLY RATE OF INTEREST/100) x MONTHLY FINANCED AMOUNT

"Are you with me so far?"
"I see it Dad. And I see you have divided by 100. That means the **MONTHLY RATE OF INTEREST** is in %."

"That's right, math whiz."

"However, the **MONTHLY FINANCED AMOUNT** is what we don't know. But we can calculate the **MONTHLY FINANCE CHARGE**. If we rearrange the equation we get the following."

MONTHLY FINANCED AMOUNT = MONTHLY FINANCE CHARGE/(MONTHLY RATE OF INTEREST/100)

"That allows us to calculate what we want. Right?"

Smirking, Nicole chimes out, "It sure does! Mr. Houdini."

APPENDIX V – CHEAT SHEETS FOR CAR LEASES AND SELECTED SOLUTIONS

CHEAT SHEET FOR CAR LEASE COSTS

GIVEN INFORMATION		CALCULATED RESULTS	
TERM (MONTHS)			
SELLING PRICE			
OPTIONS			
		CAPITALZED COST = SELLING PRICE + OPTIONS	
CASH REBATE			
CASH DOWN			
*CASH DOWN FROM TRADE-IN			
*CASH DOWN FROM SALE			
*IF NO PRESENT CAR INVOLVED: ENTER 0			
		NET CAPITALZED COST = CAPITALIZED COST - CASH REBATE - CASH DOWN - CASH DOWN FROM TRADE-IN - CASH DOWN FROM SALE	
RESIDUAL VALUE			
		NET VALUE = NET CAPITALIZED COST - RESIDUAL VALUE	
		MONTHLY DEPRECIATION FEE = NET VALUE/TERM	
		TOTAL FINANCED AMOUNT = NET CAPITALIZED COST + RESIDUAL VALUE	
*MONEY FACTOR			
*IF NEEDED, DO A SIDE CALCULATION: (MONEY FACTOR = APR/2400) AND ENTER THE RESULT ABOVE			
		MONTHLY FINANCE CHARGE = TOTAL FINANCED AMOUNT x MONEY FACTOR	
ALTERNATE CALCULATION (DONE AS A CHECK) (ROUND-OFF MIGHT DIFFER SLIGHTLY)		MONTHLY FINANCED AMOUNT = TOTAL FINANCED AMOUNT/200	
		MONTHLY FINANCE CHARGE = MONTHLY FINANCE AMOUNT x APR/12	
SALES TAX RATE (%)			
		MONTHLY TAXABLE AMOUNT = MONTHLY DEPRECIATION FEE + MONTHLY FINANCE CHARGE	
		MONTHLY SALES TAX = MONTHLY TAXABLE AMOUNT x SALES TAX RATE/100	
		MONTHLY PAYMENT = MONTHLY DEPRECIATION FEE + MONTHLY FINANCE CHARGE + MONTHLY SALES TAX	
		TOTAL PAYMENTS = MONTHLY PAYMENT x TERM	
		TOTAL FINANCE CHARGE = MONTHLY FINANCE CHARGE x TERM	

EXTENSION OF CHEAT SHEET FOR CAR LEASE COSTS

MONTHLY GAP INSURANCE COST (MGIC)			
		TOTAL GAP INSURANCE = MGIC x TERM	
MILEAGE LIMIT (ANNUAL)			
		MILEAGE LIMIT (TOTAL) = MILEAGE LIMIT(ANNUAL) x TERM/12	
ACTUAL MILES			
		EXCESS MILEAGE = ACTUAL MILES -MILEAGE LIMIT (TOTAL)	
EXCESS MILEAGE RATE ($)			
		EXCESS MILEAGE CHARGE = EXCESS MILEAGE RATE ($) x EXCESS MILEAGE	
FEES (IF ACTUALLY PAID)			
ACQUISITION FEE			
BANK FEE			
DEALER SERVICE FEE			
DISPOSITION FEE			
EARLY TERMINATION FEE			
		TOTAL FEES = SUM of FEES	
EXCESS WEAR AND TEAR CHARGE			
BOOK VALUE (0 .0 IF NO PRESENT CAR IS INVOLVED)			
		TOTAL COST TO LEASE (ROUNDED) = CASH DOWN + TOTAL GAP INSURANCE + TOTAL PAYMENTS + TOTAL FEES + EXCESS MILEAGE CHARGE + EXCESS WEAR AND TEAR CHARGE + BOOK VALUE	
		SALES TAX ON RESIDUAL VALUE = SALES TAX RATE/100 x RESIDUAL VALUE	
PURCHASE OPTION FEE (IF PAID)			
		TOTAL COST TO LEASE/PURCHASE (ROUNDED) = TOTAL COST TO LEASE + RESIDUAL VALUE + SALES TAX ON RESIDUAL VALUE + PURCHASE OPTION FEE	

SOLUTION TO: LESSON 9 - SITUATION 16

GIVEN INFORMATION

TERM (MONTHS)	36
SELLING PRICE	27500
OPTIONS	2500
CASH REBATE	1000
CASH DOWN	4000
*CASH DOWN FROM TRADE-IN	0
*CASH DOWN FROM SALE	0
RESIDUAL VALUE	16000
*MONEY FACTOR	0.0025
SALES TAX RATE (%)	8

*IF NO PRESENT CAR INVOLVED: ENTER 0

*IF NEEDED, DO A SIDE CALCULATION: (MONEY FACTOR = APR/2400) AND ENTER THE RESULT ABOVE

CALCULATED RESULTS

CAPITALZED COST = SELLING PRICE + OPTIONS	30000
NET CAPITALZED COST = CAPITALIZED COST - CASH REBATE - CASH DOWN - CASH DOWN FROM TRADE-IN - CASH DOWN FROM SALE	25000
NET VALUE = NET CAPITALIZED COST - RESIDUAL VALUE	9000
MONTHLY DEPRECIATION FEE = NET VALUE/TERM	250
TOTAL FINANCED AMOUNT = NET CAPITALIZED COST + RESIDUAL VALUE	41000
MONTHLY FINANCE CHARGE = TOTAL FINANCED AMOUNT x MONEY FACTOR	102.5

ALTERNATE CALCULATION (DONE AS A CHECK) (ROUND-OFF MIGHT DIFFER SLIGHTLY)

MONTHLY FINANCED AMOUNT = TOTAL FINANCED AMOUNT/200	205.00
MONTHLY FINANCE CHARGE = MONTHLY FINANCE AMOUNT x APR/12	102.50

MONTHLY TAXABLE AMOUNT = MONTHLY DEPRECIATION FEE + MONTHLY FINANCE CHARGE	352.50
MONTHLY SALES TAX = MONTHLY TAXABLE AMOUNT x SALES TAX RATE/100	28.20
MONTHLY PAYMENT = MONTHLY DEPRECIATION FEE + MONTHLY FINANCE CHARGE + MONTHLY SALES TAX	380.70
TOTAL PAYMENTS = MONTHLY PAYMENT x TERM	13705.20
TOTAL FINANCE CHARGE = MONTHLY FINANCE CHARGE x TERM	3690.00

SOLUTION TO: LESSON 10 - SITUATION 17 – OPTION 1

GIVEN INFORMATION	
TERM (MONTHS)	36
SELLING PRICE	23200
OPTIONS	1400
CASH REBATE	1300
CASH DOWN	1600
*CASH DOWN FROM TRADE-IN	0
*CASH DOWN FROM SALE	0
*IF NO PRESENT CAR INVOLVED: ENTER 0	
RESIDUAL VALUE	14000
*MONEY FACTOR	0.00167
*IF NEEDED, DO A SIDE CALCULATION: (MONEY FACTOR = APR/2400) AND ENTER THE RESULT ABOVE	
ALTERNATE CALCULATION (DONE AS A CHECK) (ROUND-OFF MIGHT DIFFER SLIGHTLY)	
SALES TAX RATE (%)	7

CALCULATED RESULTS	
CAPITALZED COST = SELLING PRICE + OPTIONS	24600
NET CAPITALZED COST = CAPITALIZED COST - CASH REBATE - CASH DOWN - CASH DOWN FROM TRADE-IN - CASH DOWN FROM SALE	21700
NET VALUE = NET CAPITALIZED COST - RESIDUAL VALUE	7700
MONTHLY DEPRECIATION FEE = NET VALUE/TERM	213.89
TOTAL FINANCED AMOUNT = NET CAPITALIZED COST + RESIDUAL VALUE	35700
MONTHLY FINANCE CHARGE = TOTAL FINANCED AMOUNT x MONEY FACTOR	59.51
MONTHLY FINANCED AMOUNT = TOTAL FINANCED AMOUNT/200	178.50
MONTHLY FINANCE CHARGE = MONTHLY FINANCE AMOUNT x APR/12	59.51
MONTHLY TAXABLE AMOUNT = MONTHLY DEPRECIATION FEE + MONTHLY FINANCE CHARGE	273.40
MONTHLY SALES TAX = MONTHLY TAXABLE AMOUNT x SALES TAX RATE/100	19.14
MONTHLY PAYMENT = MONTHLY DEPRECIATION FEE + MONTHLY FINANCE CHARGE + MONTHLY SALES TAX	292.54
TOTAL PAYMENTS = MONTHLY PAYMENT x TERM	10531.44
TOTAL FINANCE CHARGE = MONTHLY FINANCE CHARGE x TERM	2142.36

SOLUTION TO: LESSON 10 – SITUATION 17 – OPTION 1 – CONTINUED

MONTHLY GAP INSURANCE COST (MGIC)	5.00		
		TOTAL GAP INSURANCE = MGIC x TERM	180.00
MILEAGE LIMIT (ANNUAL)	15000		
		MILEAGE LIMIT (TOTAL) = MILEAGE LIMIT(ANNUAL) x TERM/12	45000
ACTUAL MILES	51000		
		EXCESS MILEAGE = ACTUAL MILES -MILEAGE LIMIT (TOTAL)	6000
EXCESS MILEAGE RATE ($)	0.15		
		EXCESS MILEAGE CHARGE = EXCESS MILEAGE RATE ($) x EXCESS MILEAGE	900.00
FEES (IF ACTUALLY PAID)			
ACQUISITION FEE	350.00		
BANK FEE	0.00		
DEALER SERVICE FEE	250.00		
DISPOSITION FEE	0.00		
EARLY TERMINATION FEE	0.00		
		TOTAL FEES = SUM of FEES	600.00
EXCESS WEAR AND TEAR CHARGE	0.00		
BOOK VALUE (0 .0 IF NO PRESENT CAR IS INVOLVED)	0.00		
		TOTAL COST TO LEASE (ROUNDED) = CASH DOWN + TOTAL GAP INSURANCE + TOTAL PAYMENTS + TOTAL FEES + EXCESS MILEAGE CHARGE + EXCESS WEAR AND TEAR CHARGE + BOOK VALUE	13811.00
		SALES TAX ON RESIDUAL VALUE = SALES TAX RATE/100 x RESIDUAL VALUE	980.00
PURCHASE OPTION FEE (IF PAID)	350		
		TOTAL COST TO LEASE/PURCHASE (ROUNDED) = TOTAL COST TO LEASE + RESIDUAL VALUE + SALES TAX ON RESIDUAL VALUE + PURCHASE OPTION FEE	29141.00

SOLUTION TO: LESSON 11 – SITUATION 17 – OPTION 2

GIVEN INFORMATION		CALCULATED RESULTS	
TERM (MONTHS)	36		
SELLING PRICE	23200		
OPTIONS	1400		
		CAPITALZED COST = SELLING PRICE + OPTIONS	24600
CASH REBATE	1300		
CASH DOWN	1600		
CASH DOWN FROM TRADE-IN	4500		
CASH DOWN FROM SALE	0		
*IF NO PRESENT CAR INVOLVED: ENTER 0			
		NET CAPITALZED COST = CAPITALIZED COST - CASH REBATE - CASH DOWN - CASH DOWN FROM TRADE-IN - CASH DOWN FROM SALE	17200
RESIDUAL VALUE	14000		
		NET VALUE = NET CAPITALIZED COST - RESIDUAL VALUE	3200
		MONTHLY DEPRECIATION FEE = NET VALUE/TERM	88.89
		TOTAL FINANCED AMOUNT = NET CAPITALIZED COST + RESIDUAL VALUE	31200
*MONEY FACTOR	0.00167		
*IF NEEDED, DO A SIDE CALCULATION: (MONEY FACTOR = APR/2400) AND ENTER THE RESULT ABOVE			
		MONTHLY FINANCE CHARGE = TOTAL FINANCED AMOUNT x MONEY FACTOR	52.01
ALTERNATE CALCULATION (DONE AS A CHECK) (ROUND-OFF MIGHT DIFFER SLIGHTLY)		MONTHLY FINANCED AMOUNT = TOTAL FINANCED AMOUNT/200	156.00
		MONTHLY FINANCE CHARGE = MONTHLY FINANCE AMOUNT x APR/12	52.01
SALES TAX RATE (%)	7		
		MONTHLY TAXABLE AMOUNT = MONTHLY DEPRECIATION FEE + MONTHLY FINANCE CHARGE	140.90
		MONTHLY SALES TAX = MONTHLY TAXABLE AMOUNT x SALES TAX RATE/100	9.86
		MONTHLY PAYMENT = MONTHLY DEPRECIATION FEE + MONTHLY FINANCE CHARGE + MONTHLY SALES TAX	150.76
		TOTAL PAYMENTS = MONTHLY PAYMENT x TERM	5427.36
		TOTAL FINANCE CHARGE = MONTHLY FINANCE CHARGE x TERM	1872.36

SOLUTION TO: LESSON 11 – SITUATION 17 – OPTION 2 - CONTINUED

MONTHLY GAP INSURANCE COST (MGIC)	5.00
MILEAGE LIMIT (ANNUAL)	15000
ACTUAL MILES	51000
EXCESS MILEAGE RATE ($)	0.15
FEES (IF ACTUALLY PAID)	
ACQUISITION FEE	350.00
BANK FEE	0.00
DEALER SERVICE FEE	250.00
DISPOSITION FEE	0.00
EARLY TERMINATION FEE	0.00
EXCESS WEAR AND TEAR CHARGE	0.00
BOOK VALUE (0 .0 IF NO PRESENT CAR IS INVOLVED)	6500.00
PURCHASE OPTION FEE (IF PAID)	350

TOTAL GAP INSURANCE = MGIC x TERM	180.00
MILEAGE LIMIT (TOTAL) = MILEAGE LIMIT(ANNUAL) x TERM/12	45000
EXCESS MILEAGE = ACTUAL MILES -MILEAGE LIMIT (TOTAL)	6000
EXCESS MILEAGE CHARGE = EXCESS MILEAGE RATE ($) x EXCESS MILEAGE	900.00
TOTAL FEES = SUM of FEES	600.00
TOTAL COST TO LEASE (ROUNDED) = CASH DOWN + TOTAL GAP INSURANCE + TOTAL PAYMENTS + TOTAL FEES + EXCESS MILEAGE CHARGE + EXCESS WEAR AND TEAR CHARGE + BOOK VALUE	15207.00
SALES TAX ON RESIDUAL VALUE = SALES TAX RATE/100 x RESIDUAL VALUE	980.00
TOTAL COST TO LEASE/PURCHASE (ROUNDED) = TOTAL COST TO LEASE + RESIDUAL VALUE + SALES TAX ON RESIDUAL VALUE + PURCHASE OPTION FEE	30537.00

SOLUTION TO: LESSON 11 – SITUATION 17 – OPTION 3

GIVEN INFORMATION		CALCULATED RESULTS	
TERM (MONTHS)	36		
SELLING PRICE	23200		
OPTIONS	1400		
		CAPITALZED COST = SELLING PRICE + OPTIONS	24600
CASH REBATE	1300		
CASH DOWN	1600		
CASH DOWN FROM TRADE-IN	6500		
CASH DOWN FROM SALE	0		
*IF NO PRESENT CAR INVOLVED: ENTER 0			
		NET CAPITALZED COST = CAPITALIZED COST - CASH REBATE - CASH DOWN - CASH DOWN FROM TRADE-IN - CASH DOWN FROM SALE	15200
RESIDUAL VALUE	14000		
		NET VALUE = NET CAPITALIZED COST - RESIDUAL VALUE	1200
		MONTHLY DEPRECIATION FEE = NET VALUE/TERM	33.33
		TOTAL FINANCED AMOUNT = NET CAPITALIZED COST + RESIDUAL VALUE	29200
*MONEY FACTOR	0.00167		
*IF NEEDED, DO A SIDE CALCULATION: (MONEY FACTOR = APR/2400) AND ENTER THE RESULT ABOVE			
		MONTHLY FINANCE CHARGE = TOTAL FINANCED AMOUNT x MONEY FACTOR	48.68
ALTERNATE CALCULATION (DONE AS A CHECK) (ROUND-OFF MIGHT DIFFER SLIGHTLY)		MONTHLY FINANCED AMOUNT = TOTAL FINANCED AMOUNT/200	146.00
		MONTHLY FINANCE CHARGE = MONTHLY FINANCE AMOUNT x APR/12	48.68
SALES TAX RATE (%)	7		
		MONTHLY TAXABLE AMOUNT = MONTHLY DEPRECIATION FEE + MONTHLY FINANCE CHARGE	82.01
		MONTHLY SALES TAX = MONTHLY TAXABLE AMOUNT x SALES TAX RATE/100	5.74
		MONTHLY PAYMENT = MONTHLY DEPRECIATION FEE + MONTHLY FINANCE CHARGE + MONTHLY SALES TAX	87.75
		TOTAL PAYMENTS = MONTHLY PAYMENT x TERM	3159.00
		TOTAL FINANCE CHARGE = MONTHLY FINANCE CHARGE x TERM	1752.48

SOLUTION TO: LESSON 11 – SITUATION 17 – OPTION 3 - CONTINUED

MONTHLY GAP INSURANCE COST (MGIC)	5.00		
		TOTAL GAP INSURANCE = MGIC x TERM	180.00
MILEAGE LIMIT (ANNUAL)	15000		
		MILEAGE LIMIT (TOTAL) = MILEAGE LIMIT(ANNUAL) x TERM/12	45000
ACTUAL MILES	51000		
		EXCESS MILEAGE = ACTUAL MILES -MILEAGE LIMIT (TOTAL)	6000
EXCESS MILEAGE RATE ($)	0.15		
		EXCESS MILEAGE CHARGE = EXCESS MILEAGE RATE ($) x EXCESS MILEAGE	900.00
FEES (IF ACTUALLY PAID)			
ACQUISITION FEE	350.00		
BANK FEE	0.00		
DEALER SERVICE FEE	250.00		
DISPOSITION FEE	0.00		
EARLY TERMINATION FEE	0.00		
		TOTAL FEES = SUM of FEES	600.00
EXCESS WEAR AND TEAR CHARGE	0.00		
BOOK VALUE (0 .0 IF NO PRESENT CAR IS INVOLVED)	6500.00		
		TOTAL COST TO LEASE (ROUNDED) = CASH DOWN + TOTAL GAP INSURANCE + TOTAL PAYMENTS + TOTAL FEES + EXCESS MILEAGE CHARGE + EXCESS WEAR AND TEAR CHARGE + BOOK VALUE	12939.00
		SALES TAX ON RESIDUAL VALUE = SALES TAX RATE/100 x RESIDUAL VALUE	980.00
PURCHASE OPTION FEE (IF PAID)	350		
		TOTAL COST TO LEASE/PURCHASE (ROUNDED) = TOTAL COST TO LEASE + RESIDUAL VALUE + SALES TAX ON RESIDUAL VALUE + PURCHASE OPTION FEE	28269.00

Please Note:

The content of this book reflects the author's personal approaches, experiences, thought processes, observations, and strategies. He is not a financial planner. Professional financial planning advisors might see some things similarly, others differently. Situations are hypothetical and realistic but not actual cases. All numerical work serves to illustrate the math processes involved in depicting them. It is more important to grasp the methods than the specific numbers involved. SITUATIONS are selective examples for illustration and variety only. Other circumstances can and will arise. The reader must adapt the math processes to their specific cases.

Extensive, exhaustive calculations were done behind the scenes. All numerical work was done carefully and rechecked several times, but is not infallible. It is the reader's responsibility to confirm the calculated numbers. If in doing that doubts arise, then please feel free to contact the author (via his website) about questioned values, including listed answers to any Exercise. He will confirm or correct them.

Various so-called "Cheat Sheets" are provided in Appendices. They provide the reader with a flow pattern on sequential calculations involve for the associated Lesson content. They guide the reader through providing the applicable monetary and other numerical values needed as he/or she does the sequential calculations manually. The reader is responsible for doing those steps correctly. Readers with sufficient background in spreadsheets can convert them to that format, but they alone are responsible for the end products.

Made in the USA
Monee, IL
08 November 2026

67380495R00144